# The Indian Political Service

## A STUDY IN INDIRECT RULE

*By*

## TERENCE CREAGH COEN

K.B.E., C.I.E.

*Supernumerary Fellow*
*St. Antony's College, Oxford*

1971

CHATTO & WINDUS

LONDON

Published by
Chatto & Windus Ltd
40 William IV Street
London W.C.2

*

Clarke, Irwin & Co. Ltd.
Toronto

ISBN 0 7011 1579 3

Printed in Great Britain by
R. and R. Clark Ltd.
Edinburgh

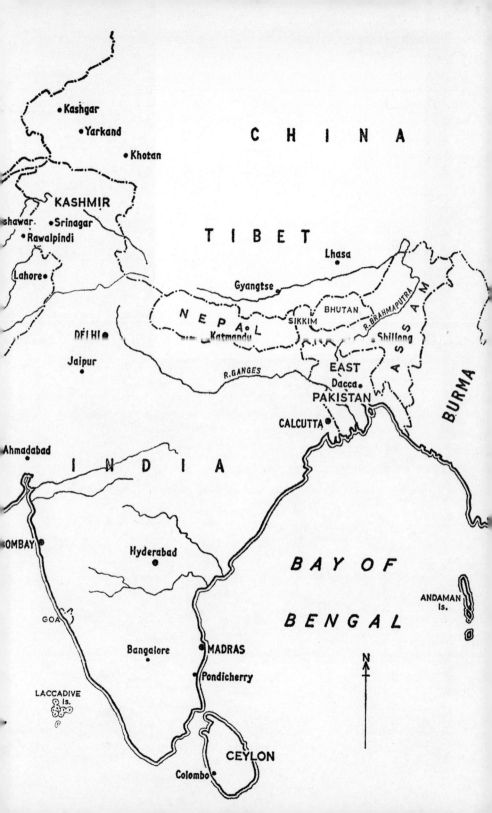

# THE INDIAN POLITICAL SERVICE

*To the Memory of*
*two great political officers and*
*good friends*

ARTHUR CUNNINGHAM LOTHIAN, K.C.I.E., C.S.I.
(1887–1962)

AND

LANCELOT CECIL LEPEL GRIFFIN, Kt., C.S.I., C.I.E.
(1900–1964)

# Acknowledgments

To my colleagues in the Indian Political Service (Retired) Association I owe my sincere thanks for choosing me to write this book and for helping me with advice on many aspects of a political officer's work. I am very grateful to the Warden and Fellows of St. Antony's College, Oxford, who elected me to a supernumerary fellowship, which greatly helped me in my research. The Directors of the India Office Library, London, and the Indian Institute, Oxford, aided me most valuably.

I would like to thank all those who provided me with information either by verbal communication or by allowing me to quote from various works. I am indebted to Colonel H. R. C. Pettigrew and Mr. G. C. S. Curtis on whose accounts of the Frontier Scouts and of the life of a frontier political officer I have drawn at length. The late Lord Hailey was of great help with his recollections of frontier policy and federation; the late Mr. Victor Butler allowed me access to the papers of his father, Sir Harcourt Butler, as did the Marquis of Zetland to his father's correspondence with the Marquis of Linlithgow.

The Hon. Lady Betjeman kindly permitted me to quote from a letter of her father's, Field-Marshal Lord Chetwode, and I would like to thank Mr. Neil Lothian for allowing me to quote from his late father's *Kingdoms of Yesterday* (published by John Murray). Mr. Nigel Nicolson kindly gave me permission to quote from Sir Harold Nicolson's *Curzon: The Last Phase, 1919–25* (published by Constable). Sir Conrad Corfield has been most helpful in allowing me to quote from an unpublished memoir, and I have also drawn on information in letters from him.

I am most grateful for permission to quote from the following: *Abinger Harvest* (the late Mr. E. M. Forster and E. Arnold & Co.); 'Sir Tej Bahadur Sapru and the First Round-Table Conference' (Professor D. A. Low); *Britain and Chinese Central Asia* (Mr. Alastair Lamb and Routledge & Kegan Paul); *Mission to Tashkent* (the late Lt.-Col. F. M. Bailey and Jonathan Cape); *The Pathans* (Sir Olaf Caroe and Macmillan); *John Jacob of Jacobabad* (Mr. H. T. Lambrick and Cassell); *The Persian Gulf States* (the late Sir Rupert Hay and The Middle Eastern Institute, Washington, D.C.); *The Indian States and Indian Federation* (Sir G. de Montmorency and Cambridge University Press); *The Integration of the Indian States* (V. P. Menon and Longmans Orient); *India: Minto and Morley, 1905–1910* (Lady Minto and Macmillan).

vii

# Contents

## PART IV
## FOREIGN POSTS

## MAPS
1 The Indo–Pakistan Sub-Continent and surrounding countries
2 Indian Empire 1858–1947
3 North-West Frontier and Afghanistan
Map 1 appears as endpapers: Maps 2 and 3 appear between
pages 148-9 and 220–21

Part I

# THE POLITICAL OFFICER

# CHAPTER 1

# Our Subject

ON 15 August 1947, the Indian Independence Act, passed hurriedly by the British Parliament, came into force. The former British Indian Empire came to an end; two new countries, India and Pakistan, achieved independence; and at least two epoch-making results ensued. First, the whole strategic set-up in Asia and the Middle East radically altered; second, a precedent was established for the voluntary abdication of rule by a metropolitan power that was to be followed elsewhere, often less willingly and less successfully, in the next few years. Great Britain has been as extravagantly praised for the manner of her departure from the Indian scene as she was extravagantly blamed for her retention of power earlier in this century; but it would be generally admitted, even by those who have not forgotten the massacres in northern India of 1947, that much credit is rightly given, all over the world, to those who secured so friendly a parting, which has led to such continued good relations between Britain and India and Britain and Pakistan.

Among the elements responsible for this good will, informed opinion pays a high tribute to the services established by the former British Government in India, and largely Indianized before independence. Those familiar with the difficulties encountered elsewhere in the world, particularly in Africa, have been loud in their praises of the good fortune of India and Pakistan in taking over their respective shares of these services, and of the good judgment of these countries in continuing, almost unchanged, their constitutional and administrative roles.

What, then, were these services ? Apart from the Indian Armed Forces, all were civil services. The best known was the Indian Civil Service, which administered British India (with the exception of the North-West Frontier Province), from its grass roots to its corridors of power. There were many others: the Indian Police, the Indian State Railways, the Indian Forest Service, to mention a few. Contrasted with the practice elsewhere, they all had two features in common. First, unlike the practice in the American hemisphere, their officers were very few in number, supported by a vast cadre of 'subordinates'–non-gazetted assistants and clerks: as in all armies, but by no means in all civil services, there was a

3

gulf in status between officers and men. Second, the proportion of European British members had been steadily dropping, slowly from before the turn of the century, rapidly from about 1920 onwards. Very broadly indeed, it might be said that by 1947 the average proportion of Europeans was 50 per cent, and that, save for a few in the Railways, all Europeans were 'officers'–European subordinates practically died out in the twentieth century. Contrast this with the vast mass of French subordinate employees in their North African territories where, right up to their independence, one would find French clerks behind the post-office counter and primary school teachers who were Frenchmen born and bred.

These services were taken over unchanged in their broad lines by India and Pakistan. But the service which is the subject of this book was not. It was wound up in August 1947, and was not, as a service, taken over by either successor State, though some of its officers were.

This book is exclusively concerned with the Indian Political Service,* formerly known as the Foreign and Political Department of the Government of India: its recruitment, composition and the nature of its work–which was, for the most part, indirect rule. What, then, was this peculiar service? An old tag has it that the Lord Privy Seal is so called because he is neither a lord, nor a privy, nor a seal. An unkind critic said that Indian Civil Servants were so called because they were neither Indian, nor civil, nor servants. This was unfair: but it would not be inaccurate to say that the Indian Political Service was neither Indian, nor Political, nor a Service. For reasons which will follow, this organization was not Indianized to anything like the extent that others were. In 1947, its sanctioned cadre stood at 170 officers, of whom there were only 124 actually serving, owing to the cessation of recruitment since the outbreak of World War II. Of these 124, only 17 were Indians: 12 Muslims, 4 Hindus and 1 Sikh.

Again, it was not 'Political' in the sense of having anything to do with party politics or with 'political activities' in the sense of espionage or anything of that kind. 'Political', as used in India, has always had a meaning of its own. Macaulay,† writing in 1841, in his essay on Warren Hastings,‡ says:

---

* *See* p. 54 on the origin of this term.

† 1st Lord Macaulay (1800–59). Politician and historian. Member of Supreme Council of India 1834–8. President of committee for composing a criminal code for India, 1835 (published, 1837; became law, 1860).

‡ Warren Hastings (1732–1818). Arrived India 1750. Resident at Murshidabad 1757–60. Governor of Bengal, 1772. Governor-General 1774–85. Impeached 1788–95, when acquitted.

The English functionaries at Fort William had as yet paid little or no attention to the internal government of Bengal. The only branch of politics about which they much busied themselves was negotiation with the native princes. . . . We may remark that the phraseology of the Company's servants still bears the traces of this state of things. *To this day they always use the word 'political' as synonymous with diplomatic.*

And 'service'? This is somewhat of a technicality, which will be further dealt with, for those readers interested in the organizational and constitutional aspect of the matter. More briefly, the Indian Political Service was a body of men, drawn 70 per cent from the Indian Army and 30 per cent from the Indian Civil Service (with, latterly, a few officers drawn from the Indian Police and Provincial Services) on indefinite secondment, which provided the quasi-diplomatic and consular representatives of the Government of India to Indian States and to certain posts in countries outside India. It also provided the administrators of the areas, now in Pakistan, known as the North-West Frontier Province and Baluchistan. Finally, it provided the officers for the secretariat at the headquarters of Government. This secretariat, under the direct charge of the Viceroy, controlled the activities of all these officers in the field.

For all practical purposes, the Indian Political Service functioned as a service, like those others mentioned above. Its title, size and composition varied through the years, but it will be our primary aim to show how it functioned and what its aims were in the twentieth century (the period immediately preceding its winding-up), adverting to the different conditions during the nineteenth century where necessary, without attempting a detailed study of the form and organization of the service in earlier periods.

Later chapters will deal with the work done by those members of the service posted to Indian States; with constitutional changes; with Baluchistan and the North-West Frontier Province and their problems; and with the work done in foreign countries, conspicuously Persia and the Persian Gulf, Afghanistan and Nepal.

At no time was any differentiation made between officers in these three sections. They were never formally constituted sub-cadres of the whole; there was never any distinction in the conditions of service; and officers were freely transferred from one area to another. It might happen that, of three officers recruited in the same year, with the same background, one officer would spend all, or almost all, his service on the North-West Frontier; one would spend it all or almost all in the States; while the third might look back, on retirement, to postings in all three of these areas. Some men happened to specialize, or to have specialization thrust upon them. Others did not; there was no fixed rule.

# CHAPTER 2

# Historical Synopsis

FROM the earliest times, the history of India has been one of a sub-continent divided into a number of smaller or larger Hindu principalities, rarely achieving anything like union, and periodically sustaining invasion by land from the north-west approaches. From A.D. 711, with the rise of Islam, those invaders were one and all Muslim; and a series of Muslim sultanates held sway for shorter or longer periods over the north-west portion of the sub-continent: usually over rather more than the area now comprised in Pakistan. Finally, the Mongols–in India, termed Moguls–seized power; a series of six powerful emperors governed that area in the north-west for two centuries, and exercised suzerainty over a number of Hindu princes, under a system of indirect rule analogous to the subject of this book, over a varying but often extensive area to the south and east.

At the beginning of the eighteenth century, with the death of Aurangzeb, the last of these six, the power of the Mogul emperors ceased. They became puppets, under Mahratta, Afghan or British control: though their dynasty was only finally liquidated in 1858, they had ceased to count long before.

But when the British first made contact with India, they were the dominant power. The date is 1600, when Queen Elizabeth I gave the East India Company its charter. This commercial organization controlled British affairs in India for just over 250 years, when it was superseded by the 'Government of India'–the usual colonial government, in structure, responsible to a Minister in London. But during that long period, the East India Company in fact ruled, though their rule developed slowly and their commercial activities long took precedence. A charter of Charles II of 1661, confirming the earlier one, gave the Company the power to make peace or war 'with any Prince not Christian'. Hence arose the Company's practice of making treaties of peace and defensive alliances, the first being anti-piracy treaties with the maritime States of Sawantwadi (1730) and Janjira (1733).

This treaty-making power was exercised by delegation by the Company's representatives in India till 1773, when Parliament curtailed it by

7

saying that, save in emergencies, approval must be obtained from London. Later there were further changes.

Directed at first by a President, later known as Governor, later again as Governor-General, the organization in India–a small Council of traders who eventually became civil servants–was based in Calcutta and controlled by the Court of Directors in London, who theoretically possessed unlimited power, save that the Board of Control might over-rule them. In fact, the 'Secret Committee' of the Board of Control (whose President was in the Cabinet) was all-powerful; and though, from 1858, both Governor-General and Secretary of State were assisted and re-stricted by Councils which had certain statutory powers, the tendency is constantly seen to recur of Governor-General and Secretary of State bypassing their respective Councils. More will be said of this later, when we discuss the private and personal correspondence between these authorities.

The British went to India to trade, not to conquer; and again and again expansionist policies in India were severely criticized or even forbidden by the home authorities. Many Governors-General genuinely tried to exercise a self-restraint which later events made it hard to apply. The Company was, at first, purely a trading organization not, indeed, confined to India: much of its revenue at one stage came from China. When, very gradually, some of its officials began to look up from their ledgers to the land around them and the problems of its rule, it was not as civil servants administering British 'districts'–there were few or none to administer. All around them were the 'country powers' as they were called, headed by the legitimate sovereign, the Mogul emperor, but increasingly con-sisting of upstart authorities who had broken away from his rule. It was as diplomatic representatives to these powers, not as direct administra-tors, that the Company's non-commercial officers served: thus there were 'politicals' before there were 'civil servants'. Though the service with which we deal was not constituted as such (still less under its latest title, the Indian Political Service) till much later, the activities of the earliest Company officers were political, in Macaulay's sense. Many of them were soldiers, and this military preponderance prevails throughout its history. The career of such a man as Warren Hastings was that of a diplomatist as well as of a ruler. Direct rule came slowly, round these nuclei: Madras (founded 1641), Bombay (founded 1665), Calcutta (founded 1690). The area round Bombay was, till long after, insignificant: that round Calcutta (transferred by the Emperor earlier but finally taken over in 1772) was the largest and most productive area. But apart from the criminal jurisdiction of Bengal, assumed in 1790, and customs' offices, the executive and judicial activities, as opposed to the commercial activities of the Company's staff, were long limited in extent.

Between, say, 1770 and 1813, when the Charter Act plainly claimed sovereignty for the Crown, the Company while continuing to trade became, largely owing to the need for self-protection from the French in south India, more and more a governmental body. Always the home authorities, and several Governors-General, tried to restrain the process of acquisition of territory, not from any fear of what now would be called colonialism but from a desire to save money. But during these years large tracts became what was later called British India: an area ruled directly by the Company on behalf of the Crown in full sovereignty; and other tracts became what were later called Indian States. In particular, Lord Mornington (1798–1805), later Lord Wellesley, and brother of the Duke of Wellington, who came out at the early age of thirty-seven as Governor-General, followed a forward policy. In brief, he turned territories which had been independent powers, allied to the British, into subsidiary States, under British suzerainty. These areas, some originally independent States, others off-shoots of older States or territories of successful rebels from the Mogul emperors, entered into relations with the Company which we shall examine later; for the present it suffices to say that, in this early period, the extension of Company control might take the form either of annexation or of treaty relationship. Later, this treaty relationship became one of paramountcy–again, a matter to be discussed fully later–but in this period, it was often not yet clear of many areas whether they were independent 'country powers', linked by treaty, or Indian States under the paramountcy of the Company.

In the 1814–15 settlement after the Napoleonic wars, France and Holland for the first time recognized British sovereignty over the Company's possessions. From about 1800, especially during the Governor-Generalship of Lord Moira (1813–23), created on his retirement Lord Hastings, the map was tidied up. With few exceptions, those States which were going to be swallowed up by their neighbours or by the British had, by the time of his departure, been so swallowed up; at all events, none – save a handful of powers on the external frontiers like Burma, Nepal, Sind or the Sikh State in the Punjab–remained whose status was not, from 1821 to 1947, what was known as a native, later an Indian, State. Between 1821–the key date when it becomes possible to draw the map of India with some certainty–and 1857, the date of the Mutiny, there was a period, when Lord Dalhousie was Governor-General, when a few States were absorbed for failure of heirs, in application of the notorious 'doctrine of lapse'. During this same period (1821–57), the punishment for gross misrule was annexation; later, there was a radical change, and for annexation of the State was substituted deposition of the individual ruler of the day and his replacement by another member, however distant, of the same family, This policy of annexation led to a certain diminution in the number of States. Annexations were in fact, few; but each caused terror to survivors.

In 1839, Ranjit Singh, who had created the Sikh State of the Punjab, died; and after a period of confusion, which included two hard-fought wars, the Punjab was annexed in 1849. Similarly, in 1843, Sind was finally conquered and annexed. In 1856 the King of Oudh, a large State whose future had long been a problem, was deposed and his State converted into a British Indian province. This, following the annexation of Poona (1818), Satara (1849), Nagpur (1853) and Jhansi (1853) concluded the tidying-up process – and was followed by the Mutiny. Between 1857 and 1947, there were practically no changes in the map of Indian States (the annexation and later excision of Burma being omitted), save the inclusion of Kalat and a few other frontier states and the artificial creation of Benares in 1911.

In 1857 occurred the Mutiny, the effects of which were profound psychologically but, from our point of view, important only in two ways. First, it led to the final transfer of the powers of the Company to the Crown (thus completing a process of greater control from London which had been going on for some time, at each decennial renewal of the Company's charter). Next, the almost universal loyalty of the States led to a fresh approach to them, marked by the grant of the Canning *Sanads*,* which gave expression to a determination to freeze the map of India and have done with the annexation of State territory for whatever cause.

The annexation of Sind and the Punjab had the most important effect, for our purposes, of moving back the north-west frontier of British India to a point which, save for the acquisition of Baluchistan and some minor modifications, it held until 1947. The move brought the Government of India face to face no longer with two settled States, but with a congeries of warlike and unorganized tribes and what has ever since been known as the Frontier Problem, which we shall discuss in due course. Its peculiar difficulty lay in the fact that, behind the tribes, was the enigmatic Afghan-

---

* These were unilateral documents issued after the Mutiny by Governor-General Canning to all the major rulers, guaranteeing the right of succession according to Hindu or Muslim law where direct heirs failed.

istan and behind her, again, the continually advancing and greatly suspect power of Russia.

After the Mutiny, relations with the States became more uniform. Broadly speaking, Government control over them was strengthened and standardized from 1857 to 1905, the date when Lord Curzon resigned the Governor-Generalship. This was followed by an immediate relaxation of control, announced in 1909 in Lord Minto's Udaipur speech; and shortly afterwards, from about 1920, began the transition period when all eyes were fixed on constitutional reform. In 1937, the penultimate constitutional change was made with the introduction of the Government of India Act, 1935, by which relations with the States were transferred from the Governor-General in Council to the Crown Representative (a post in fact held by the Governor-General), and the North-West Frontier Province, which had become a Governor's province in 1939, was like other Provinces granted full provincial autonomy.

# CHAPTER 3

## Indirect Rule

IN the last chapter, we outlined the steps by which the British achieved control, by the mid-nineteenth century, of practically the whole of the Indo-Pakistan sub-continent. By this date, there were two clearly defined areas: British India and Indian States (with which we here equate tribal territory on the north-west and north-east frontiers). The States covered approximately two-fifths of the area of India, and contained more than one-fifth of its total population. British India was divided into Provinces and governed (except for the North-West Frontier Province), by the Indian Civil Service, in a system of direct rule. Its autocratic powers were substantially and increasingly curtailed, from about 1920 onwards, by Indian ministers operating through democratic parliamentary institutions. The States, sometimes called Indian India, lay wholly outside the legislative powers whether of the various Indian legislatures or of the British Parliament.

What the States' special status was–whether they, or some of them, retained any measure of sovereignty or jurisdiction–was hotly contested in the nineteenth century; but by the end of that century a series of legislative enactments, judicial decisions and executive rulings, all analysed in the constitutional writings of Sir W. Lee-Warner,* and Sir Charles Lewis Tupper,† established the position clearly. The Simon Commission, in 1930, described the Indian States as 'without precedent or analogy elsewhere'. This is going rather far: the Malay States, the States in the former Netherlands East Indies, the constituent States (Baden, Bavaria, Saxony, Würtemberg etc.) in the German Empire between 1870 and 1919, all presented interesting analogies for comparison.

Yet another analogy is to be found in pre-British Indian history. Even so early as the days of the Mauryan empire, in the account of Megas-

* Sir W. Lee-Warner (1846–1914), G.C.S.I., Indian Civil Service, 1869, Bombay. Collector and Political Agent, Political Secretary to Bombay Government. Secretary, Political and Secret Department, India Office, 1895. Member, Council of India, 1902–12.

† Sir Charles Lewis Tupper (1848–1910), K.C.I.E., C.S.I. I.C.S., 1871, Punjab. Chief Secretary, Punjab, 1890. Financial Commissioner, 1899.

thenes, Seleucus' envoy to Patna, in the fourth century B.C., we find a number of subordinate rulers subject to the suzerainty of the emperor. In the eleventh–thirteenth centuries A.D., we find that the Turkish Sultans were adopting similar methods. Akbar, again, made full use of the remarkable willingness of most of the Rajput rulers to transfer their loyalty to the Mogul throne, and to serve their suzerain in military campaigns designed to crush the resistance of Muslim rulers, whom, unlike their Hindu fellows, he regarded as a permanent obstacle to Mogul rule.

But the crucial feature of the set-up in the Indian States and Tribal Territory was paramountcy. De Montmorency* in 1941, in a short but able work[1] defined the doctrine of Paramountcy thus:

> In very general terms it may be said to be the taking of action by the British authority for the common weal in a direction not specifically covered by treaty or engagement, and the formulation of policy by reading treaties as a whole and taking usage and sufferance also into consideration.

The author would define Paramountcy in another way as the power exercised by a suzerain State over an area which

a. that State's own laws and courts recognize as not amenable to its legislative authority;

b. foreign countries recognize as having no international status (such as, essentially, the power to make peace and war) and as being by them approachable only through the diplomatic channels of the suzerain State.

In India, the States, though they retained a measure of sovereignty and were permitted to exercise varying degrees of jurisdiction over their subjects (comparatively few were permitted to execute sentences of death without the concurrence of the British Resident), were all equally–though some tried to deny this–under the paramountcy of the British Government. That is to say, however much, for reasons of policy, that Government may have endeavoured to avoid interference, in the ultimate resort it could and did, even in the case of Hyderabad, the greatest of the Indian States, interfere to prevent misrule. When the Nizam of Hyderabad raised this issue, he received in 1926 a reply from Lord Reading, the

---

* Sir Geoffrey de Montmorency (1876–1955), G.C.I.E., K.C.S.I., K.C.V.O., C.B.E. I.C.S., Punjab, 1899–1933. Private Secretary to Viceroy, 1922–6. Governor of the Punjab, 1928–33.

Viceroy, acting on the authority of the British Cabinet, in which he wrote:

> The sovereignty of the British Crown is supreme in India, and therefore no Ruler of an Indian State can justifiably claim to negotiate with the British Government on an equal footing.

This was followed by a series of measures, in the shape of 'authoritative advice', little known at the time or even later to most of the outside world, by which the Nizam's autocratic rule was radically curtailed.

This example, the most extreme available, is mentioned to show that, if challenged, the British Government acted, in Indian States, by no mere reference to treaties or usage but by the strength of its right arm. The same was even more crudely the case in Tribal Territory. On the North-West Frontier, whether the British Government could induce a tribe to, for example, restore prisoners carried off from British India in raids, ultimately depended on what force the Government had available and were prepared to use. *Vis-à-vis* foreign powers, an area such as Waziristan was under British control. A Wazir tribesman going to a foreign country could obtain a passport describing him as a 'British protected person'. At the same time, his country was often described, to the distress of the legal pundits but with much relation to the facts of life, as 'independent territory'. At all events, there was no settled rule in Waziristan, either by the British or by a tribal leader, since there were no real leaders, but anarchy.

If, then, there was no outside rule in such areas, how were relations between the British and the tribesmen regulated? The answer is, by Indirect Rule, the operation of which, in its various forms, is the subject of this book. Between the two extremes – the well-recognized day-to-day advice and correspondence, through the Political Agent as a channel of communication, between Government and an Indian State, and the far more hazardous relations between the Wazirs or Mahsuds and their Political Agent – there is a long road. But the principle is one. Indirect rule does not, in law, give orders; it gives advice. In one area, things may be so well regulated and so long established that the distinction is unimportant, the advice being automatically accepted. In others, as was sometimes the case in the larger States and often the case in the more turbulent tribes, the advice-pill had to be gilded: in a State, by courteous but persistent argument; in a tribal area, gilded with pleasant financial inducements, or forced down with a military operation.

Indirect rule is a system of Government so wide and varying in its application even to India that to compare in detail its operation elsewhere would be far beyond the scope of this work. There is matter for a number of books on its operation in the British Colonies in East and West Africa, in Malaya and the Netherlands East Indies, in French North Africa and lastly in Burma, where conditions similar to those obtaining in India were handled through a different agency.

When, in 1928, a major attempt was made by those rulers who constituted the dominant party in the Chamber of Princes to obtain, from the Butler Committee, a definition of Paramountcy in accordance with their claims to semi-independence, based on treaty rights, they were met with the monumental snub: 'Paramountcy must remain paramount.' Indeed, it was best to face facts; and this was done so early as 1894 by Lee-Warner. He wrote:[2]

> What is a Native State? That is a question to which some answer must be supplied at the very threshold of an inquiry into rights and duties annexed to that status of writing or usage. A Native State is a political community, occupying a territory in India of defined boundaries, and subject to a common and responsible ruler, who has, as a matter of fact, enjoyed and exercised, with the sanction of the British Government, any of the functions and attributes of internal sovereignty. The indivisibility of sovereignty, on which Austin insists, does not belong to the Indian system of sovereign states.

So much emphasis was laid, over about a century, on courtesy and the preservation of diplomatic forms that it was often overlooked that the mailed fist still lay within the velvet glove; that if, after 1857, annexation even in the gravest cases of misrule ceased and was replaced by deposition, this was in pursuit of a particular policy, not by constraint of doctrine. It was not till after the removal of British paramountcy, in 1947, that the stark facts of life became apparent to the States. Once policy changed because of a change of rulers, and it was no longer desired to retain a system of indirect rule, the successor Government of India created its own paramountcy and swallowed up the States with the merest form of agreement by consent. Tacitus's *Oderint dum metuant* was not confined to the Roman Empire.

But if we have emphasized the theoretical all-powerfulness of paramountcy, that is not to say that the practical application of indirect rule was harsh or crude. On the contrary, episode after episode in the history of our service shows the velvet glove most in evidence. From the earliest days, the precepts of the controlling body in London, the policy of the

Governor-General, with rare exceptions such as Lord Wellesley, and the day-to-day practice of the Residents and Political Agents on the spot, converged on one point: the importance of avoiding friction coming to a head: the desirability of avoiding a row and settling disputes by quiet diplomacy. Again and again this doctrine was preached, and was applied; and because much of this diplomatic activity was done in secrecy, to save the faces of the Rulers concerned, the occasional unavoidable intervention for gross misrule attracted more attention than was reasonable.

Indirect rule varied so much in its application in our three disparate areas that it can best be studied in its separate operation when we examine each area: the States, the Frontier and foreign posts. But there are certain common features which must be mentioned before we move on to an examination of how the service was organized and functioned, since it is indirect rule and the theories underlying it which inspired the service.

All through the history of the British in India the claim has been made –not by all, but by an important group of statesmen and historians–that much was lost where State territories were annexed and made into British Indian provinces. Henry Lawrence believed that the people were happier under their own rulers than under the Company. What may be called the Henry Lawrence as opposed to the John Lawrence strategy has always claimed adherents. They would say that the British Indian method was harsh, rigid, and did not till it was too late allow adequate scope for Indian talents. That in the search for the efficiency ensured by large units it forgot that, in Fisher's* words, most that is remarkable in the history of culture has been produced by small States. That, in terms of Frontier policy, only those areas, notably Baluchistan and the Malakand, where rule was indirect, i.e. through natural tribal leaders, were ruled peacefully and cheaply; and–though this is hotly disputed–that the Sandeman† system which is, after all, the local application of indirect rule, could have been extended to areas such as Waziristan had they been caught early enough.

So late as 1910, Butler,‡ who as Foreign Secretary from 1907–10 became head of the service direct from the Indian Civil Service in British

* The Rt. Hon. H. A. L. Fisher (1865–1940), O.M. Historian and politician. President of the Board of Education, 1916–22. Warden of New College, Oxford, 1925–40.

† Lt.-Col. Sir Robert Sandeman (1835–92), K.C.S.I. Punjab Commission, military political. Deputy Commissioner, Dera Ghazi Khan, 1866. Agent to the Governor-General in Baluchistan, 1877–92. Created Baluchistan.

‡ Sir Harcourt Butler (1869–1938), G.C.S.I., G.C.I.E.; I.C.S., U.P., 1890–1929. Foreign Secretary, 1907–10. Lt.-Gov. of Burma, 1915–17. Lt.-Gov. and Governor of U.P., 1918–23. Governor of Burma, 1923–7.

India, without any previous political experience, wrote in his 'private and secret' handing-over note to his successor:

> It has been one of my desires to see junior civilians sent from provinces for a short course of training in selected Native States under selected political officers. And I think that the experiment might be tried now. This would help in time to lessen the gulf between British India and Native States and would broaden the outlook of the younger generation of Indian civilians.
>
> And we have much to learn from Native States. The indigenous system of Government is a loose despotic system tempered by corruption, which does not press hard on the daily lives of the people and relies for its sanctions on occasional severe punishments of erring or offending individuals. Our system is a scientific system which presses steadily on the people in their daily lives, controls them, regulates their actions, attempts to be preventive and through its hordes of subordinates makes itself everywhere felt. The advancing Native States generally adopt our methods, because it is easy to get good men trained in our school and difficult to get good men of their own school with modern training. Imitation is abroad. Our system of education has officialised the people. But he would be a bold man who said that our system was always the better. And my own belief is that we shall see some reaction of ideas. A system which would maintain the simpler executive form of Government and adopt independent judicial courts would suit most States very well.

Another argument in favour of indirect rule much urged in the pre-Mutiny period was what we may call the object-lesson argument. Crudely expressed, it claimed that princely rule was so bad that it was necessary to preserve specimens of it to show the rest of India how lucky they were to be under British rule. Sleeman, a great political officer, writing to Lord Dalhousie in 1848, a decade before the Mutiny, urged:

> While we have a large portion of the country under native rulers, their administration will contrast with ours greatly to our advantage in the estimation of the people; and we may be sure that, though some may be against us, many will be for us. If we succeed in sweeping them all away, or absorbing them, we shall be at the mercy of our native army, and they will see it; and accidents may possibly occur to unite them, or a great proportion of them, in some desperate act ... the best provision against it seems to me to be the maintenance of

native rulers, whose confidence and affection can be engaged, and administrations improved under judicious management.

Yet another argument was that, based on the loyal reaction of most of the princes during the Mutiny of 1857, which regarded the States as bulwarks against possible future risings. This theory persisted, in terms of constitutional development rather than risings, into the twentieth century, and inspired the feeling that the proposed federation of the conservative States and the Muslim bloc with the Congress-dominated provinces of British India would achieve a synthesis which would solve the problem of the protection of minorities under Indian self-rule.

What chance this had of achievement will be examined in our later discussion of federation. We now turn to the organization of the Indian Political Service.

CHAPTER 4

# The Organization of the Service

FROM about 1820, when the political situation in India was more or less stabilized, until 1947, when the sub-continent was partitioned, the Indian Political Service functioned in broadly the same fashion but in very varying areas. If we take two lists of posts filled by our officers, one of 1820 and one of 1947, we shall find that, with the exception of Hyderabad, Mysore, and some posts in Rajputana and Central India, practically none of those existing in 1820 persisted in 1947, while at the latter date numerous posts unheard of before find place in our cadre. And yet the political map had hardly changed, except for the acquisition of the North-West Frontier Province and Baluchistan. How is this explained?

In the first place, the progress made in the standard of administration in the States and the improvement in communications made several of the earlier posts, e.g. in Rajputana and Central India, unnecessary. Second, and more important, the earlier practice of exercising political control over States through Provincial Governments, ceased, on the recommendation of the Montagu-Chelmsford report, in the 1920s and 1930s, and numerous provincially-controlled areas, such as the Punjab States, the Bombay States and the Eastern States, were transferred to the control of the service in the last few years of British rule.

Lastly, the posts outside India varied greatly according to world political developments. At one time, there were Political Agencies, staffed from India, in Canton, Mauritius, Penang, Sumatra, Baghdad and Basra. An important post was 'the Political Resident in Turkish Arabia' at Baghdad–a title to which the Young Turks much objected;[3] and at one time eastern Persia was an area of great significance to the service. On the other hand, the posts, existing in 1947, of Agents-General for India, each with a First Secretary and Third Secretary, in China and the U.S.A. were, like the Mission to Lhasa and consulates at Goa and Pondicherry, recent developments; while Aden, for long controlled by a Resident under the Bombay Government, became for a time a Chief Commissionership under the Government of India, to change subsequently to a Governorship

19

under the Colonial Office and, yet later, to a High Commissionership.

The whole elaborate organization in the North-West Frontier Province was part of the Punjab until Curzon's reorganization at the turn of the century; and Baluchistan was foreign, or at least wholly unadministered territory until 1854, when a loose suzerainty was assumed over Kalat by the Bombay Government. Later, Sandeman's moves in the sixties brought under the Political Service this huge if largely desert area, divided into six Political Agencies presided over by an Agent to the Governor-General.

Working back from 1947 is like tracing up from its mouth a large river which, every few miles, is joined by tributaries and grows smaller and smaller. Without delving into minute differences of status or nomenclature, we may state the position immediately before Partition in 1947 as follows.

There were, broadly, three classes of officers:

a. First-class Residents, paid Rs. 4,000 per mensem, and given the title of 'The Honourable'.

b. Second-class Residents, paid Rs. 3,000 per mensem. (The rupee was worth 1/6d., so that pay at so many rupees per mensem = £ per annum less 10 per cent.)

c. Time-scale officers, whose pay rose by annual increments from Rs. 500 to Rs. 2,250 per mensem, and who, if European, also drew a small sum known as 'overseas pay'.

These were divided into superior and inferior posts. Civil and military officers from 1925 onwards drew the same salary–the same as the Indian Civil Service; but whereas the former drew a fixed pension of £1,000 per annum, whatever the last post they held, military officers' pensions were rather lower unless they had held the post of first-class Resident for some years. Secretarial posts and some others carried small allowances. The External Affairs Department, still usually known as the Foreign Office, and the Political Department were the headquarters' organizations at Delhi in winter, at Simla in summer, for the two main branches of the service, the former controlling both Frontier and Foreign cadres. Total numbers varied between 100 and 150; allowing for leave and deputation, there were seldom more than 100 officers on duty even after the expansion which took place in this century. Until 1914, the headquarters' staff consisted of the Foreign Secretary, Deputy Secretary, Under Secretary and Assistant Secretary. A Political Secretary (in charge of the States) was added in 1914, a second Deputy Secretary after World War I. When federal negotiations greatly increased work in the 1930s, some temporary posts were created; and lastly the post of Political Adviser to the Crown Representative came with the new constitution in 1937. This staff was astonishingly small.

CHAPTER 5

# The Tributaries

WORKING back from the 'river's mouth' of 1947, we shall examine in inverse chronological order the various new posts brought on to the cadre of the service, and the reason for the addition.

## (1) AGENCIES GENERAL, CHINA AND U.S.A.

During World War II, the Government of India felt that the time had come to bring India into diplomatic touch with certain foreign powers of peculiar importance to her. The diplomatic formula previously adopted for Canada and Australia, when they began to set up diplomatic services, was to attach a 'Canadian Counsellor' or 'Australian Counsellor' to the British Embassy in question. For purposes of protocol, he was on the British Ambassador's staff; in practice he handled his own country's affairs largely independently. The same practice was, broadly, followed by India; but India's representation was at a higher level, that of Agent-General, ranking as a Minister. His staff was drawn partly from the Indian Political Service.

## (2) PONDICHERRY AND GOA

There had long been consular officers in these two posts, controlled respectively by the Governments of Madras and Bombay; but it was only in 1936, as war approached, that the necessity was felt of placing them in relations with the Government of India. In that year, the post of H.B.M.'s Consul-General in the French establishments in India was created, and in November 1939 he was given jurisdiction also in the Portuguese possessions in India. Later this post was split, and a separate Consul appointed to Goa. These posts were normally held by officers of the Indian Political Service, though the first occupant of the Pondicherry post was a retired army officer. Their creation seems to have been largely due to the needs of wartime security, though smuggling had long been a problem on the Pondicherry border.

## (3) EASTERN STATES AGENCY

The Montagu–Chelmsford report recommended the abolition of the method by which many States were in political relations not with the

Government of India through a Resident (or an Agent to the Governor-General acting through Political Agents) but with a Provincial Government. This method, the last trace of which was abolished by the creation of the Eastern States Agency, is described by de Montmorency[4] as follows:

A third method of agency, however, was in operation where states lay within the geographical orbit of a Province in British India; and in that case the relations of the States with the Government of India were conducted through the agency of the Provincial Government concerned. This method was employed in the case of a large number of States geographically included in the boundaries of Madras, Bombay, the Punjab, Bengal, the United Provinces and the Central Provinces. This system was no doubt based on its apparent convenience and displayed some economies in cost as compared with the two former.

i.e. the system of relations with Residents or Agents to the Governor-General.

The change was inevitable, for constitutional reasons. What has not always been noticed is whether the Political Department, handicapped, as we shall see later, by the policy decision conveyed in Lord Minto's Udaipur speech of 1909, was not slacker in its control than the Provincial Governments had been. Keyes\* comments, in an unpublished note on the States, that when the Government of India, in 1909, adopted a policy of less intervention in States' affairs, the Bombay Government did not follow their lead. As a result, in his view—and he was very far from being an interventionist in Hyderabad—the States formerly in relations with the Government of Bombay were the best administered in India. It is an interesting point, which will no doubt be studied by historians in due course, how far transfer from provincial control led to deterioration in administration. The fact, often overlooked, that States' administration was steadily improving during all this century probably compensated for such deterioration as might otherwise have ensued.

The States comprised in the Eastern States Agency, set up in 1933, were a group of forty mostly quite small States, only three of which

---

\* Brig.-Gen. Sir Terence Keyes (1877–1939), K.C.I.E., C.S.I., C.M.G. Military political. Served in Persia; Russia, 1917–20; Baluchistan, 1921–8; Nepal, Gwalior, Western India, 1928–9; Hyderabad, 1930–3.

enjoyed a salute,* and the isolated States of Tripura and Cooch Behar, formerly in relations with the Government of Bengal (added in 1936). These forty States comprised two groups: those (except Makrai, transferred to the Bhopal Agency) formerly in relations with the Government of the Central Provinces, with a Political Agent at Raipur; and those formerly in relations with the Government of Bihar and Orissa, with a Political Agent at Sambalpur. The Agency, set up after an exhaustive enquiry by Lothian,† was a good deal played about with. It was the object of an unsuccessful experiment (soon dropped) by which the Political Agent at Sambalpur acted also as Secretary to the Agent to the Governor-General for his own States. Its headquarters, first at Ranchi, were eventually admirably housed in a historic house at Alipur, a suburb of Calcutta, once occupied by Warren Hastings, whose ghost was said to haunt it. (The wife of one of the Residents claimed to have seen it and had it exorcised.)

The status of the States in this Agency was the matter of much dispute in the 1880s. Doubt existed whether some of them were in British India or were States, and this fell to be determined in 1881–2 by the Calcutta High Court in regard to one of the largest of these States, that of Mayurbhanj. A divisional bench of the Court held that Mayurbhanj formed part of British India specially exempted from the ordinary law. On reference, however, to a full bench of five judges, the Court decided in 1882, by three judges to two, that Mayurbhanj was not in British India. The Government of India recommended to the Secretary of State in 1888 that a similar decision should formally be given as regards all the States in this Agency; he agreed, and *sanads* were distributed to them. An Act was passed to repeal Regulations wrongly applied to them and to condone past irregularities. Until their transfer, however, to the Government of India in 1933, they were ridden by the Provincial Governments concerned on a very tight reign; most Rulers' powers were far more curtailed than was the case in other States, partly because of the large proportion of aboriginals in these States.

## (4) DECCAN STATES AGENCY AND KOLHAPUR RESIDENCY

This consisted of the large State of Kolhapur, which had always had a Resident (though, until 1933, he was subordinate to the Government of

---

* See p. 72.

† Sir Arthur Lothian (1887–1962), K.C.I.E., C.S.I.; I.C.S., Bengal, 1911; political. Entire political service in States. Special representative of Viceroy in federal discussions, 1935–7. Resident, Rajputana, 1937–42; Hyderabad, 1942–6. Author, *Kingdoms of yesterday*.

Bombay), and of 16 small States, 4 only of which were Salute States. These, from which Janjira was so recently as in 1946 withdrawn and transferred to the Gujarat States Agency, had until 1932 been in political relations with the Government of Bombay, exercised in seven cases through the Collectors of neighbouring districts, while eight, known as the Southern Mahratta Country States, had as their Political Agent the Resident at Kolhapur. The Government of Bombay until 1924 had its own quite large Political Department, staffed by about twenty-eight officers drawn almost entirely from the Indian Army, who were responsible for relations with Kolhapur, and some Deccan States: Cutch, Kathiawar and Aden. Other States in the Deccan, as some in Gujarat, were in relations with Collectors of neighbouring districts, who were of course in turn subordinate to the Government of Bombay.

Thus the Political Service had no relations at all with this extensive area between the abolition of the Peshwaship in 1819 and 1933. The same will be seen to be the case with Kathiawar and Cutch, and (with the exception of Baroda) with the area comprised in the eastern part of the charge of the 'Resident at Baroda and for the States of Western India and Gujarat', to give him the title by which he was known in 1947.

## (5) ADEN

Aden, from its capture in 1839 until 1932, was under the Bombay Government. In 1932, the Settlement of Aden was transferred from Bombay to the Government of India and made a Chief Commissioner's Province, and the Resident became the Chief Commissioner and Commander-in-Chief so far as the Settlement was concerned. At this time, officers of the Bombay Political Department were replaced by the Indian Political Service. In 1937, the Chief Commissioner's Province of Aden was transferred from the Government of India to the control of the Colonial Office, and became a Crown Colony under a Governor and Commander-in-Chief, and yet later, a High Commissionership.

## (6) WESTERN INDIA STATES AGENCY

Originally, the whole area covered by the geographical terms Cutch, Kathiawar, Baroda and Gujarat (with a British Indian enclave consisting of the Northern Division, Bombay) was in political relations with the Government of Bombay—with one exception: the large and advanced Mahratta State of Baroda, which early broke away from the Mahratta Confederacy and settled down to the status of an Indian State. From before 1830 and up to 1854, Baroda had a Resident drawn from the Bombay cadre and in political relations with the Government of Bombay. Baroda several times changed its relationship; by 1908 a Resident had replaced the A.G.G., as the Agent to the Governor-General was known. In 1933, the States in the northern part of Bombay Presidency were transferred to this officer who, till 1937, was known as the 'A.G.G., Gujarat States, and Resident at Baroda'.

The peninsula of Kathiawar consisted of a large number of States, some so small that they were known as 'Estates' and did not exercise any criminal or civil jurisdiction. This was exercised on their behalf by officials called Deputy Political Agents with magisterial powers, similar in status to the Extra Assistant Commissioners of the North-West Frontier Province and Baluchistan. Beneath them again were officers called *thanadars* who were not, as in British India, policemen but revenue and magisterial officers of status comparable to that of *tahsildars* in British India.

In 1902 the title of the political officer was changed from 'Political Agent' to 'Agent to the Governor' (of Bombay); this in its turn, in 1924 when the Government of India took over from the Government of Bombay, was changed to 'Agent to the Governor-General'. This term remained in force until 1937 when, as explained later, all Agents to the Governor-General in States became Residents.

Between 1924 and 1944, the set-up in Western India was as follows.[5] A first-class Resident was stationed at Rajkot, and was in direct relations with the 17 Salute States and one non-Salute State. The three Political Agents – for Western Kathiawar, Eastern Kathiawar and Sabar Kantha – were in relations with those of the above large States which geographically adjoined their Agencies for only a few routine purposes such as boundary disputes, passports, extradition, marriages and trials of European British subjects, etc. These Political Agents, whose headquarters were respectively at Rajkot, Wadhwan and Sadra, were also in full relations with a number of non-Salute States (46, 15 and 32 respectively), which enjoyed limited jurisdiction, and a huge number of non-jurisdictional Estates grouped in *thanas*, as explained above. An estate owned jointly by two shareholders with a total annual income of Rs. 3,000 and a population of 174 was by no means exceptional; and it was above all this area, with its ridiculously fragmented map, that was responsible for the size of the officially approved total figure (562) of Indian States. Indeed, almost any figure could be produced with good arguments for it: it depends on how many shareholders are included.

In 1944, a radical reorganization of this political charge and its neighbour Baroda and the Gujarat States) took place. The second-class Residency of Baroda, carved out of Bombay in 1933 (before which most of the states had Bombay Collectors as their Political Agents), was abolished and merged in that of Western India, with dual headquarters at Baroda and at Rajkot. The Sabar Kantha Agency was abolished, and all the salute States formerly in the charge of the Resident for Baroda (with the exception of Baroda itself, which the Resident retained) were transferred to a new Agency, that of the Political Agent, Gujarat States, with headquarters at Bulsar, in Surat district. To him were also transferred the non-salute States for which the Secretary to the Resident for Baroda had been responsible. There were 11 Salute States, 16 semi-jurisdictional States, and 54 non-jurisdictional Estates (further subdivided, however, into 98 shareholders). The majority of these were 'attached' to Baroda.

At the same time, all Salute States formerly in relations with the Rajkot Resident were placed in relations with the Political Agents, W. and E. Kathiawar, with the exception of Cutch, which the Resident retained, and Idar which was transferred to Rajputana.

This rearrangement was carried out largely in the interests of a scheme, known as the Attachment scheme, to be discussed later, which made it logical to include this sprawling but linguistically homogeneous area in one Residency. It lasted, however, less than three years and there were only two Political Agents in the whole history of the Gujarat States Agency which, with all the rest, ceased to be in 1947.*

## (7) GWALIOR RESIDENCY

Gwalior had long had a Resident of its own, though one subordinate to the Agent to the Governor-General in Central India. In the changes introduced in the 1920s (based on the desire of the larger States for 'direct relations' and for as few links as possible in the chain leading to the Viceroy), the Gwalior Residency was cut off from Central India and became an independent charge. In pursuance of the requirements of the Government of India Act, 1935, the States of Rampur and Benares, formerly in political relations with the Government of the United Provinces, were transferred to the charge of the Resident at Gwalior in spite of the strong objection of Hailey,† Governor of the United Provinces. In

* This 1944 reorganization is wholly overlooked by V. P. Menon in Appendix 1 of his usually most accurate book, *The Story of the Integration of the Indian States.*

† Lord Hailey (1872–1969), O.M., G.C.S.I., G.C.M.G., G.C.I.E.; I.C.S., Punjab, 1895. Finance Member, S. of I., 1919. Governor of Punjab, 1924–8; of U.P., 1928–30 and 1931–4. Author of *An African Survey* and other works on Africa.

1936, the former United Provinces State of Tehri-Garhwal was transferred to the Punjab States Agency, through the Political Agent, Simla Hill States. Benares, incidentally, was unique in having been created so recently as 1911, from territory formerly part of British India.

## (8) PUNJAB STATES AGENCY

These States were brought under the Indian Political Service in 1927. They had previously, with two exceptions, been in relations with the Punjab Government, through Commissioners, in the case of the larger States, and Deputy Commissioners, in the case of the smaller. The exceptions were Tehri-Garhwal (see (7) above), and Khairpur, an enclave in Sind which, until the 1935 Act required a change to be made, was in relations with the Bombay Government through the Collector of Sukhur and the Commissioner in Sind. The Agency consisted of 17 Salute States; 3 smaller States formerly in relations with the Commissioner, Ambala; and 18 States, some very small and primitive, in the Simla Hills. These last were, until 1937, in relations with the Deputy Commissioner, Simla, who had an Indian Civil Service Assistant specially attached to him for this purpose. He originally reported to the Commissioner, Delhi, but after Delhi was cut off from the Punjab was placed under the Commissioner, Ambala.

## (9) MADRAS STATES AGENCY

This Agency in 1947 contained the two important States of Travancore and Cochin, and the much smaller ones of Banganapalle, Pudukottai and Sandur. All these were previously in political relations with the Government of Madras, through Collectors (Kurnool for Banganapalle, Trichinopoly for Pudukottai, Bellary for Sandur), and one Resident for the two important maritime States. The Government of India had many occasions to interfere and, particularly in early times, the officers posted as Residents may be deemed to have been 'politicals', having come from cadres other than the Madras Government's. But it was only in 1923 that the Agency was constituted and the Madras Government's superintendence ceased.

## (10) BURMA STATES

Burma constitutes an exception to the rule we have noted that more and more States flowed in as tributaries to the political river as 1947 approached. The province of Burma was in 1937 cut off from India by the Government of India Act, 1935, and such areas as constituted States in

Burma ceased to be the concern of the Governor-General in Council. Our Service was never concerned with them.

## (ii) KABUL LEGATION

Although technically, like Washington and Chungking, this post was not on the cadre of the service, from its creation in 1922 until 1947 it was, by convention, almost invariably staffed by officers seconded from the I.P.S. A Minister, a Counsellor and a First Secretary were the normal complement, and they were almost always drawn from officers with long experience of the North-West Frontier Province. Before 1919, the British Government by treaty controlled the foreign relations of the Afghan Government. The two disastrous and unnecessary Afghan wars in 1839 and 1878 had left the Afghan rulers and people united on one thing: detestation of the sight of an Englishman; and the Government of India, taught perhaps by the massacre of their envoy, Cavagnari,* and his staff in 1878, did not till 1922 resume the posting of British officers to Kabul.

Not that they were not urged to do so. Salisbury,† when Secretary of State for India–and a great one–seems to have felt very strongly on this subject. In his private correspondence with Northbrook, the Viceroy, in 1874, he constantly reverts to the lack of adequate intelligence from Herat and Kabul. Spend more on agents there, he urges in June, 1874. Later, he positively directs the Viceroy to send an agent to Herat, if the Amir agrees. He keeps pressing the necessity of a 'resident Englishman' in Afghanistan since, though he doubts the likelihood of a Russian invasion, he thinks Russia may well push the Afghans on. Every other country, he points out, allows it as a right to have an envoy: why should Afghanistan refuse? It appears that the Amir was wise, and that in the nineteenth century it would have been hard to guarantee his life. Burning of embassies is not exclusively a post-World War II habit; in 1874, Salisbury wrote to the Viceroy about Chinese Turkestan:

> We are a little troubled at Mr. Shaw‡ calling himself envoy and plenipotentiary. Our apprehension is that if, as is not impossible, he

* Sir Pierre Louis Napoleon Cavagnari (1841–78), K.C.B., C.S.I. Naturalized, 1857. Lieutenant, Indian Army, 1860. Punjab Commission, 1861. D.C., Kohat, 1866–77.

† 3rd Marquess of Salisbury (1830–1903). Secretary of State for India, nine months in 1866, and 1874–8. Secretary of State for Foreign Affairs, 1878–80. Prime Minister, 1885–1902, with intervals in opposition.

‡ R. B. Shaw (1839–79). A remarkable career. Ill-health preventing his joining the army, he arrived in India in 1859 and became a tea planter in Kangra. In 1868–1869, he went as a merchant to Yarkand and Kashgar–the first Englishman to do

gets his throat cut by the Chinese, we shall have to avenge him as the Queen's representative which might be difficult not to say impossible.

Next month,

> Sir G. Clark frightened us with a description of the unmentionable fate which awaits the Envoy, if he should fall into the hands of the Chinese.

It was not till after the 3rd Afghan War, when Afghanistan secured control of her foreign relations, that a legation was established in Kabul and, reciprocally, as the Amir Abdul Rahman had wished, in London.

### (12) THE NORTH-WEST FRONTIER PROVINCE

Curzon's action in creating this province, in 1901–the year, incidentally, of Amir Abdul Rahman's death–had important effects on the Indian Political Service. With the exception of the Malakand agency which, surprisingly, from its creation had been in direct relations with the Government of India, the whole area comprised in what was in 1947 the North-West Frontier Province had, before 1901, been the responsibility of the Government of the Punjab. The Punjab was an integral part of British India. With the exception of the Isa Khel *tahsil* of Mianwali and of the Baluch district of Dera Ghazi Khan and a few villages in the Dera Ismail Khan district, transferred to Dera Ghazi Khan to prevent any Baluchis being left behind in the new province, the whole trans-Indus territory, British Indian and tribal territory alike, was in 1901 cut off from the Punjab, as was the non-Pashtu speaking cis-Indus district of Hazara (which, incidentally, provided a hill-station) and made into a Chief Commissioner's province. This involved a large addition to the cadre, expanded *ad hoc* mostly by the recruitment of Punjab Commission officers (mainly civilians, some Army officers) already serving trans-Indus.

The change had been under consideration for many years. In 1877, Salisbury thought that there should be a Chief Commissioner in charge

---

so. He made friends with the 'Amir' Yakub Beg who, on his advice, sent to ask for an envoy to arrange a treaty. Shaw returned by the Karakoram pass and volunteered to accompany Forsyth, the envoy in question. (Sir Thomas Forsyth (1827–1886), K.C.S.I., C.B.; I.C.S. Punjab, 1849. Visited St. Petersburg, 1869; Yarkand 1870 and Kashgar, 1875. Envoy to Burma, 1873.) Shaw was appointed to the Political Service, as British Joint Commissioner in Ladakh. In 1875 he returned to Yarkand in charge of the ratified copy of the treaty made by Forsyth in 1874. 1878, Resident, Mandalay.

of Tribal Territory, the Punjab keeping the plains–the worst possible compromise. Earlier, Northbrook considered several schemes. One was for a new province stretching from the Himalayas to Karachi, to include Baluchistan and Sind, for the loss of which Bombay was to be 'compensated' by the addition of the whole or at least the Mahratti-speaking districts of the Central Provinces. Another scheme was to take Sind, create an Agent to the Governor-General for Baroda and Gujarat, and reduce Bombay to a Lieut.-Governorship. In his next letter, to Salisbury, Northbrook thinks that there will never be peace (between the Governments of Bombay and the Punjab) till Sind is taken from Bombay and transferred to the Punjab. Other Viceroys toyed with similar schemes. A unified North-West Frontier–Baluchistan might have had much to be said for it, but the inclusion of Sind seems to have been rightly regarded from an early date, as impracticable.

It has been said of Curzon that everything he did was right but was done in the wrong way. Certainly the partition of the Punjab was carried out with little tact, the Lieut.-Governor of the Punjab being by-passed in the negotiations with scant courtesy. But what concerns us here is the effect on the cadre. The time had perhaps come for a radical reconsideration of the composition of the service. In fact, that did not escape Curzon's eagle eye, as we shall see later, where several schemes for altering the recruitment system will be discussed.

## (13) KASHMIR RESIDENCY

The history of Kashmir has been so much in the limelight since Partition that it may be a matter of some surprise to the reader to know that this Agency too, well-established under a second-class Resident in 1947 (with a Political Agent in Gilgit in loose subordination to him, though reporting direct to the External Affairs Department), was not always under the Political Department. In 1848, the Governor-General wrote to the Maharaja, suggesting the posting of a Resident to Kashmir. The Maharaja claimed that an oral promise had been given him that no Resident would be appointed. In 1851, the proposal was revived, but until 1885 only a part-time man, under the Punjab Government, was sent each summer to keep control over European visitors.[6] In 1873 India pressed strongly for the appointment of a Resident, but the Secretary of State declined to overrule the Maharaja, merely extending to eight months the periods of the Officer on Special Duty's stay. In 1884, St. John,* then

---

* Lt.-Col. Sir Oliver St. John (1837–91), K.C.S.I. Military political; Agent to the Governor-General in Baluchistan and Resident at Mysore.

Officer on Special Duty, reported that the Maharaja was near to death and the heir-apparent unfit to govern. The Government of India therefore asked the Secretary of State once more for authority to appoint a Resident. In reply, he wrote:[7]

> As to the urgent need of reforms in the administration of the State there is unfortunately no room for doubt. It may, indeed, be a question whether, having regard to the circumstances under which the sovereignty of the country was entrusted to the present Hindu ruling family, the intervention of the British Government on behalf of the Muhammadan population has not already been too long delayed; but, however this may be, Her Majesty's Government are satisfied that, upon a fresh succession, no time should be lost in taking whatever steps may be requisite in order to place the administration upon a sound footing. The same occasion would, in the opinion of Her Majesty's Government, be a suitable one for introducing a change in the present arrangement, under which Your Excellency's representative remains in Kashmir for a portion only of the year . . .

Accordingly, on the death of Maharaja Ranbir Singh, a Resident was appointed; and Maharaja Partab Singh, who succeeded to the Chieftainship, was informed, in reply to the protests which he promptly submitted, that 'the change had been made in compliance with the wishes of Her Majesty's Government and could not be the subject of further discussion.'

So a Resident was appointed, in 1884, and Kashmir was thereafter in direct relations with the Government of India.

## (14) THE REST

So what remained? The Assam States, Baluchistan, Bhutan, Central India, Hyderabad, Mysore, Rajputana, Sikkim and Nepal. No organizational change occurred in the Hyderabad or Mysore Residencies during their long history; none in Baluchistan in its short history (save, in 1937, the small change in nomenclature mentioned above). Rajputana and Central India originally had more subordinate Political Agencies; even that in Haraoti and Tonk had remained in abeyance for years before 1947. Right up to 1940, the posts at Jodhpur, Jaipur and Udaipur continued to be called residencies; in that year, their titles were brought into line with their status, and they became Political Agencies. Otherwise, the Great Sloth Belt, as jealous frontier officers called this area, remained unchanged.

The Political Officer in Sikkim held charge of a Mission in Lhasa in the years of World War II, and Sikkim enjoys the singular distinction of having been upgraded instead of downgraded since Partition by the Government of India. Sikkim ended up as a Protectorate when all her sisters had been mediatized. Bhutan, though in political relations with the Bengal Government, through the Commissioner of Rajshahi, from 1896 to 1903, was later recognized to have a very special status, though its relations were with the Political Officer in Sikkim from 1905 to 1947. The Maharaja is now a King; so Sikkim is not alone in its promotion.

The Assam States Agency consisted of Manipur and sixteen small States in the Khasi and Jaintia Hills and, with the North-West Frontier States, was a relic of the old days when Provincial Governments superintended such areas. From 1 April 1937, the Governor of Assam was constituted 'Agent to the Crown Representative' in his personal capacity, for Manipur and these sixteen States; the Government of Assam, which from 1937 on enjoyed provincial autonomy under elected ministers, had no say in their affairs. The reason why this exception was made was presumably that Manipur was very remote and on the Burma frontier, while the sixteen small States, whose income varied from a maximum of Rs. 35,470 p.a. (under £3,000) to a minimum of Rs. 320 (£25), were not only very small and primitive but hopelessly mixed up with British India. Indeed, in some cases, they were even more mixed up with Shillong, the capital of the province, than were some of the Simla Hill States with Simla. Their population varied from the maximum of 43,588 to a minimum of 57. They gave the Political Department few, if any, headaches, it may well be believed, until one day in 1947, when we were faced with the problem of the transfer of power and stand-still agreements. There was literally no solution in view for this patchwork-quilt area; the matter was referred to the Agent to the Crown Representative (Sir Akbar Hydari,[*] a son of the Hyderabad statesman of that name), who solved the problem by not replying, and leaving the States to be dealt with later by Patel[†] and V. P. Menon.[‡]

[*] Sir M. S. Akbar Hydari (1894–1948), K.C.I.E., C.S.I.; I.C.S., Madras, 1920; Governor of Assam, 1947.

[†] Sardar Vallabhai Patel (1875–1950). Deputy Prime Minister of India with portfolios of Home, Information and Broadcasting and States, 1947–50.

[‡] Vapai Pangunni Menon (1894–1966), C.S.I., C.I.E. Joined Government Service as a clerk, 1914. Reforms Commissioner to Government of India, 1942–7; Secretary to Government of India; Ministry of States, 1947–8; Adviser in ditto 1948–9; Secretary in ditto 1949–51. Governor of Orissa, May–July 1951; retired 1952. See Bibliography.

As for Nepal, its status has always theoretically been that of an independent country. But, *de facto*, it was treated very like an Indian State. From 1816 to 1920, the British representative in Katmandu (drawn from our service until 1947) was called Resident. In 1920 his title was changed to Envoy, and from 1934 to 1947 he was a Minister. Since 1947, he has been an Ambassador.

## CHAPTER 6

## Recruitment

IN spite of a proposal which dragged on from 1928 to 1940, the system followed for many years, and up to the end, for recruiting officers was as follows. Army officers who had passed their promotion examination, were unmarried and were under twenty-six, could apply through their commanding officers for permanent transfer to the political service. Indian Civil Service officers who had passed their departmental examinations, were unmarried and had less than five years service, could similarly apply, through their Provincial Governments. The precise recruitment formula was '2 members of the I.C.S. every year subject to a reduction by 1 in every 5th year, and 4 or 5 military officers in alternate years'. The applications always exceeded the vacancies available, but commanding officers and provincial Governments were often unwilling to let their best officers go, and friction sometimes arose over this. In certain cases, the Viceroy had to overrule Governors who were unwilling to spare officers. Owing to the scarcity of British officers, from the 1920s onwards, the rules were amended to admit Indian Police officers on terms similar to military officers.

In selecting military officers, candidates who had obtained their commission through a university or who showed evidence of exceptional linguistic ability were favoured. Certain Provinces and certain regiments provided an exceptionally high proportion of recruits. Among the former, the Punjab and the United Provinces, among the latter, the Central India Horse were conspicuous. But it cannot be denied that the claim which above all weighed was relationship to a member or retired member of the service. Reading the history of India, one comes across the same surname among politicals again and again, from the earliest times. Four officers, serving in 1947, well illustrate this tendency. Russell* represented the last of five generations in direct descent from Claud Russell (b. 1732) who joined the Company's service at Madras in 1752, and whose successors served in India in the Army, Civil Service and lastly, Political

---

* Lt.-Col. A. A. Russell (1898–1967), M.C. Military political; Resident, Madras States, 1945; Gwalior, 1946–7.

Service. Cotton* was descended from five generations, father and son, of Indian Civil Servants. Hancock's† father and grandfather, like him, were political officers in Kathiawar, while his great-grandfather was Adjutant-General of the then Bombay Army. St. John's‡ father and grandfather (whom we have already met in Kashmir) were military political officers who reached the rank of first-class Residents. Thus in this service, appointment by nomination, which was abolished for the Indian Civil Service in the mid-nineteenth century, survived. All candidates had, of course, passed competitive selection tests: the Indian Civil Service officers the open competitive entrance examination to that service, the military officers the entrance and passing out examinations to and from Sandhurst or Woolwich or a university, followed by promotion and language examinations in the Indian Army.

A moderate dose of nepotism never did a cadre any harm, and most of those officers who had relations in the service stood out as certainly above the average in efficiency. At the same time, doubts were sometimes felt about some aspects of this system of recruitment: felt, indeed, for forty years, though no change was ever made until 1938 when a slight variation was made in the N.W. Frontier Province.

In 1900, on the basis of proposals worked out by Daly,§ himself a military political, Curzon wanted to have the cadre composed two-thirds of Indian Civil Service officers, on the ground that they were more suitable for States work than military officers, and one-third from the army, who were required mainly foɪ the Frontier and ex-India posts on the foreign side. These proposals were blocked by the Finance Department, not on their merits, but because this change would have led to considerably increased expenditure owing to the then higher cost of Indian Civil Service officers. For the rates of pay of military officers on the political time-scale, although considerably higher than those in the army, were then lower than those of their Indian Civil Service colleagues, whose pay had to be equated with that of Indian Civil Service officers in the pro-

---

* Major Sir J. H. Cotton (b. 1909), K.C.M.G., O.B.E. Military political. After Partition, appointed to Diplomatic Service; Ambassador to the Congo, Kinshasa, 1965–9.

† Lt.-Col. Sir Cyril Hancock (b. 1896), K.C.I.E., O.B.E., M.C. Resident, Western India States, 1944–7.

‡ Major O. C. B., St. John (b. 1907) C.M.G. Military political. After Partition, served under U.K. Foreign Office.

§ Lt.-Col. Sir Hugh Daly (1860–1939), K.C.S.I., K.C.I.E. (son of General Sir Henry Daly, G.C.B., C.I.E., Agent to the Governor-General in Central India, 1871). Military political. Agent to the Governor-General in Central India, 1905–10; Resident in Mysore, 1910–16.

vinces. This differentiation in pay was a source of grievance until its abolition in 1925, on the Lee Commission's recommendation that officers doing the same work should draw the same pay. In 1900, therefore, the proportion was left at 70 and 30 per cent; nor was it reconsidered in 1925 when it became technically possible to do so.

On the creation of the North-West Frontier Province in 1901, a large number of Punjab civilians were retained, so that the usual 70:30 ratio was, for some years, not observed on the Frontier. O'Dwyer,[8] one of these officers, points out that the North-West Frontier Province had about thirty-five British officers after it was cut off from the Punjab, of whom roughly two-thirds were civilians and one-third soldiers.

Butler, in his 1910 handing-over note referred to earlier, wrote:

> The ideal arrangement would be to combine the Bombay Political Department with our own and to have one big Internal Department for Native States. In the Foreign Branch, we could then indent on the Civil Service and the Army for officers, who would be seconded for a term of years. We want [a] totally different class of men for frontier and internal work and one of the great difficulties ahead at [sic] the frontier will be the securing of trained men for judicial and administrative work. The North-West Frontier Province is unquestionably a very small ground for training. But the difficulties in the way of so large a change are at present insuperable.

As has been mentioned, the Bombay Political Department, consisting of some twenty-eight officers, was not amalgamated with our service until 1924. It was not in this note, but elsewhere, that Butler summed up his views as follows:

> We want lean and keen men on the Frontier, and fat and good-natured men in the States.

The question of Indianizing the cadre arose in the 1920s as a result of the Montagu*–Chelmsford† and the Public Services Commission reports: but little progress was made, and the case was inextricably confused with a revival of Butler's scheme outlined in the last paragraph. The ruling Princes who had been consulted about Indianization, with the exception of the Maharaja of Gwalior, were unanimously adverse, on the

* The Hon. E. S. Montagu (1879–1924). Parliamentary Under-Secretary of State for India, 1910–14; Secretary of State for India, 1917–22.
† 1st Viscount Chelmsford (1868–1933). Viceroy of India, 1916–21; Warden of All Souls, 1932–3.

theory that, as their relations were with the British Crown and not the Government of India, British officers were the more suitable inter-mediaries. There were difficulties, too, over the posting of Indian officers to consular posts on our cadre. With the great increase in Indianization of the Indian Civil Service in consequence of the Lee Commission's report, and constant pressure in the Legislative Assembly, this question became a live issue again. Indianization of the department therefore had to come, in spite of the negative attitude of the ruling Princes. The Finance Member's own proposals, which were those eventually sanctioned by the Secretary of State, worked badly, as they involved too rapid Indianization and had later to be modified with his permission.

In practice, comparatively few Indian officers served in the States, though K. P. S. Menon was Under-Secretary at Hyderabad and Dewan of Bharatpur; Iskander Mirza,* Political Agent, Orissa States; while Saeed Alam Khan† held several posts in Kathiawar and was Secretary at Kolhapur. Khurshid was Assistant Political Agent in Chitral, and Muiz-zudin Ahmad Under-Secretary, Eastern States. More served on the Frontier, which was doubtless why a larger number of Muslims than non-Muslims was recruited, several Muslim officers being taken from the Provincial Civil Service, and permanently promoted into the Indian Political Service. They thus formed an exception to the rule that all officers were drawn from the Indian Civil Service, the Indian Army or the Indian Police.

The question of Indianization was again examined in detail in 1927. Opinion was generally against it, but Bray‡ noted:

> Confining myself to the Frontier, I see no reason to regret the Indianization of the Department. It is not the poorer for including or having included men like Abdul Qayyum,§ Mir Shams Shah, Sharbat, Muzzafar and Lehna Singh. Nor am I concerned at the failure of our efforts to confine the Indianization to the martial races of northern India, for, apart from the fact that all entrants are

* Major-Gen. Iskander Mirza (1899–1969), c.i.e., o.b.e. Military political. Served mostly on frontier. Joint Secretary and Secretary, Ministry of Defence, Government of Pakistan. Later, Governor-General and President of Pakistan.

† Nawabzada Saeed Alam Khan (1892–1933). Provincial Civil Service, Bombay, 1923. Political, 1928. Served in N.W.F.P., Punjab States and Western India.

‡ Sir Denys Bray (1875–1951), k.c.s.i., k.c.i.e., c.b.c.; i.c.s., Punjab, 1898. Foreign Secretary, 1920–30. Numerous writings on Baluchistan of which he conducted the first census. Member of Council of India, 1930–7.

§ Abdul Qaiyum, etc. These were all officers of the Provincial Civil Service who were promoted, at a fairly ripe age, into the Political Service.

selected by H.E., Sandeman's first lieutenant, Hitu Ram,* was none the less a great Empire builder for being a *bunia*.† Nor does he stand alone.

In 1928, however, Birkenhead‡ writing to Halifax, observed:

How much I regret that our predecessors agreed to any indianization of the Political Department.

In 1929, the Butler Committee (presided over by the same officer who had been Foreign Secretary, by then a Governor) recommended,§ though the recommendation after immense consideration was not adopted, that the cadre of political officers dealing with the States be separated from the Frontier and foreign cadre and in future recruited neither from the Indian Civil Service nor the Indian Army, but direct from England, presumably by the Civil Service Commission. It is interesting to speculate how this system would have worked. In the previous year, 1938, Glancy,‖ who was officiating as Political Secretary, pressed this proposal (of which he appears to have been the author) as getting round the extreme difficulty of obtaining sufficient European I.C.S. officers from the provinces. It was examined and approved by Bray, the Foreign Secretary; and Halifax, the Viceroy, to whom it was mentioned, 'was disposed to consider it favourably'. The Home Department, who were in charge of personnel matters, were consulted in July 1928; when reminded in October 1929, they were found to have taken no action. They then suggested dropping the matter as provincial Governments and the Secretary of State would have to be consulted and some would probably oppose the scheme: an extraordinary excuse. It looks as though the Indian Deputy Secretary who handled the file there meant to sabotage the scheme.

* Rai Bahadur Hitu Ram, c.i.e., A Dera Ghazi Khan Hindu who was secretary to Sir Robert Sandeman and Regent of Las Bela, and for years presided over the Shahi *jirga* in Baluchistan.

† Money-lender.

‡ First Earl of Birkenhead (1872–1930). Lord Chancellor, 1919–22. Secretary of State for India, 1924–8.

§ Discussing the I.C.S. and the Indian Army as services they wrote: 'These sources of supply are now limited. Both the I.C.S. and the Indian Army are short-handed. Thoughtful Political Officers are concerned as to the future recruitment for their department. They think that the time has come to recruit separately from the universities in England for service in the States alone. We commend this suggestion for consideration. . . .'

‖ Sir Bertrand Glancy (1882–1953), g.c.i.e., k.c.s.i.; I.C.S., Punjab. Political Secretary, 1933–7. Political Adviser to the Crown Representative, 1938–41. Governor of the Punjab, 1941–6.

In September 1930 Halifax and his executive council sent a very clear and definite despatch which, while specifically opposing any recruitment by nomination, as used for the Sudan, strongly advised recruitment by competitive examination, followed by a selection board, to a special Political–I.C.S. cadre. Two-thirds of the States' cadre should be staffed from this source, one-third from the army. The Frontier and foreign cadre should be staffed 50 : 50. The Viceroy should retain the right to nominate provincial I.C.S. officers in quite exceptional cases. The despatch felt that it was premature to say whether men should be asked to opt for one or the other branches of the cadre, and opposed the idea of attaching them to embassies for training.

The India Office stalled, and the red herring of 'nomination' kept creeping in. Clearly what was needed was to add to the competitive examination, which already covered, for example, the Diplomatic and Home Civil Service, a new category–the Indian Political Service. There was no hurry about deciding to split the service or not. The case was deplorably handled; when in doubt everyone seems to have played for safety and the *status quo*. In 1931, Patrick minuted that the India Office had passed no orders as the Government of India had asked for none. In a long printed note of July 1932 we find the Reforms Office taking a hand, and suggesting that the Home Government must pay for the Political Department–at a cost of about Rs. 1 *crore* yearly ( = about £750,000). In 1933, Morley* wrote an immense minute, clearing up the status of the service which he correctly described as a 'Central Service, Class 1.'

It was considered essential that, for the settled districts of the North-West Frontier Province, where provincial autonomy would be introduced, a cadre should be built up gradually of I.C.S. officers recruited, like all other I.C.S. officers, for service under the provincial Ministry. This was done, and, from 1938 to 1940 officers were assigned direct to the North-West Frontier Province. Recruitment thereafter stopped, on account of the war, and was never resumed. The main case dragged on; in December 1936 we find Glancy writing that the decision to postpone the constitution of a separate cadre for the North-West Frontier Province means that the present joint cadre will continue with the present system of recruitment until more experience is gained. Finally, in May 1940, the Secretary of State approves the latest proposal and adds that he is 'disposed to think' (the phrase is so typical of this case) that the Crown Representative might properly make a somewhat fuller use of his discretion to appoint to Selection and, in special cases, to Superior or

* Sir Alexander Morley (b. 1908), K.C.M.G., C.B.E. India Office, 1930.

Inferior posts in the Political Service specially qualified officers, i.e. I.C.S. officers, from provinces, a practice to which resort seems to have been had less frequently of late than it was some years ago. (He ignored the fact that even if these budding Durands and Metcalfes had been there, and willing to transfer, no province would have spared them in 1940.) He also suggested a few minor changes, e.g. recruiting civilians with a minimum, not a maximum, of five years' service.

By now (1940), as we shall see, Linlithgow had for a year been inclined to recruit the whole Political Service from the ranks of the provincial I.C.S. This extraordinary idea, entertained first in early 1938, ran up against two objections. Apart from the great practical difficulty of getting the provinces to part with their good men, his proposal overlooked a further difficulty. The I.C.S. was recruited on a basis of 50 per cent Europeans and 50 per cent Indians for the whole cadre, and it was clearly not practical politics in 1938 to expect that the percentage of Europeans could be increased. It was therefore clear that, if the Political Service weighed in with a heavy demand for European I.C.S. officers, which would completely upset the provincial distribution, this would immediately and acutely raise the question of Indianizing the Political Service to the same extent. The objections to this, fully considered in 1927, were felt to be even greater when the States' cadre was no longer under the Government of India. Eventually, with a war-time ban on recruitment and the approach of the dissolution of the service, the matter was, of course, dropped. If the ghost of Curzon were around, he must have summed up this long-drawn ineffectiveness in some lapidary and damning phrase.

The 70 : 30 per cent ratio and the early recruitment (it will be remembered that Indian Civil Service officers had to have less than five years' service and military officers to be under twenty-six, to enter the Political Service) survived unchanged for many years. It must have often been thought that, while such insistence on early recruitment was logical in the stirring days of Malcolm and Elphinstone, when an officer had often fought two or three campaigns before settling down, still young, as a political, in the twentieth century it had disadvantages. Many excellent army officers who specialized in frontier service, often by years of secondment to the Frontier Scouts, where they acquired a remarkable knowledge of Pashtu and of tribal mentality were, because of their age, not available for recruitment, though there were often great shortages of officers with such qualifications. On a few occasions in this century such officers were seconded on long contract; but this was wholly exceptional.

The establishment difficulties involved in anything but a strictly defined recruitment system were, of course, great. There were too many junior posts on the Frontier and too many senior posts in the States for a well-balanced service. But, looking back, it certainly seems that, with the much increased specialization which this century saw, both in States and Frontier work, and the great increase in the area covered by the service, there was at least a case for splitting this service into a States' cadre and a Frontier cadre, as suggested by Butler in 1910 and Glancy in 1928. This would have avoided the loss of specialized knowledge by transfers necessitated by the imbalance referred to. The frontier cadre could have staffed the North-West Frontier Province and Baluchistan,* and foreign posts like Kabul and the few Persian posts that it was really necessary to retain, and could have been recruited largely from the Indian Army, at varying ages, a few Punjab civilians being borrowed primarily for work in the settled districts.

The system was never changed; but doubts remained. So late as 7 February 1939, Linlithgow, the Viceroy, writing to Zetland,† the Secretary of State, suggested that they should perhaps abolish the Political Service as such and get States work disposed of by the posting of officers from the ordinary Indian Civil Service cadre with experience of work in the districts. Nothing short of a shake-up of this kind would, he thought, purge the Political Service 'with its large proportion of somewhat second-rate men' of their mediaevalism. It is interesting to contrast his comment with Curzon's‡ remarks on leaving India, in a farewell speech delivered at Simla on 5 September 1905:

> Perhaps I may be allowed to interpolate a word in this place about the particular branch of the Service of which I have been more especially the head. I allude to the Political Department. The Viceroy, as taking the Foreign Office under his personal charge, has a greater responsibility for the officers of that department than for any other. A good 'Political' is a type of officer difficult to train, indeed, training by itself will never produce him, for there are required in addition

* Many officers have felt that, leaving aside so radical a change as splitting the service in two, more transfers between the N.W.F.P. and Baluchistan would have been salutary.

† 2nd Marquess of Zetland (1876–1961). Member (as Earl of Ronaldshay) Royal Commission on the Public Services in India, 1912–14, and Governor of Bengal, 1917–22. Secretary of State for India, 1935–40.

‡ 1st Marquess Curzon of Kedleston (1859–1925). Under-Secretary of State for India, 1891–2. Viceroy of India, 1899–1905. Secretary of State for Foreign Affairs, 1919–24.

qualities of tact and flexibility, of moral fibre and gentlemanly bearing, which are an instinct rather than an acquisition. The public at large hardly realises what the 'Political' may be called to do. At one time he may be grinding in the Foreign Office; at another he may be required to stiffen the administration of a backward Native State; at a third he may be presiding over a *jirga* of unruly tribes on the frontier; at a fourth he may be demarcating a boundary amid the wilds of Tibet or the sands of Seistan. There is no more varied or responsible service in the world than that of the Political Department of the Government of India. And right well have I been served in it, from the mature and experienced officer who handles a Native chief with velvet glove, to the young military 'Political' who packs up his trunk at a moment's notice and goes off to Arabia or Kurdistan. I commend the Political Department of the Government of India to all who like to know the splendid and varied work of which Englishmen are capable, and I hope that the time may never arise when it will cease to draw to itself the best abilities and the finest characters that the Services in India can produce.

# CHAPTER 7

# Training

AFTER recruitment, the Indian Civil Service officer, who had already had some years of civil and judicial experience and had passed his departmental examinations, faced only a simple examination, after six months, in the Political Department Manual and one or two historical books. The military political had to spend eighteen months on civil (largely magisterial) training in the Punjab or the United Provinces and to pass the Indian Civil Service departmental examinations as well. This was a sound arrangement, provided he served under a Collector who had the time and the keenness to supervise his training at every step. This was not always the case. Both civil and military officers were placed on probation for three years, during which six-monthly confidential reports were submitted on them by their superior officers. Failure to confirm was rare, but became commoner in the 1930s when there was some tightening-up of standards.

The *Manual of Instructions to officers of the Political Department of the Government of India*,[9] to give it its full title, was a remarkable work: 'variously judged', as Karl Baedeker says of hotels found to be less than universally admired.

Butler seems to have been largely responsible for the post-Curzon reaction against close supervision of the States, which Minto's Udaipur speech embodied, and no doubt his hand is to be seen in this Manual.* The rest of the book is a useful compilation of rules about correspondence, ceremonial, minority administration, extradition and so on; but the Introduction is an eloquent though controversial plea for a light hand on the reins. Its most famous or notorious paragraph reads:

> He [i.e. the political officer] should leave well alone; the best work of a political officer is very often what he has left undone.

More will be said of this doctrine when we come to discuss policy towards the States.

This was the formal training laid down, and frankly it was not good

* For a picture of this distinguished Foreign Secretary, *see* Woodruff's *The Men Who Ruled India*, Vol. 2, pp. 288, 289.

enough. The officers at, say, the headquarters of a Residency or a district headquarters on the Frontier, did not get adequate scope for training in secretariat methods. And so, in the '30s of this century, two interesting reforms were carried out which were intended, and successful in their intent, to raise the standard of officers in this respect. One was a rule that no officer would be promoted to a first-class Resident's appointment who had not served for two years as Secretary to a first-class Resident. The other was the establishment, for junior military political officers in Simla during some weeks of each summer, of a training class in Secretariat methods. This owed its origin and successful organization to the zeal of Prior,* when Deputy Secretary in the Political Department.

Surprisingly, no encouragement was given to officers to see anything of indirect rule outside India, e.g. when on leave. The Government of India compared, say, with the Government of the Netherlands Indies, were always singularly blind to the advantages of a wider view. Political officers did not get around enough. Though diplomatists, they were never attached, even for a few weeks, to an embassy abroad. Though responsible for relations with Tibet, no one was encouraged to visit China; though concerned to solve a tribal problem in the North-West Frontier Province, no one went to Morocco to see what Lyautey† was doing. It was no political officer but a political journalist, Valentine Chirol,‡ who went to see for himself in Morocco. Writing to Hailey, he said:

> The French have done great things there in the short space of 12 years . . . and they have been fortunate enough to find in Marshall Lyautey something very like another Cromer,§ possessing at any rate Cromer's rare combination of energy and patience and more than Cromer a good knack of handling orientals . . .

The fact that Morocco presented in fact a very different problem from Waziristan, owing to the absence of Afghanistan and an organized arms traffic, does not excuse the failure to study it.

* Lt.-Col. Sir Geoffrey Prior (b. 1896), K.C.I.E. Political Resident, Persian Gulf, 1939. A.G.G. in Baluchistan, 1946–7.

† Marechal Hubert Lyautey (1854–1934), G.C.M.G. Resident General in Morocco, 1912–25, where his policy was based on his studies of Sandeman's 'system' in Baluchistan.

‡ Sir Valentine Chirol (1852–1929). Traveller, journalist and author. He wrote three books on India, which he visited seventeen times.

§ 1st Earl of Cromer (1841–1917). Royal Artillery, 1858. Private Secretary to the Viceroy of India, 1872–6. Egypt, 1877–80. Finance Member of the Executive Council of the Governor-General of India, 1880–4. Agent and Consul-General in Egypt, 1888–1907.

But if training was practically exclusively 'on the job', it was good training. On the Frontier, a young officer would do the same vastly varied work as done by an Indian Civil Service officer in a province – trying cases, checking revenue documents, inspecting *tahsils*, visiting disputed sites, sitting on district boards and committees, learning Pashtu or Baluchi or Brahui, and qualifying to have charge of a sub-division and often to act, quite early in his career, as Political Agent or Deputy Commissioner and District Magistrate. But besides all the work common to other provinces, in the North-West Frontier Province every district had its ration of tribes, quite apart from the major tribal conglomerations under political agents. And so a young officer was brought into touch with the problems of indirect rule – administration of tribesmen, passing orders on *jirga* reports, and the constant law and order problem. This last was much sharper than in other provinces, where it was almost exclusively left to the police. Here, raids and dacoities were a constant anxiety, and as they had their 'political 'side, were a matter for the Deputy Commissioner and his assistants to an extent unknown in normal times in other provinces.

In the States, the newly appointed officer often worked for six months or so as Personal Assistant to a first-class Resident: a post broadly equivalent to that of an aide-de-camp to a Governor. He then lived in the Residency, enciphered and deciphered telegrams, organized the social side of Rulers' visits and worked for his examination. He probably toured extensively with the Resident to States other than that where the Residency was.

# CHAPTER 8

## Control of the Service

THE headquarters' secretariat dates back to long before there can be said to have been any regular cadre. Roughly, up to the Mutiny (1857), officers might be commanding troops one day and performing diplomatic functions the next. Keatinge, a soldier who served from 1863 to 1870 in purely political posts in States, went on to be Chief Commissioner of the Central Provinces and the first Chief Commissioner in Assam. Lyall's, Elphinstone's and Temple's careers were similarly mixed, while, as we have seen, R. B. Shaw came into the service (if one can use the term) in the 1870s after spending fifteen years as a tea-planter.* But from 23 September 1783[10] the 'Secret and Political Department' was created in the Supreme Government by Government Resolution, Mr. Edward Hay being appointed Secretary. From 1784 to 1842, the department was divided into three distinct branches: secret, political and foreign; in May 1843 the title of the entire department was changed to that of 'Foreign department'. On 1 January 1914, it was split into two, and renamed the 'Foreign and Political department', a Political Secretary being created to supervise the States, since the work had become too much for one officer. The Viceroy (also known as the Governor-General) remained, as always, in charge of both portfolios, foreign affairs and States, frontier matters being included in the former.

In 1937, a fresh post of Political Adviser to the Crown Representative, was belatedly added. (Belatedly, because the Viceroy was consistently overworked and seldom devoted enough time to his Foreign and Political portfolio.) This post carried higher pay and status and, in Wavell's† time,

---

* An even stranger example of mixed function was William Fraser, a civil servant who was an intimate friend of James Skinner and commanded the 3rd corps of Skinner's Horse. Jacquemont mentions his 'perfect monomania for fighting. Whenever there is a war anywhere, he throws up his judicial functions and goes off to it.' He had no rank and could not wear uniform. He was political officer to General Martindell in the Gurkha war of 1814, and was given the rank of major after the war, while Commissioner, Hill States. Later he was A.G.G., Delhi and was murdered there.[11]

† 1st Earl Wavell (1883–1950). Field-Marshal, 1943, Viceroy of India, 1943–1947.

on the suggestion of Corfield,* its holder began to attend meetings of the Executive Council or Cabinet, when any matter concerning the States was to be discussed, and to see all Executive Council papers in circulation. This was necessary to ensure that departments of the Government of India, when discussing matters of all-India interest, were not deprived of the States' point of view when making decisions. If this practice had been introduced many years earlier one might have avoided a legitimate grievance of the States: that their interests were not consulted until a decision, often unwelcome, had been reached on economic matters of mutual concern.

The establishment problems of the service were far from easy, as they involved the operation of one cadre but three areas. They were solved in personal discussions between the Foreign and Political Secretaries. The one grave error was the tendency to leave officers in their posts too short a time, on compassionate grounds or on considerations of seniority. Dera Ismail Khan† was, compared with many British Indian stations, a civilized and interesting post; but it certainly lacked the climatic amenities of almost all other Frontier stations. As a result, officers posted there made haste to ask for a transfer elsewhere with appalling results to continuity and efficiency. (How many, if any, of its Deputy Commissioners between 1901 and 1947 could speak a word of the local language, Jatki or Hindko?)

Once an officer was posted off by headquarters, whether to the Frontier or a Residency, his immediate control rested in the local authority there. In the case of Baluchistan or the States, his exact posting was settled in Delhi. The services of an officer posted to the North-West Frontier, were, however, 'placed at the disposal of the Chief Commissioner' (later, Governor); and he could be posted by him to any district or agency without reference to Delhi. The blame for too frequent transfers must therefore be laid firmly in Peshawar.

Earlier, men seem to have been left longer in their posts. We may note Sandeman's nine and a half years in Dera Ghazi Khan and Warburton's‡

* Sir Conrad Corfield (b. 1893), K.C.I.E., C.S.I., M.C.; I.C.S., Punjab, 1920. Political Adviser to H.E. the Crown Representative, 1945–7.

† '75 officers were posted as Deputy Commissioners from 1901 to 14th August, 1947. This number includes 16 officers who were posted again and again and as such 59 officers actually held the charge of the post of Deputy Commissioner, Dera Ismail Khan, during the said period.' (Letter no. 273/PA(G) of 31.3.1965 from the Commissioner, Dera Ismail Khan division, to the Establishment Secretary to the Government of Pakistan, who kindly made this enquiry at the author's request.

‡ Col. Sir Robert Warburton (1842–99), K.C.S.I. Military political. P.A., Khyber, at intervals from 1789–82, and 1882–90. His father, an artillery officer, married an Afghan princess.

eighteen in the Khyber Agency as examples of the advantages of long residence. Other cases of long tenure were as follows: Cobden-Ramsay, a Bihar and Orissa I.C.S. officer, was Political Agent and Commissioner, Orissa Feudatory States, from 1906 to 1922. Earlier, B. H. Hodgson, the ethnologist and Buddhist scholar, was Assistant to the Resident in Nepal from 1823 to 1843; while Pelly was Political Resident in the Persian Gulf from 1862 to 1871. Macaulay was seventeen years in Dera Ismail Khan, Cavagnari ten in Kohat; Jacob was eleven years in Jacobabad.

So much for control of individuals. Whence came the over-all control of high policy, the decision whether or not to engage in a Frontier war, whether or not to depose a Maharaja, to allow or to disallow an oil company to explore in the Persian Gulf? Whence but from the Government of India, i.e. the Governor-General acting on the advice of his Executive Council, or possibly from the Secretary of State, similarly advised by *his* Council?

Whence, indeed, one would think. But the reader would be surprised, reading some comments by Viceroys and Secretaries of State, to see how in practice matters were handled. Right through the period, dating from 1820 to 1937, when the political service was theoretically controlled by the organization mentioned above, policy was decided in advance by long private and personal letters of very great importance, between Governor-General and Secretary of State. These letters (which were taken away on retirement) were later supplemented by telegrams, and finally took the form of air-mail letters, sometimes, in Linlithgow's time, fifteen pages long when printed, which were exchanged weekly or oftener. By this time, the Viceroy, as Crown Representative, was entirely correct in not consulting his Executive Council. Earlier, it is with some shock that one reads time and again how both authorities—Morley,* the doctrinaire Liberal, no less than Salisbury, the high Tory—combined to settle things behind the backs of their Councils.

'Their encroaching tendency,' wrote Salisbury to Northbrook† in 1874 of the Governor-General's Council,

> is not wholesome and ought not to be encouraged. . . . They are subordinate portions of an executive hierarchy. An *official* remonstrance from them against what the Queen's advisers recommend to

* Viscount Morley of Blackburn (1838–1923). Secretary of State for India, 1905–10, in which capacity he interfered more actively than his predecessors in Indian administration.

† First Earl of Northbrook (1826–1904). Under-Secretary for India, 1859–64. Viceroy, 1872–6.

Parliament seems to me to involve a wholly inverted view of their position.

Later, after Lytton* had succeeded Northbrook, Salisbury wrote to him criticizing Northbrook's tendency to follow his Council, and added:—

> I suppose from time to time you will have to report officially: and for that purpose to take the Council's opinion. But most of the management can be arranged demi-officially.

When, however, the administration–medical in particular–of the expeditionary force to Iraq during World War I broke down so badly that the British Government set up a Commission to enquire into responsibility, this question of private and personal correspondence was criticized. Austen Chamberlain,† was so sharply blamed for confining his supervision to such a channel and not using official correspondence that he resigned. The Viceroy (Hardinge) had just handed over, or he too would probably have had to go.

At all stages, Viceroys also corresponded freely with the Permanent Under-Secretary of State at the India Office, the Civil Service head of the London end of the administration. The Under-Secretary often wrote privately to let the Viceroy know how cases were progressing, warning him of the likelihood of delay or parliamentary opposition, etc. This channel of correspondence was mostly a discreet and useful supplement to the Secretary of State's letters. Viceroys also wrote privately to the Monarch, and Secretaries of State sometimes to Presidency Governors (i.e. Governors of Bengal, Bombay and Madras).

The importance of this 'private and personal' correspondence between Secretary of State and Viceroy can scarcely be exaggerated. It would not be going too far to say that from the Mutiny to Partition, policy towards the States and the Frontier and relations with India's limitrophe countries was controlled by this channel though, when we deal with Waziristan, we shall see how the Executive Council could, and did in 1922, stand up to the Viceroy. Very regrettably, the Viceroy never visited England during his tour of office until Curzon's reappointment gave him the opportunity for a home visit. A regular period of leave (once only) during his term of office was instituted after World War I, but no Secretary of

* 1st Earl of Lytton (1831–91). Diplomatic service. Viceroy of India, 1876–80. Ambassador to Paris, 1887–91.

† Sir Austen Chamberlain (1863–1937). Secretary of State for India, 1915–17; for Foreign Affairs, 1924–9.

State save Montagu and Crewe\* ever visited India till Pethick-Lawrence†
led the 1946 mission. Clearly, misunderstanding and bureaucratic controversy would have raged had there not been this soothing series of
private letters to ease the path for official proposals. Hoare[12] quotes Dalhousie's apt comment on the practice. In a letter dated 28 June 1854, to
the President of the Board of Control, he wrote:

> My experience has taught me that men who correspond over a space
> of 10,000 miles should watch their pens, for ink comes to burn like
> caustic when it crosses the sea.

One cannot fail to be impressed by the sympathy and tact shown in
their correspondence by a series of statesmen, sometimes of opposing
political parties, and their commonsense and unpompous approach to
problems of administration. Aristocrats undoubtedly have their virtues
as administrators. Nor did they lack the light touch. Amery, writing to
Zetland on 1 July 1940, shortly after he had taken over from him as
Secretary of State, at a grim moment in the war, added as a postscript to
an important private and confidential letter giving him advance information of a Viceregal statement:

> A propos of the efforts of the public schools in the war, Winston at
> lunch yesterday said: 'Harrow: myself, Gort and Amery. Eton:
> King Leopold and Captain Ramsay.‡ Winchester: Oswald Mosley§
> and Sir Stafford Cripps.'

And then there was the Crown. Especially in regard to the Princes,
there seems to have been a long history of interference from the Palace,
usually, as one would expect, on the side of preservation of their rights.
It does not, however, appear that, in a clear case of a decision to intervene
against a Ruler, misgivings in the palace were regarded as more than
matters to be got out of the way with the least possible fuss. When Salar

---

\* 1st Marquess of Crewe (1858–1945). Secretary of State for India, 1910–15.
Attended King George V at Delhi Durbar, 1911. Ambassador to France, 1922–8.

† 1st Lord Pethick-Lawrence (1876–1961). M.P. (Labour), 1923–45. Secretary
of State for India, 1945–7.

‡ Captain A. H. M. Ramsay (1895–1955). M.P. Detained from 1940–4 under
Regulation 18B of the Defence (General) Regulations, 1939, made under Section
1(2)(a) of the Emergency Powers (Defence) Act, 1939. This authorized the
detention of persons believed by the Secretary of State to have been recently concerned in acts prejudicial to the public safety or the defence of the realm.

§ Sir Oswald Mosley (b. 1896), 6th Baronet. Former M.P. Similarly detained
under Regulation 18B.

Jung* was doing extensive propaganda, backed by large sums of money, in England for the restoration of Berar, Salisbury warned the Viceroy from time to time. In 1874:

> The Nizam is a danger and I would never willingly strengthen him. But he has powerful friends here. I think I told you that the Queen had interfered and questioned me about him.

Later:

> I have just heard that the Nizam has sent over 10,000 solid reasons to support his claim in the Press and the House of Commons,

and:

> Salar Jung has had access to the Prince of Wales for some time.[13]

More legitimately, Queen Victoria–whose great personal interest in India is well-known–was exercised about the Prince of Wales' visit to India in 1875. On 22 July Salisbury wrote:

> The Queen is still very anxious about the possible conduct of some of the Prince's suite. They are lively personages, well known probably to you by reputation–and I think the Queen has visions of zenanas escaladed on ladders of ropes, and all the resulting scandal ... You will not need to be told which are the members of the party of whose mercurial temperament the Queen is apprehensive.

Later, in 1899, Curzon wrote to the Queen–they corresponded weekly, though she was in the very last months of her life–about the eccentric Maharaja Holkar of Indore. He had been ripe for deposition for some time but never quite overstepped the mark. Then one day he rashly offered to accept a plan of control which later ended in his abdication. Curzon snatched at the opportunity and told the Queen with some glee what had happened. 'The Queen,' came the freezing reply on 15 June 1899,

> ... is very glad that no strong measures were thought necessary to bring Holkar to reason. She is always doubtful of the policy, and even right, of too much interference in the internal affairs of the Native Princes. Holkar is a strange, not very satisfactory person, but he sent the Queen direct (as the Princes she knows generally do) a very kind telegram for her birthday, so she at once answered. She likes these direct communications, and thinks it [sic] does good.

* Sir Salar Jung (1829–83). Prime Minister of Hyderabad, 1853–83. Perhaps the greatest of all Indian State officials, he was a fanatic on the question of Berar; some of the methods he adopted in order to get it reopened aroused criticism.

Then on 28 July 1899:

> The Queen is very sorry to hear that Holkar is giving so much trouble. She is anxious that a person of some military standing should be found who was firm but cautious. So many of the Political Agents are . . . often less able.

[The omission is not ours but that of Curzon or whoever edited his correspondence. We are spared the full blast of the royal comment on the service.]

The tradition of personal links with the Crown survived. King George V and, after his death, Queen Mary, corresponded regularly with Bikaner,* a very prominent politician-prince who first launched and then back-pedalled on the abortive scheme of federation. Earlier, King Edward VII was shocked, as was the Secretary of State, when Curzon not merely issued to his officers, but actually published in the Gazette, a circular laying down that Rulers were not to leave India without asking leave. 'Schoolmasterly,' commented Hamilton,† the Secretary of State. 'Just what we ought to be,' replied Curzon. King Edward showed much reluctance, as did some of Curzon's Council, towards accepting Curzon's scheme for an Imperial Cadet Corps.

But interesting though these sidelights on royal concern in the affairs of Indian States are, this concern never seems to have seriously affected the control of the service. This was vested in the Governor-General in Council, overruled at times by the Secretary of State. This was the position down to 1 April 1937, when a change came into force. The Butler Committee had recommended that 'In view of the fact of the historical nature of the relationship between the paramount power and the Princes, the latter should not be transferred without their agreement to a relationship with the new Government in British India responsible to the Indian legislature.' They therefore proposed–and this proposal was embodied in the Government of India Act, 1935, which emerged from the three Round-Table Conferences–that a new post should be created, that of Crown Representative, to replace the Governor-General in Council. This

---

* H.H. Maharaja Ganga Singh of Bikaner (1880–1943), G.C.S.I., G.C.I.E., G.C.V.O., G.B.E., K.C.B. Succeeded as Ruler, 1887. Served in World War I. First Chancellor of the Chamber of Princes. A prince of great personality and charm, whose state was not, however, administered so efficiently as his sand-grouse shoots.

† Lord George Hamilton (1845–1927). Son of the Duke of Abercorn. Under-Secretary for India, 1874–80, Secretary of State for India, 1895–1903, during most of Curzon's viceroyalty.

post was always in fact held by the Viceroy through this was not compulsory. This change seemed to be of a radical nature, and was expected by those concerned to be so. It was hoped that the Departments of the Government of India (which constitutionally ceased after 1937 to have any more control over the States than the Government of France) would, in fact, lose their grip on matters such as finance, defence and communications, the Political Department being able to advise the Crown Representative, in absolute impartiality, on matters in dispute between the Government of India or Provincial Governments and the States. It did not work out like that at all, as we shall see when we discuss the lapse of Paramountcy. In particular, the Finance Department retained, through a Crown Finance Officer placed in the Political Department with the status of Joint Secretary, the minutest control over its finances. All occupants of the post were Hindus. But the constitutional theory, for the brief ten years that saw the *Götterdämmerung* of the Indian States, was that the Viceroy, as Crown Representative, was solely responsible to the British Government, through the India Office and the Secretary of State for India, for all matters concerning the Indian States. India Office control, very light where British India was concerned, was always present where the States were concerned. They had a handful of officials who specialized on States' affairs and remained for years on end on this task. The name of Patrick* will occui to many political officers as the supreme expert in this century on this subject.

Once admitted to the service, a political officer whether civil or military by origin, normally stayed in it until the day of his retirement, when his 'services were replaced at the disposal of His Excellency the Commander-in-Chief' or 'of the Government of the Punjab', (or whatever province he originally hailed from), if a civilian. This meant that military officers obtained a military pension only and this was usually lower than the £1,000 p.a. which was the pension universally drawn by Indian Civil Service officers, unless High Court Judges. This discrepancy rankled and lacked justification.

But all officers were theoretically on deputation and not members of a separate service. Indeed, the term Indian Political Service, which we use throughout, was only coined, at the suggestion of Lothian, and with the demi-official approval of the India Office, in 1937, when the Government of India Act, 1935, made the old designation impossible. This had been 'the Foreign and Political Department of the Government of India',

---

* Sir Paul Patrick (b. 1888), K.C.I.E., C.S.I. India Office, 1913 and, on return from war service, 1919–49.

usually abbreviated to 'F. & P.' Since, after 1937, the State's portion of the service came under the Crown Representative and not the Government of India, the term had to be changed.

Anyone interested in the exact status of our service before the passing of the Government of India Act, 1935, and the setting up of the office of Crown Representative, should not overlook the Civil Services (Classification, Control and Appeal) Rules issued as Statutory Rules and Orders, 1930, no. 524 (H.M. Stationery Office). Little known to the average officer, they were important where discipline was concerned. Issued under the rule making power given by subsection (2) of section 96B of the (1919) Government of India Act, they cancelled certain rules made in 1926 and set out what the various services were, and what punishments could be awarded and by whom. (Broadly, no one could be removed or dismissed by an authority lower than the authority who could appoint.) The public services in India were to consist of six groups, of which (1) the All-India Services and (2) the Central Services, class 1, concern us. The I.C.S. fell under (1) and 'officers holding the King's commission on the active list of the Regular Army' are given analogous rights. Under (2) we find twenty services, such as the Indian Ecclesiastical Establishment, the India Audit and Accounts Service and the Imperial Customs Service. At no. 13 of (2) we find the 'Political Department of the Government of India'. The text has little to say of it save that all first appointments to it 'shall be made by the Secretary of State in Council. Provided that the Governor-General in Council may appoint a member of the I.C.S. or an officer holding the King's commission in the Indian Army, or, for special reasons and with the prior approval of the Secretary of State in Council, a member of any other all-India Service–' e.g. the Indian Police.

An important result of the fact that officers were seconded from the I.C.S. and Indian Army and did not constitute a Secretary of State's service was that they carried with them their basic superannuation rule. Army officers were required to retire at fifty-five; I.C.S. officers on the expiry of thirty-five years' service. Depending on the age at which the latter passed the entrance examination, this period of thirty-five years took them to fifty-eight or fifty-nine. Thus if an I.C.S. political elected to stay on for his whole permitted period he often shut out a military political colleague who had to retire at fifty-five. This caused resentment, and perhaps partly accounts for the fact that, of the twenty permanent Foreign Secretaries from 1867 to 1947, only two were military politicals, while of the ten permanent Political Secretaries from the creation of the post in 1914 to 1947, all were I.C.S. officers.

# CHAPTER 9

# They Also Served...

THE Service was assisted by a number of officials outside it whose work we must briefly record. A great many of the inferior posts, and occasionally some of the superior, were at times held temporarily by officers outside the cadre of the service. This was particularly frequent in the North-West Frontier Province and Baluchistan where, when there was a shortage of political officers, Extra Assistant Commissioners, as members of the Provincial Civil Service (who were practically always Indians) were called, were often put in to act in their posts. The importance of the role played by such officers cannot be over-stressed. For good and for ill, their power was very great. They were mostly local men, with vast knowledge of the customs and policies of the tribes. The Political Agents, too often frequently transferred, would have been as blind leaders of a blind and distant Government without the skilled advice of their Muslim and Hindu assistants. And when, after Partition, the Frontier was suddenly left almost denuded of its higher cadre, which being British mostly retired, and the Government of Pakistan was left to fill these vital posts on its borders, the Provincial Civil Service took over and, with efficiency and loyalty, carried on in a still provincial grade until the young officers of the newly formed Civil Service of Pakistan had acquired sufficient experience to take over from them.

For ill: many were reputed corrupt, and many are the stories told of how they pulled the wool over the eyes of the not always wise Deputy Commissioner or Political Agent. But when all is said and done, the record of the various officials and clerks who assisted the officers of the Indian Political Service is a most notable one, and has not been adequately acknowledged. At headquarters, in the Foreign Office and the Political Department, there were a large number of clerks, assistants and higher officers who spent their whole service there, and acquired in some cases a profound knowledge of their subject. Those political officers who, after 1947, joined the British civil or diplomatic service, were emphatic in testifying how superior their old, Indian clerical staff were to what Whitehall or the Embassy could provide.

In the States, executive work by subordinates was not so noticeable as on the Frontier. In them, it mostly took the form of skilled and devoted service by clerks and assistants in small offices – the secretariats of the Residents – where knowledge of local political law and practice was all important. Precedents lay scattered on files which, recorded in a manner that would astound western filing experts, were somehow always found when wanted. Here, again, there was an evil side to the great influence exercised by 'the office'; especially in Western India, where the Bombay Government's traditions lasted long, it was sometimes felt that the dead hand of bureaucracy hampered an ideal relationship with the States.

Indeed, in Western India, local 'political practice' had grown up and become ossified to such an extent that, though there were very few actual lawsuits tried before Political Agents, there was a flourishing bar at Rajkot which drafted petitions for petty chiefs and their relations at considerable profit to themselves, on all sorts of subjects: maintenance allowance to widows, boundary disputes, etc. Officers were bound by an infinity of precedents based on the rulings of previous Agents to the Governor-General. All orders were appealable – and usually appealed. It was pleaders' raj *in excelsis*.

And then there were the doctors. The Indian Medical Service was an integral part of the Indian Army, like the Royal Army Medical Corps in the British Army. But, over a long period of years, it had seconded a number of officers to the civil line, retaining the right to recall them in time of war. Not only did these officers man the more important hospitals in British India, and provide the posts of Civil Surgeon and Director-General in each province, they also had a cadre specially attached to the Political Service. This cadre, apart from staffing the more important medical posts in the North-West Frontier Province, Baluchistan and the Persian Gulf, provided posts at the various residencies in the States.

But perhaps the group of men most directly associated with the Political Service was that which staffed the five Chief Colleges, as they were known: institutions based on English public schools, which were founded in the days when few boys of ruling families received an education that was not vitiated by *zenana* influence and lacking in the western character which contemporary upper-class Indians were getting in British India. There were five of these institutions – at Ajmer, Indore, Rajkot, Raipur and Lahore – and most of them owed their foundation or improvement to Curzon. They were, until the thirties of this century, reserved for members of ruling families or British Indian families which passed the test of inclusion in the local Indian 'Debrett'. The life of these boys was rather sybaritic in the beginning, with servants and polo ponies galore. It was felt that this social test, however necessary originally to induce shy and exclusive princes to enter their sons, was altogether too snobbish and anachronous for the 1930s; and so, at a period when Indian public schools were being founded in many provinces, this test was abolished, with general approval. These schools have, largely as a consequence of this change in policy, survived the States for which, and often largely by which, they were founded. In present-day, post-Independence Pakistan (in the case of Lahore) and India (in the case of the other four), they have expanded and greatly flourish.

These schools had an English principal and usually one or two other English masters; the rest were Indian, and were largely drawn from the States. The standard of English, manners and sports, especially riding, was high; that of other subjects markedly below that obtaining in the best schools in British India. But some young princes were a distinct credit to their teachers. The story is told[14] of one who had to write an essay on hills – a subject of which he knew nothing. He wrote: 'Hills are good things. Where there are hills there are trees. Where there are trees there are jungles. Where there are jungles there are tigers. Where there are tigers, the Viceroy comes. The roads are mended; the Chief gets a K.C.I.E. and everyone is happy.' This passage illustrates (a) how to write good, clear English prose; (b) how a clever boy can switch painlessly from a subject which he doesn't know to one he does; (c) how some people thought the States were administered.

It was another Indian princeling whom Walter Lawrence quotes as writing: 'The horse is a noble animal, but when irritated he will not do so.'[15]

An interesting body was the Crown Representative's Police, a force one battalion strong, controlled by officers borrowed from the police or the army. It was stationed at Neemuch, an administered area in Central India, and was raised early in 1941 as a result of the difficulties caused by the unwillingness of Congress-controlled Governments in the provinces to restrain political movements in their areas from creating trouble in small States, still less to lend police to such States in time of need. After the elections held under the Government of India Act, 1935, Congress Governments had been elected in most of the provinces, and agitations had arisen in Mysore, Kashmir, Hyderabad, Jaipur and the Orissa States, amongst others. In Orissa, there was a serious outbreak in the small State of Ranpur, in which Bazalgette,* the Political Agent, was

---

* Major R. L. Bazalgette (1900–39). Military political. Political Agent, Orissa States. Killed by mob during disturbances in 1939.

killed. As a result, it was decided in 1940 to create this force which, during its short life, did most admirable work in preserving law and order wherever detachments of it had to be sent. A tribute from an unexpected source is to be found in *The Integration of the Indian States* by V. P. Menon, who writes:

> When I took over the States Ministry we stopped the disintegration of this force and changed its name from the Crown Representative's Police to the Central Reserve Police. It was one battalion in strength at that time. We increased it to two battalions. This was the only effective force which the States Ministry had at its disposal. It was very well trained, and but for the discipline, efficiency and devotion to duty of its officers and men, we would not have been able to maintain order, particularly in the small States and in the border areas, during the crucial period following the transfer of power.

Previously, there had been a number of small forces of armed police, under political control, in areas where an aboriginal population had presented problems beyond the power of the local rulers to cope with. Most of these had been wound up long before 1947, but the Malwa Bhil Corps, stationed at Indore, remained to the end.

Apart from these para-military police, there were bodies of ordinary police wherever there were any Administered Areas. Nearly all Agencies contained some, the Punjab and Eastern States Agencies being notable exceptions. In Hyderabad Residency lands there was quite a large body, amounting to well over a thousand men, under two Superintendents of Police, borrowed from the Central Provinces and controlled by the Secretary to the Resident, who held the post of Inspector-General of Police, *ex officio*. The same occurred in the civil and military Station of Bangalore, in Mysore State, and on a smaller scale in the Abu and Indore administered areas in Rajputana and Central India. There were twenty such areas in all, some, e.g. the Civil Lines, Nowgong, being extremely small. But perhaps the most interesting case of the use of Residency-controlled police in State territory was in Western India. There, apart from the small administered areas in Rajkot and Wadhwan, there were a number of very small States grouped, as we have seen, into *thanas*, which had no courts of their own, nor police. For the maintenance of law and order in these scattered but quite extensive territories, a large Police Force was maintained under a Deputy Inspector-General of Police, borrowed from Bombay. And Rajkot contained a large gaol where prisoners from these *thanas* were detained, as well as prisoners from States whose judicial powers were limited, e.g. to three years' imprisonment.

Much earlier, the Central India Horse–a unit which supplied many officers as recruits to the Political Service–had been permanently stationed, with similar duties, in Central India. And the Hyderabad Contingent, a large force which was amalgamated with the Indian Army early in the century, during Kitchener's reforms, had been stationed at a number of cantonments in Hyderabad State, under the overall control of the Resident at Hyderabad.

# Part II

# THE INDIAN STATES

# CHAPTER 10

## The Work of Political Officers in the States

LOOKING at the work of a Resident or Political Agent in an Indian State, we find that he had a quantity of day-to-day routine work, common to all Agencies; certain problems (for example, those arising from the death of a Ruler) which were liable at any time to arise in any Agency but which were occasional in their nature; and certain problems permanent, indeed, but confined to certain Agencies only. (Such were those arising out of the existence of ports, in the maritime States in Western India.)

Towards the end there were two grave problems that affected all States:

a. The federal problem, acute between 1930 and 1940, i.e. whether or not the States would join an all-India federation.

b. The lapse of Paramountcy: the problem which arose in 1946, and was not yet fully solved on the Partition of the sub-continent in August 1947, of the future of the States after British India gained independence.

First, we must explain a few terms. Using those in force from 1937, practically all States were in relations with a Resident, usually assisted by a Secretary and Under-Secretary. With the exception of a few large States, these relations (after 1937) were not direct but through Political Agents, who each had a group of States in their charge. A Resident's charge was known usually as an Agency—a throw-back to earlier nomenclature—but when there was only one State involved, as with Hyderabad, Mysore and Kashmir, the term Residency was used. (Compare a Legation with its Minister and Secretaries.)

The Resident had a small secretariat, and the Political Agents even smaller ones. Relatively small, that is; in the Western India States Agency there were no fewer than 145 clerks. Attached to Residents' offices would sometimes be a small group of technical experts with their clerks: an executive Engineer, a doctor known as the Residency or Agency Surgeon, a Military Adviser on deputation from the Indian Army to assist and inspect the forces of those larger States which had contingents of Indian State Forces. Sometimes there would be a Superintendent or higher officer of police in charge of administered areas (of which, more below) in the States, such as railway lands and cantonments; where the administered lands were extensive (as in Hyderabad and Mysore) there would almost certainly be a magistrate and a district and sessions judge, probably borrowed from British India, to lighten the burden and raise the quality of judicial work, which would otherwise have had to be done by a too junior Under-Secretary, or a too busy Secretary.

Though diplomatic relations with Rulers had always to take first place in importance, the day-to-day out-turn of files might well be 75 per cent Administered Area and 25 per cent States work proper. Residents and their staff often found themselves weighed down with a mass of tiresome detail arising from municipalities, schools, hospitals and various institutions, in places like Secunderabad, Bangalore, Rajkot or Abu, in addition to their political work proper. And a Resident's social obligations were comparable to a Governor's. At Secunderabad in Hyderabad, there were 10,000 troops stationed; and entertaining their officers and the numerous State nobles and civil servants formed part of the work of the Resident and his staff.

Two Residents, Rajputana and Mysore, were *ex-officio* Chief Commissioners for very small British Indian provinces: Ajmer and Coorg. Though constitutionally their status was different, in practice the work of supervising them was similar to the supervision exercised over Administered Areas. But each had a resident Commissioner: in Ajmer always, till the 1940s, a political officer; in Coorg an officer borrowed from Madras.

Originally, there was a ban on States corresponding with and entering into agreements with other States. This century saw a great loosening of control in this matter. In recent times, the States corresponded freely *inter se* without any objection; indeed, the creation of the Chamber of Princes, officially encouraged, made this inevitable. V. P. Menon and other authors have drawn a quite wrong picture of political officers frowning on inter-state co-operation. They are a century or more out of date.

Extradition was a matter of common occurrence, which seldom caused difficulties. Extradition to and from countries outside India was rare, and was treated in the same way as if the case arose in British India. In inter-state extradition, save when special agreements existed, all that one State could reasonably ask of another, or the paramount power could be expected to help in obtaining, was such cooperation as was consistent with the principles of comity. There remained two other classes of extradition: to India States from British India and vice versa.

Extradition to States from British India was simple, and covered by the Extradition Act of 1903. The Political Agent examined the *prima facie* evidence produced by the State, holding a preliminary enquiry to this end, and then issued his warrant which the British India authorities were bound, under the Extradition Act, 1903, to execute unless, on appeal to the Provincial Government, the Governor-in-Council set it aside.

In cases of extradition to British India from States, no Act applied. The Political Agent acted in the exercise of Paramountcy, though he normally only requested a State to extradite for an 'extradition offence' as defined in the Extradition Act (i.e. a fairly grave offence). The States were usually wholly cooperative; the Political Agent had to examine the *prima facie* evidence forwarded by the magistrate in British India before passing on the warrant to the State for execution.

No hard and fast rules were laid down regarding what a Political Agent should do immediately before and after the death of a Ruler. In early days, it was often necessary to take stern measures to prevent *sati* (suicide by burning of the Ruler's widows). If a Ruler left a clear heir, the Political Agent had nothing to do save to report through his Resident to Government the name of the heir; recognition then followed as a matter of course. At one time, this question of recognition was a thorny subject of controversy. The Political Department laid down in 1891, what had been the practice since about 1834, that 'Every succession to an Indian State holding direct relations with the British Government must be recognized by, or on behalf of, the British Government, and no succession is valid until recognition has been given'. This was resented by many of the Princes, but their feelings were assuaged by a pronouncement in 1917 which, while not abrogating the 1891 decision, read: 'Where there is a natural heir in the direct line, he succeeds as a matter of course; and the recognition of his succession by H.M. the King-Emperor will be conveyed by an exchange of *kharitas* of a complimentary character between the new Prince or Chief and the Viceroy or other high authority concerned.' (A *kharita* was a formal letter written by the Viceroy in a flowery Persian, and one of the few surviving relics of earlier diplomatic courtesies. Its use was confined to occasions like successions, and to those Rulers who were entitled to correspond direct with the Viceroy.)

The States did not deny that, in the case of a disputed succession, the political authorities had to intervene. Who else was there? Democratic public opinion in the State? Perish the thought! A family conclave? Impossible! So the much-maligned but recognizedly impartial Political

Agent was brought in when there was no clear heir. He was enjoined to consider, when a Ruler was believed to be dying, whether he should not be encouraged to declare his wishes as regards his successor. If a serious dispute was feared, the Political Agent was to consider whether extra police and troops need be asked for. After death, in such a case, he had to take precautions for the security of State and personal property, particularly treasure and jewels, if possible visiting the State personally and affixing his seal. He had, of course, to report as quickly as possible to higher authority who, in his opinion, should succeed, not failing to mention whether there was any chance of a posthumous son. Provisional arrangements for carrying on business must be made–a difficult and delicate matter this. The Political Agent had further to make sure that no ceremony, religious or otherwise, purporting to recognize accession, was performed until Government orders were received.

In early times it was not uncommon for a decision about the succession to be reached well before a Ruler's death. Eventually this practice was abandoned. It had many inconveniences; Rulers had a habit of changing their minds not only once but even oftener. They also produced sons long after this was expected; they quarrelled with their recognized heirs; they discovered convenient legal flaws in the adoption which they had already made.

There were two exceptions to the general rule that eldest sons succeed automatically. One was the matriarchal rule of succession in two States, Travancore and Cochin, in the extreme south. The other was that of the offspring of marriages with foreigners. In this century, amongst others, the Ruler of Kapurthala married a Spaniard, the Rulers of Pudukkottai and Palanpur, Australians, and the Ruler of Rajpipla an Englishwoman. Such marriages, rare at first, became almost frequent after 1947. In these cases, the offspring was not allowed to succeed (in most cases there were heirs by an Indian wife as well): and in addition, the foreign wife was refused the title of Her Highness or Maharani, and the privilege of presentation to the Viceroy or other high official. This last ruling seems unnecessarily harsh; but it was a ruling that had the strong support of King Edward VII and, perhaps for that reason, was always enforced.

A change of religion raised problems on which there was no such clear-cut decision. Two curious cases spring to mind. The predecessor of the Maharaja of Kapurthala who married the Spaniard for long had no son, and the heir presumptive was his brother. This brother became a Christian at a time, not long after the Baroda deposition, when Government were anxious not to give avoidable offence to the feelings of States' subjects. Since shortly after this conversion a son was born to the long-childless Maharaja, all was well and no need for action to exclude the brother arose. The fact remains that it was widely believed that this was a supposititious child, and that a blind eye was turned by Government to the proceedings.

The other case, that of Baoni, occurred in 1871, when the Hindu Raja became a Muslim, and it was decided that 'although the Chief has abandoned the Hindu religion yet the relations between him and his subjects have in no other respects been changed'. Later, in 1902, Bane Singh, this Chief's younger son, succeeded his elder brother who had reverted to Hinduism and adopted a Hindu relative on his death-bed. Bane Singh was a Muslim, but known to be keen to renounce that religion and secure readmission to his Hindu caste. This he was allowed to do, and the claims of two adopted sons were turned down.

The right, granted to all States of any size after the Mutiny, by what were known as the Canning *Sanads*, of adopting heirs in the absence of a son to succeed, was of great importance. It created many problems. Hindu law treats a child duly adopted by a son-less man from the appropriate caste and sub-caste, and complying with various rules (e.g. he must not be an only son, or have been already adopted elsewhere) as in all respects equivalent, for purposes of succession to ordinary property, to a son of the body. And this applies equally to a son adopted after the father's death by his widow, if he has failed to exercise this right in his lifetime. But–and this was an important exception–this absolute right to adopt applied only to private individuals and not to Rulers. Thus, before the Mutiny, Dalhousie made use of the veto which this gave him in several cases to refuse to recognize adoption, instead escheating the State to the British Government. Afterwards, in the belief that this was one of the causes of the Mutiny, policy was reversed, and in solemn promises made in Queen Victoria's name, the Princes were informed that

> Her Majesty being desirous that the Governments of the several Princes and Chiefs of India, who now govern their own territories, should be perpetuated, and that the representation and dignity of their Houses should be continued, I hereby, in fulfilment of this desire, convey to you the assurance that, on failure of natural heirs, the adoption by yourself and future rulers of your state of a successor according to Hindoo law and the customs of your race will be recognised and confirmed. Be assured that nothing shall disturb the engagement just made to you, so long as your house is loyal to the

Crown, and faithful to the conditions of the Treaties, grants and engagements which record its obligations to the British Government.

This was the text of the Canning *Sanads* referred to above. In the case of Muslim Rulers the words after 'natural heirs' were altered to 'any succession to the Government of your state, which may be legitimate according to Mahomedan law, will be upheld'.

Thereafter, there was no dispute about the right to adopt. But often, when a Prince died leaving an adopted son, collaterals would weigh in with petitions drafted by the most eminent lawyers in India alleging a flaw here or there in the adoption and pressing their own claims. Of course, if there had been no adoption, the case was further complicated. It required some legal ability and good knowledge of local conditions and personalities to advise on these cases, which, if the State were of importance, were not finally decided by the Viceroy but went on to the Secretary of State.

When a Ruler died leaving as his heir a minor, many problems arose for the Political Agent. A young child was usually selected. This undoubtedly led to good results so far as the Ruler's character was concerned, as there was thus time to educate him properly. The greatest care was taken in choosing a tutor-cum-guardian for the young Princes; and with rare exceptions the choice was successful. Some men made almost a profession of it: Fraser,[*] tutor both to His Highness of Kolhapur and His Highness of Mysore (as also to the Chief of Kagal and the heir to the Ruler of Bhavnagar) and Harvey-Jones,[†] tutor to His Highness of Dhar and others, were conspicuous examples. It was a matter of regret that it was seldom possible to spare officers: apart from Fraser, and later Gaisford[‡] and Trevelyan[§] in Gwalior, very few politicals in this century

[*] Sir Stuart Fraser (1864–1963), K.C.S.I., C.I.E.; I.C.S., Bombay, 1884. Political, 1889. An officer of great distinction who died a few weeks short of 100 years old after serving as Resident in Kashmir, Resident in Mysore, and Resident in Hyderabad. In the first two of these posts he was followed by his son, Lt.-Col. Sir Denholm Fraser (1889–1956), K.C.V.O., C.S.I., C.I.E., who after retirement was Political A.D.C. to the Secretary of State for India, 1945–8.

[†] Captain M. S. Harvey-Jones (1893–1968). Indian Army, retired, served as tutor with conspicuous success to the Ruler of Dhar. Later, employed in Junagadh State, and left in charge when its accession to Pakistan was unsuccessful.

[‡] Lt.-Col. Sir Philip Gaisford (b. 1891), Kt., C.I.E. Indian Army, 1911–19. Guardian to H.H. the Maharaja Scindia of Gwalior, 1929. Resident in Western India and at Mysore, 1942–6.

[§] Humphrey, Lord Trevelyan (b. 1905), G.C.M.G., C.I.E., O.B.E.; I.C.S., Madras, 1929; Political, 1932. Joint Secretary External Affairs Dept., 1946–7. Diplomatic Service, 1947–65; Ambassador, Egypt, Iraq and Moscow. High Commissioner, Aden, 1967.

served as tutors, though many more were lent to States as *Dewans*, the term usually used for Chief Minister. Officers thus loaned were known as being on 'Foreign Service', and an officer could be sent to a State (though not against his will) without losing seniority. He usually drew 25 per cent extra pay and certain easements, especially freedom from British Indian income tax. Such deputations were thus popular.

The actual administration of a State during a minority might be carried out in many different ways. The local political authorities were expected to have thought out an appropriate scheme before the Ruler's death. Tupper,[16] in his unpublished *Political Practice*, summing up numerous precedents in 1895, laid down the principles to be followed.

These were that, during a minority, the position of the British representative should be 'one of commanding influence and power', no interference by relations of the minor Ruler being allowed. Reforms should be introduced; the minor Ruler educated and trained; a Superintendent selected who, for reasons of economy would normally but not always be an Indian; a Council of Regency might be appointed in a large State, but strictly under the directions of the Political Officer. Rulers normally got their powers at eighteen–but this could be delayed if necessary or, up to twenty-one, powers might be limited, e.g. he might be required to employ a Chief Minister selected by Government.

But during the period after Curzon's departure, when there was a marked reaction against what might be called his 'forward policy' towards the States, a very different code was laid down, and later published in the Manual of the Political Department. In over 1,000 words it laid down that anything like pressure on States during minorities to introduce British methods of administration was forbidden. Administrative efficiency was at no time the only or indeed the chief object to keep in view. Conservation of the customs of the State was our primary duty. 'Customs' included the performance of religious ceremonies and exchange of presents with other States. Local talent was always to be employed, where available. No constitutional changes were allowed, nor alteration of currency, of the court language or the postal system. The privy purse should continue to be paid in full and kept in trust for the minor Ruler. State jewellery should not be sold. Shooting rules and restrictions should be strictly enforced.[17]

The change of policy was marked, and the above brief précis from a long and strongly worded ruling shows how closely the hands of Political Agents were tied, when they wished to use a period of minority rule to modernise and improve administration. Had they followed this code closely, the condition of the States in 1947 would have been greatly inferior to what in fact it was. In practice, it was remarkable how many reforms were carried out, in spite of the 1917 code. But it was there, for all to read, in the Political Department Manual. There was some good sense in it, and it was a valuable curb on the zeal of an officer who would have totally upset the traditional methods current in a State; but it was also a charter of reaction, and one feels that, to its drafters, tigers came before schools.

Under British Indian law, all British subjects, European and Indian alike, were amenable to British Indian jurisdiction for crimes committed in Indian States. In practice, this procedure was very seldom adopted: British Indian subjects were tried by State courts, and European British subjects were tried by the Political authorities.

This is somewhat reminiscent of the capitulations which formerly governed the trial of foreigners in China, Turkey, etc.; but there was not the rigid insistence on special courts which marked the capitulatory system.

Great variety existed in regard to the judicial powers which States could exercise outside these special categories. The largest States were allowed to try all persons, whether their own subjects or subjects of other States, for all offences, including those punishable by death. In less important States, various restrictions began to be imposed, the first being that which required death sentences to be confirmed by the Resident. Further down, offences punishable by death were reserved to the Residency courts; and lower again, offences punishable with so many years imprisonment, till eventually the small Estates were reached which, consisting of a village or even less, were not considered fit to try even a parking offence—in the unlikely event of their possessing a road on which a car could be parked.[18]

Tupper records a large number of cases in which barbarous practices —female infanticide, torture, sati, impalement, burial alive of lepers, execution without trial—were severely punished, whether by deposition of the Ruler concerned or otherwise. But right up to 1947, different ideas were held on what was reasonable to treat as a crime; and it was notorious that in Kashmir, a State overwhelmingly Muslim in population, the Hindu dynasty punished cow-killing severely, the law permitting a sentence of up to seven years' rigorous imprisonment until some modification was introduced in the late thirties.

Boundary disputes between States were of constant occurrence, and there were few Agencies where there were not some long-standing files which no one seemed in any great hurry to settle. In early days, great importance was attached to the prohibition of States entering into agreement with other States, save through the medium of the Political Officer concerned. In most Agencies there was a regular procedure for the settlement of boundary disputes. In 1877, a code of rules which had been in force for some time in Central India was amended and extended to Rajputana as well. The main principle of this code was that, first, every opportunity should be given to the parties to settle the dispute by agreement or arbitration. If this were not found possible, then a representative of each State was to attend a Boundary Officer at the disputed boundary and mark out his claim. If they disagreed, the Boundary Officer determined the case on such evidence as was available. An appeal lay to the Agent to the Governor-General. Almost identical rules existed for the Punjab States and for Baroda and the Western India States.

Ceremonial matters—titles, salutes, and forms of address—were of great interest to many Rulers and were among the subjects which all political officers had to master. The grant by the British of titles direct, i.e. not through 'the pageant court of Delhi' began, Tupper[19] tells us, with Hastings,\* but was rare. The systematic grant of titles started with Amherst,† and some rules were laid down by Bentinck‡ in a Resolution of 30 May 1829, the principle feature of which was that they should not be hereditary.[20] In 1859, Canning§ obtained the Secretary of State's approval that all grant of titles should be made by the Viceroy.

Earlier, on 27 June 1770, King George III, when he wished to invest Sir John Lindsay and Major-General Eyre Coote with the K.C.B., wrote a personal letter[21] to the Nawab of Arcot, and asked him to conduct the ceremony, and in so doing 'to represent Our Person upon this solemn occasion, and that you will perform these Functions for Us which We always perform Ourselves when the circumstances will admit'. (The Nawab's successor was created a Prince by Letters Patent in 1870[22]—the only Indian to be given that title until the late Nizam's eldest son was created Prince of Berar in 1936).

This is far removed from 1895, when Tupper summarized the precedents regarding titles. Though he took care to emphasize that, 'In the

---

\* 1st Marquess of Hastings, 2nd Earl of Moira (1754–1826). Governor-General, 1813–22.

† 1st Earl Amherst (1773–1857). Governor-General, 1823–8.

‡ Lord William Cavendish Bentinck, (1774–1839). Governor-General, Bengal, 1827. Governor-General India, 1833–5.

§ 1st Earl Canning (1812–62). Governor-General, 1856–62.

grant of titles in India, care should be taken to avoid too much system. Much is left to the unfettered discretion of the Representative of the Queen,' he laid down these rules, amongst others :[23]

a. The power to grant titles in India to Ruling Chiefs and, except as implied below, to Native British subjects rests exclusively with the Viceroy.

b. Titles may be granted by Ruling Chiefs to their own subjects 'so long as they are granted with discretion'.

c. Titles conferred by the Rulers of Native States on European British subjects without the previous sanction of the Queen cannot be recognized.

d. Ruling Chiefs may not confer titles upon Native British subjects without the consent of the Government of India; and should not grant to Native British subjects in their service titles the same as those which are usually conferred by the Viceroy.

e. The Viceroy has full authority to grant Indian titles to the subjects of Native States, and it is not ordinarily the practice to consult the Rulers of States before proposing titles for their subjects.

Rule e. at least was rescinded in recent times. And the tone of these commandments was, perhaps, somewhat personal to Tupper, a Punjab civilian who was not in the political service and only spent a few years in the Government of India on special duty for this work.

The gun salutes to which the leading States were entitled formed a rough-and-ready guide to the importance of States.[24] They varied from nine to twenty-one. Ceremonial varied in these leading States; but their tendency was constantly to try to make it more elaborate and exacting and that of the British authorities to restrict it, if not to a uniform system, at least to a reasonable scale. The worst disputes centred round questions of the manner in which a succession to a princely throne was to be recognized, how the attainment of full ruling powers by a minor was to be signalized and publicly celebrated, and what should be the participation of the British representative in these events. Acute wrangles sometimes resulted; but as a result of the deliberations of the Chamber of Princes an agreed procedure was evolved which covered the more important points.[25]

Great care was, of course, always taken when addressing a Ruler to give him all his titles. Many had long-standing hereditary titles in addition to that of Maharaja, for example, and such English titles as were given for life. For example, the Nizam's full titles were: 'Lieutenant-General His Exalted Highness Asaf Jah Muzaffar-ul-Mulk wal Mamalik,

Nizam-ul-Mulk Nizam-ud-Daula, Nawab Sir Mir Usman Ali Khan, Bahadur, Fateh Jang, Faithful Ally of the British Government, G.C.S.I., G.B.E., Nizam of Hyderabad.' To prevent any omission by oversight, envelopes were kept in the Hyderabad Residency with these full titles printed on them, the envelopes being nearly covered by the print. These were invariably used when the Resident wrote to the Nizam.

Patiala came near to the same quantity of titles with his: 'Lieutenant-General His Highness Farzand-i-Khas-i-Daulat-i-Inglishia Mansur-i-Zaman Amir-al-Umra Maharajadhiraja Rajeshwar Sri Maharaja-i-Rajagan Sir Bhupindar Singh Mahindar Bahadur, G.C.S.I., G.C.I.E., G.C.V.O., G.B.E., LL.D., A.D.C., Maharaja of Patiala.' And Jaipur and Alwar had the interesting titles of 'Sawai', meaning one and a half. They were 'one-and-a-half Maharajas'—whatever dignity any colleague had, they had half as much again, was the idea.

Not merely precedence, not merely the firing of guns, but modes of address were a source of anguish. Princes with salutes of only 9 guns, alone of all their fellows, were refused the title of 'His Highness'. The fact that their subjects and shopkeepers in British India used it, without authority, did not compensate the lack of official recognition. Some Residents were insistent on enforcing this restriction, and distress resulted, until, in 1942, Fitze* gave orders 'to suspend operations against solecisms which, in my view, the British Crown could well afford to ignore.'[26] This whole subject seems, in 1970, so remote and so ridiculous as scarcely to be worth recall. But it may be suggested that, had we been less rigid over ceremonial and stricter over misrule and insisting on radical administrative reforms in, for example, finance and the judiciary, we might have benefited the subject more and been no more hated by the Prince. The writer recalls his surprise when, on a visit to Java, he saw the wives of leading Dutch officials curtseying to the Sultans (who were not even, by our tests, Rulers of States, but mediatized landlords). What did this politeness cost them?

To continue the personal note, the sad story of the 9-gun Princes has a happy ending. A few weeks before the end of British rule, Mountbatten† announced at a Residents' conference that his experience of his own German relations was that they were inordinately addicted to titles. He felt that this should be borne in mind in handling the Indian States. The

---

* Sir Kenneth Fitze (1867–1960), K.C.I.E.; I.C.S., Central Provinces, 1911. Secretary to the Crown Representative, 1940–4.

† Earl Mountbatten of Burma (b. 1900). Viceroy of India, March–August 1947. Governor-General of India 1947–8.

writer thereupon revived a proposal which he had made, but which had previously been turned down, for the grant of the title of 'Highness' to 9-gun Rulers; supported by his departmental superiors and the Viceroy, the proposal came back from the India Office approved in record time, just before Partition.

But 'Highness' was not the only forbidden word. At the time of the Butler Committee, the grievances of some of the Rulers on these and many other subjects were ably set out in a book, Nicholson's *Scraps of Paper*,[27] which lists the taboos. 'Closed' crowns on writing-paper, 'throne' instead of *gaddi*, 'royal family' for 'Ruler's family'–so the lamentable list continues. The pity of it! The book is valuable as showing what an important group among the Princes thought of these restrictions.

It was all really rather ridiculous. Sometimes the funny side of etiquette showed itself openly. The late E. M. Forster[28] tells a tale of a former Maharaja Holkar of Indore:

> One or two of them, e.g. the Gaekwar of Baroda, exact and accord the minimum of ceremonial, but the rest try to get it both ways, in spite of the practical disadvantages. There is a story about Holkar (not the present Ruler of Indore, but a predecessor) who wished to visit Hyderabad, but could not go because the ceremonial which the then Nizam accorded him was insufficient. He therefore planned an oriental joke. He went to Hyderabad secretly, and drove in a shabby carriage along the route that the Nizam was accustomed to frequent. When the Nizam's carriage approached, he managed to graze against its wheels and fling himself out, as if dislodged by the concussion. The late Nizam had a compassionate nature, and, seeing a stout old gentleman rolling in the dust, jumped out to assist him. 'At last,' he said, 'the Nizam of Hyderabad has descended from his carriage to greet the Maharajah of Indore.' Fortunately, the host thought the joke equally delightful. Roaring with laughter, he seated his mischievous guest beside him, and they drove on to the palace together.

This particular Maharaja–the one who remembered Queen Victoria's birthday–was a great eccentric. For years he did things (e.g. harnessing six leading money-lenders to his carriage and himself driving them through the town) which were scandalous but just not enough to earn him deposition. Eventually, in a rash moment, he volunteeered his abdication, which Curzon was not slow to accept. Thereafter, he lay low and little was heard of him until Curzon himself was practically forced to resign owing to the failure of the Cabinet to back him up in his dispute with Kitchener, the Commander-in-Chief. Then Holkar's chance came; he sent a telegram to the outgoing Viceroy which read: 'I deposed greet you deposed.' Curzon, in his *Leaves from a Viceroy's Note-book*, has much to say about the Maharaja of Indore: he does not mention this telegram.

Wherever in the States a Political Agent might be serving, certain features would be common to his work. He would, especially if the Agency contained many States, spend a considerable time on tour, sometimes joined by his Resident. He would probably aim at visiting each State, on a very broad average, about twice a year, for three or four days at a time. If any State were under minority administration he would probably need to go much oftener.

When States were remote and isolated by poor communications, these visits sometimes had strange features. A certain Ruler in Western India, when his Resident and his Secretary paid their first visit, entertained them to tennis, after which they sat out in the Ruler's garden. This contained a number of marble female statues, all in the nude, and calculated in the Ruler's eye to make a bad impression on his new Resident. He therefore fitted them all out in bathing dresses.

It was to an even smaller and remoter state in the same part of the world that the writer paid an official visit as Political Agent in the winter of 1944–5. The young Ruler, educated in a Chiefs' College and himself very westernized, laid on a programme of athletics in which his aboriginal subjects did not greatly distinguish themselves. When he apologized for this, the P.A. said that what he was really looking forward to was the archery; the men in this State were famous for this, and even at times killed tiger with arrows. To this the Ruler replied: 'I sent out a few days back to summon all the best archers for today. When they heard this they said: "We remember that, in September 1939, we were clearly told that there would be no conscription in this war. And now, with Rundstedt counter-attacking in the Ardennes, you send for the *best archers* for a P.A.'s visit. We're not quite so dense."' . . . and they disappeared into the jungle till he had left.

But normally, visits to the States lacked such highlights. The Rulers' standards of hospitality were high, and the atmosphere in most States was that of an old-fashioned English country-house party. Some Rulers indeed deliberately laid on so much shooting or other sport that there was insufficient time to visit institutions like schools and prisons.

To curb this tendency, Linlithgow issued instructions that all P.A.'s after visiting a State should send in a brief report for the Viceroy's information. It was prepared in quintuplicate–an office copy, a copy for the Resident (who added his comments occasionally); copies for the Political Department, Viceroy and Secretary of State. They were intended to be informal and, if possible, amusing. They often were. Shortly before Partition, a Resident reported that he had just visited a very remote State where the Raja was an alcoholic. He met the Resident in a rather formal gathering of officials, with the words: 'I hear you're going to quit India. When you do, old man, take me with you, will you?'–and then fell flat on his face.

Much in this book will show the friction which existed between the Political Department and Rulers accused of misgovernment, or which arose from two different views of State rights. But though undoubtedly many Rulers in their heart of hearts resented the whole set up of paramountcy to an extent which made them look upon their Political Agent as their opponent, it would be wrong to suggest that there were not many instances of the reverse. Often, a close personal friendship, analogous to that which sometimes arises between a Head of State and a foreign ambassador, existed between a Ruler and his P.A. Again and again a Ruler would ask his P.A. privately for advice on some grave matter like federal negotiations, and it was a tribute to the service that the Rulers, as a whole, trusted the word of their P.A.s and, even when the matter at issue was some controversy with Government, would fully confide in them.

Indeed, they would sometimes ask advice in personal and family matters in which a P.A. was not permitted to advise. Political officers were not supposed to take part in negotiations for marriages, but it was not unknown for Rulers to ask their advice about the suitability of a matrimonial alliance with some State where the officer had previously served.

In every State there was an official usually known as the *Dewan*, if the State were Hindu or Sikh, or the *Wazir*, if it were Muslim, who was the Chief Minister and head of the administration. In large States, there might be a Council of Ministers, but it was rare for these to assert themselves strongly against the *Dewan*. On his efficiency, much depended, and on the whole they were a fine body of men. In some States it was the convention that the advice of the political authorities was sought to appointments of *Dewans*, even if far from blindly accepted. This was not necessarily confined to small States. On the contrary, in the largest of all States, Hyderabad, there was a long-standing tradition that the Viceroy's approval was required to the person selected by the Nizam as his Chief Minister; and when later this post was put into commission and an

Executive Council of half a dozen or so Ministers created, the Viceroy continued to exercise his paramountcy–given veto on individual ministers. Even that champion of Hyderabad prerogatives, Sir Salar Jang the first, had invoked the aid of the British Government to prevent his own downfall.

The choice of *Dewans* in the major States in the years preceding 1947 played a very great part in the 'final solution', to borrow a phrase from Nazi nomenclature, of the States' problem. More and more in the last few years did these Rulers give up employing their own subjects, and imported *Dewans* on high salaries, often from South India, of exceptional ability, usually lawyers or civil servants by training. Many of these Rulers were, it so happened, men of quiet and even nervous temperament, unlike the generation that preceded them who may some of them have been scoundrels, but were men of great drive and sure of themselves. These imported *Dewans* were often a marked success as administrators, and if resistant to proposals like federation, nevertheless gave the impression that a good lawyer gives of being reasonable and willing to negotiate. What no one anticipated was that, in some cases, their not unnatural personal convictions as sincere Indian nationalists–in one case, K. M. Panikkar, as a Communist fellow-traveller–would lead them at the last moment to show their true colours and advise their masters to adopt a course which, for good or for ill, meant the liquidation of their rule.

Certain problems which gave a good deal of work in early days, had in this century fallen into a seldom disturbed routine. One was the employment by States of Europeans (which, in India, included Americans and Australians). Every such case had to be referred for approval, but in recent times this useful check on the employment of scoundrels seldom caused friction. Similarly designed to protect Princes from themselves, some restriction on the taking of loans was always enforced. Inter-State loans had to receive Government approval; loans by British Indian–still worse, British-European–money-lenders were regarded with less than sympathy.[29] Political Agents used to be bombarded with requests from shopkeepers and others in British India for intervention to induce Rulers to pay their debts. This was always refused, nor did the law of British India permit them to be sued in its courts, any more than they could be prosecuted criminally, save with the consent of Government.

There was a complete ban on foreign consuls being accredited. This was well-recognized; and when in 1873 the German Government defined the limits of their Karachi consulate as extending 'over provinces of Sind and the Punjab *with the Native States within them*', the British chargé d'affaires in Berlin was promptly instructed 'in a friendly spirit to draw the attention of the German Government to the fact that under no circumstances are any Native States permitted to enter into relations with other States or with Foreign Powers except through the medium and with the knowledge and sanction of the British Indian Government.'[30]

During the Fascist regime in Italy, several attempts were made by the Italian Consul-General at Bombay to bluff his way into visiting the States. And during the war, though he was admittedly an ally, the Chinese Consul-General at Calcutta was held to have acted irregularly in visiting Bhopal State without permission.

In the nineteenth century much work arose over the question of Customs. Great efforts were made by the Government of India to induce States to abandon internal customs barriers, and the unfair opportunity sometimes taken of minorities—when the State was under the direct authority of the Government of India—to secure their reform, however desirable, was one of the practices which the Chamber of Princes put forward as a grievance. In this century, it was excise rather than customs which caused trouble. A major grievance of the States was that when, abandoning free trade, the Government of India in the 1920s and 1930s, under the pressure of nationalist opinion in the Assembly, passed legislation increasing the duty on imports, the States were, in fact, indirectly taxed without getting anything in return. When, then, certain excise duties were introduced, notably on sugar and matches, both of which by 1930 had begun to be produced in large quantities in British India, the States took the view that, even if it were too late to remedy their customs grievance, they should not be done down on excise as well. Here, the Government of India agreed; and a formula was devised, based on the population of the States, for the sale of sugar and banderolled* matches, by which the States were given a rebate which was in some cases quite considerable.

Lastly, all Political Officers serving in States had a variety of routine administrative work such as issuing passports, gun licences and so on. Since the States had no direct contact with foreign powers, passports were issued exclusively by the political authorities. They certified that the holder was not a 'British subject' but a 'British protected person'. During both wars, especially the second, controls of various kinds were introduced, more particularly in World War II over food. There was an

* Bearing certificate of payment of excise.

excellent food scheme which depended for its success on direct cooperation between the Government of India and the States. Here, too, the political authorities did all in their power to secure cooperation, free from red tape; and the criticism of the department and its officers as trying to Balkanize India was unfair and inaccurate.

# CHAPTER 11

## Matters Affecting certain States Only

A MONG the day-to-day work of the political officer in some, but not all, Agencies, a high place must be given to what were generally known as Administered Areas. They fell into three categories: railway lands, cantonments, and others. All these areas were integral parts of the State and could at any time be retroceded to the State if no longer required. (This was done in regard to a number of small cantonments in Hyderabad and Central India, as well as to half the larger cantonment of Secunderabad: when troops were moved elsewhere, by mutual agreement a notification was issued in the Gazette of India and they resumed their original status.)

What was this notification? It was one issued under the Foreign Jurisdiction and Extradition Act (No. XXI of 1879), an act of the British Indian legislature.

Under similar legislation, by Order in Council in the U.K., large territories (e.g. Tanganyika) were absorbed, as Protectorates, in the British Empire in Africa and elsewhere. The effect of these notifications in India was that, while no legislation by either the Home Government or the Government of India was automatically applicable to any territory within an Indian State, it could be and frequently was applied to an Administered Area by the mere issue of a notification, whether in full or curtailed or amended before issue. These notifications gave the Administered Areas a complete set of laws, the text of which was printed in a six-volume work, MacPherson's *British Enactments in force in Indian States* which was to be found in every Political Agent's office, along with the similarly full and instructive Aitchison's *Treaties*. From these, read with the long and well-indexed *Unrepealed General Acts of the Government of India*, a Political Agent with little legal training could in a minute or two lay his hand on the exact law applicable in any Administered Areas. There was no procedure for applying State laws to them, nor was this ever done.

Early on, when railways were being constructed up and down the country, it was found that they must inevitably cross State territory. In fact, the main line from Bombay via Baroda to Delhi crossed State frontiers thirty-eight times. The States, it must be remembered, were scattered over the map of India, usually in the less fertile and more hilly and wooded areas. It was soon realized that, to prevent thefts in trains, it was very desirable that British Indian controlled police and British Indian administered laws should operate unchecked by State authorities on lines which crossed State frontiers *en route* to other points in British India. In a few small cases where a line was built purely inside a State and did not link up with other territories, no objection was raised to that State's police operating. But otherwise, railway lands were always administered by the Political Department.

Cantonments – by which were simply meant places where troops were garrisoned – were similarly treated. There were large cantonments at Secunderabad, Bangalore and Quetta. There were smaller ones at Mhow in Indore and at Baroda.

In both Secunderabad and Bangalore, a large and prosperous civil station had grown up next to the barracks, and by this century was an anachronism. The intention was that the troops should have ample elbow room but not that their presence should be made an excuse for a large body of merchants to trade and avoid payment of State taxes. In fact, Secunderabad had grown so large and prosperous because the Indian merchants concerned did not trust the Hyderabad State Courts. When in the 1930s these two States asked for the return of such part of the cantonments as was extra to the needs of the garrison, Government readily agreed, though there was some difficulty in agreeing with Mysore precisely where the boundary should run, in the case of Bangalore.

Another function that was exercised by some but not all Agencies was the collection of tribute. Tribute was a historical anachronism, though it added to the problems which arose to defeat federation in the 1930s. Some States paid tribute to Government, some to other States. Some States paid it to one neighbour and received it from another. The sums, mostly very small, had long ago been settled and no one troubled about this survival.

A subject confined to a small but important group of States was that of maritime customs. In spite of the lengthy coast line of India, no States had a seaport except Cochin, Travancore, Janjira, several States in Kathiawar, Kalat and Cutch. The Kathiawar group and Cutch all had small ports which handled a certain amount of coastwise traffic by dhows, which even made trips to East Africa and the Persian Gulf. Their activities were of minor importance until, early in this century, the gradual but substantial rise in customs rates imposed by the Government of India, in pursuance of a policy of protection, made it worth while to import to British India through these ports, thereby undercutting Bombay by charging lower dues. At the request of the Government of India, Cutch and the Kathiawar States (Bhavnaghar, Junagadh, Porbandar, Baroda, Nawanagar and Morvi), agreed to charge rates no lower than Bombay in return for the abolition of a very tiresome customs cordon which the Government of India had established at Virangam, the land entrance to Kathiawar. This worked for a time, until the Government of India realized that imports through these ports were far higher than their local consumption would justify and revived the Virangam cordon. It was found that, while these States kept to their word over the rates of duty levied, they gave at the same time various easements–free porterage, waiving of port dues, etc.–which still made these ports more popular than Bombay. Government insisted that this practice should cease. It was reduced–it was scarcely capable of complete extinction.

Many States originally coined in mints of their own. Over the years, gradual persuasion of the Government of India induced most to give up this valuable sign of sovereignty in the interests of the economic unity of India. By the end, only Hyderabad had an elaborate currency with banknotes printed in England, but there were eight States which minted their own rupee currency, and some more which minted copper coins or special ceremonial issues.

Some work arose in large States which had Indian States Forces, i.e. which had earmarked certain units in their army for loan to the British Government in time of war. Most of the work in connection with this was carried out by the Military Adviser–an Indian Army Officer seconded for these diplomatic duties.

Certain States had a number of *jagirdars* (known also by various other titles) who were apt to invoke the assistance of Political Agents against their Ruler. A *jagirdar* was a noble or landlord who had been made exempt, for certain reasons, from the liability to pay land revenue on the land situated in his *jagir*. (Land revenue meant the tax or rent universally paid in India to the Government, British or State.) Many of these *jagirdars* would have been princes but for the luck of the throw in the early nineteenth century, when the pieces began to be set out on the board. Some had guarantees from the then representative of the Governor-General: often they were Rajputs, perhaps claiming descent from the sun or the moon, who had been overrun by the Mahrattas. Again, they might be collaterals of the Ruler. In any case, there was scarcely a large State that had not many hereditary *jagirdars*, some guaranteed by the British, some not. Where there was a clear guarantee embodied in a treaty, it was impossible not to interfere. In other cases, a wise Political Agent would be very loth to be involved in any way in a dispute between a non-guaranteed *jagirdar* and his Ruler.

Now the guaranteed *jagirdar*—prominent above all in Gwalior and Kolhapur—had very definite rights which could be a great nuisance to the State Government. It might be engaged on some wholly admirable piece of modernization—say, for example, the introduction of compulsory education or the enforcement of measures of control against undue felling in forests. They would run up against the *jagirdar* who might be a thoroughly bad landlord, and a clash would result, followed by appeals to the P.A. Many of these problems had been thrashed out by modern times and the *jagirdars'* exact rights agreed upon. But occasionally the eighteenth century would impinge on the twentieth, and one would get a glimpse of a scene reminiscent of the days of the Mahratta rise to power. One such episode, which astonished a world which thought that armed revolt was a thing of the past, was the extraordinary rising in 1938 in Sikar, which, with Khetri and Uniara, was one of the three great *jagirs* which had semi-independent jurisdiction in Jaipur, itself one of the principal States in Rajputana, and far from being a backward, feudally-minded State. In his memoirs[31] *Kingdoms of Yesterday*, Lothian, who was Resident for Rajputana at the time, gives a full account of the affair.

What was practically an armed rebellion broke out in April 1938, lasting till September. Relations between Jaipur, the suzerain State, and Sikar had long been bad. The Rao Raja of Sikar had a sixteen-year-old son whose parents wished to marry him early. The boy did not want this and the Maharaja of Jaipur thought it would be best to take him with him unmarried to Europe. Out of this petty family matter there nearly arose a civil war. The Rao Raja, as the *jagirdar* was called, was an uneducated man whose administration was so bad that all his judicial powers had been taken away in 1933, though he was allowed to live in Sikar and was paid the customary honours. But he and his followers resented the position and were glad of any excuse to get it upset. When, therefore, the Maharaja told the Rao Raja that he intended to take his son to England, the Rao Raja retired to his fort, entrenched himself with about 10,000 armed men, closed the gates of the town and declared a *hartal* (protest strike). The State, failing to persuade him to behave sensibly, sent police and troops to Sikar.

Armed as they were with modern weapons, the Jaipur troops could have settled the matter in a few hours, but at the cost of considerable loss of life. Although, therefore, it was a matter of internal State administration, Lothian volunteered his good offices to go to Sikar in his personal capacity and try to bring about a settlement, since he knew the Rao Raja well. The Maharaja of Jaipur agreed. Lothian was able to induce the Rao Raja to come away with him to Abu (the Resident's headquarters) on promises of a safe-conduct, but as they left Sikar, where by now not less than some 30,000 excited armed men were gathered, there were anxious moments. But this was not the end. The Jaipur State added fuel to the fire by declaring the Rao Raja incapable of managing even his private property, which they placed under the Jaipur Court of Wards. A so-called public committee seized power; the Rani took her husband's place in the fort and several months elapsed before order was restored. The Indian National Congress meanwhile took a hand, and tried to secure immediate responsible government in Sikar. After long negotiations, a settlement was reached. As Lothian summed it up: 'The whole episode was interesting as perhaps the last dying flicker of mediaeval India, mixed up at the same time with modern all-India politics.'

# CHAPTER 12

## The Chamber of Princes

THE principle on which the East India Company insisted, that States hold no correspondence direct with other States, long since became obsolete. Lytton had, indeed, suggested the creation of an Imperial Privy Council, Curzon a Council of Ruling Princes, and Minto an Advisory Council of Rulers and British Indian landlords. But nothing came of these proposals, and all that was done before 1921 was to call *ad hoc* conferences of Princes from time to time.

It was not until after World War I that a concrete step was taken to encourage cooperation between the States. The Montagu–Chelmsford report recommended the establishment of a Chamber of Princes; and it was set up in 1921 by Royal Proclamation, read on behalf of King George V by his uncle, the Duke of Connaught, at a ceremony in Delhi fort. On this occasion, not for the first time, reference was made by the highest possible authority to the

> assurances given on many occasions by My Royal Predecessors and Myself ever to maintain unimpaired the privileges, rights and dignities of the Princes of India ... the Princes may rest assured that this pledge remains inviolate and inviolable.

The Chamber of Princes was a consultative body which played no role in the legislative procedure by which laws were made for British India. The Legislative Assembly and the Council of State were the rough equivalent of the House of Commons and the House of Lords; they had, however, nothing whatever to do with State territory. The composition of the Chamber of Princes was as follows:

a. 108 members in their own right, i.e. Rulers of States who *either* enjoyed permanent dynastic salutes of 11 guns or over, on 1 January 1920, *or* enjoyed such full or practically full internal powers as in the opinion of the Viceroy qualified them for admission.

b. 12 representatives selected by 127 other States.

The really small Estates or *talukas* were not represented at all.

When the Chamber was first constituted, it could only discuss the agenda framed for it by the Viceroy. In 1928, however, it was given power to frame its own agenda through its Standing Committee, subject only to disallowance of objectionable items by the Viceroy. This greatly increased the importance of its functions.

At first an almost solely decorative body–weakened, too, from the start by the refusal of Hyderabad, Mysore and a few other very large States to take any part in its work–its Standing Committee became more and more important. Residents and Political Agents had no direct functions in connection with the Chamber, whose leaders dealt with the Political Department and its officers in Delhi (indeed, the Chamber provided a great deal of work for the latter). An important clause in its constitutions excluded from consideration by the Chamber:

> Treaties and internal affairs of individual States, rights and interests, dignities and powers, privileges and prerogatives of individual Princes and the actions of individual Rulers.

It was also laid down that the institution of the Chamber did not prejudice in any way the engagements or relations with the Viceroy of any State, or the right or freedom of any State to address the Government of India in regard to any matter. Whatever the Chamber might recommend was not binding on any individual State or Ruler.

In 1928, seven years after the foundation of the Chamber, the Indian Statutory Commission (commonly known from its chairman as the Simon Commission) began its three-year study of India which included the question of future links between British India and the States. Federation was in fact in the air, though it was not formally discussed as much more than a distant ideal until the first Round-Table conference (May 1930). The Commission made three concrete proposals regarding the States. First, they advised a serious and business-like effort to draw up a list of matters of common concern to the States and British India. They tentatively suggested–

1. The Customs tariff of British India.
2. The Salt tax.
3. Any other form of central taxation affecting the Indian States.
4. Railway policy.
5. Air communications.
6. Trunk roads.
7. Posts and telegraphs.
8. Wireless.

9. Currency and coinage.

10. Commerce, banking and insurance, so far as the matters raised affect both the States and British India.

11. Opium policy.

12. Indians overseas.

13. Matters arising in connection with India's membership of, and participation in, the League of Nations.

14. Such other subjects of common concern as the Viceroy from time to time certifies as suitable for consideration by the Council for Greater India (see below).

Second, they recommended for inclusion in the preamble of the next Government of India Act

> a recital which would put on record the desire to develop that closer association between the Indian States and British India which is the motive force behind all discussions of an eventual Federal Union,

making it plain, however, that such association could only come about if and so far as the Indian States desired that it should.

Third, and most important, they proposed a standing consultative body of, perhaps, thirty members, of whom ten might be representatives of the States, the remaining twenty being partly drawn from the Central Legislature, partly nominated by the Viceroy. (It was contemplated that the Political Secretary would be a member *ex-officio*.) Five years was proposed as the tenure of office of all members. The title suggested for this body was 'The Council for Greater India'. 'The whole scheme for this Council, as we conceive it, is designed to make a beginning in the process which may one day lead to Indian Federation.' They described it as 'a throwing across the gap of the first strands which may in time mark the line of a solid and enduring bridge'.

It is a remarkable fact that this Council, which had obvious possibilities, was never set up. Instead–a poor substitute–the Standing Committee of the Chamber of Princes and their able if not universally trusted secretariat remained permanently in touch with the Political Department.

# CHAPTER 13

## Treaties and Gross Misrule

W E have described something of the day-to-day work of a political officer. There might be a difference of approach to some of these routine problems by him and the State; it would usually be easily resolved. But the problem which we shall now examine was a never-resolved one, regarding which probably no Ruler, however liberal or selfless, saw eye to eye with a political officer, however sympathetic and treaty-conscious. It was the problem of Paramountcy. Hear E. M. Forster[32] forty years ago on this problem:

> The Princes have studied our wonderful British Constitution at the Chiefs' Colleges, and some of them have visited England and seen the Houses of Parliament. But they are personal rulers themselves, often possessing powers of life and death, and they find it difficult to realize that the King-Emperor, their overlord, is not equally power-ful. If they can exalt and depress their own subjects at will, regard the State revenue as their private property, promulgate a constitution one day and ignore it the next, surely the monarch of Westminster can do as much or more. This belief colours all their intercourse with the Government of India. They want to get through or behind it to King George and lay their troubles at his feet, because he is a king and a mighty one, and will understand. In the past some of them nourished private schemes, but today their loyalty to the Crown is sincere and passionate, and they welcomed the Prince of Wales, although his measured constitutionalisms puzzled and chilled them. Why did he not take his liegeman aside and ask, in his father's name, for the head of Gandhi upon a charger? It could have been managed so easily. The intelligent Princes would not argue thus, but all would have the feeling, and so would the reader if he derived extensive powers under a feudal system and then discovered that it was not working properly in its upper reaches. 'His Majesty the King-Emperor has great difficulties in these days': so much they grasp, but they regard the difficulties as abnormal and expect that a turn of the wheel will shake them off. However cleverly they may discuss

democratic Europe or revolutionary Russia with a visitor, they do not in their heart of hearts regard anything but Royalty as permanent, or the movements against it as more than domestic mutinies. They cannot understand, because they cannot experience, the modern world.

Let us state the case for the Princes, as it would be put by a member of that Standing Committee of the Chamber of Princes just discussed. The Prince would begin by referring to the Treaties. It cannot be denied that, in some of them, it was laid down in the most explicit terms that there should be no interference. Article 15 of the 1800 treaty with the Nizam of Hyderabad[33] reads:

> As by the present Treaty the union and friendship of the two States are so firmly cemented as that they may be considered as one and the same, His Highness the Nizam engages neither to commence nor to pursue in future any negotiations with any other power whatever without giving previous notice and entering into mutual consultation with the Honourable East India Company's Government; and the Honourable Company's Government on their part hereby declare that they have no manner of concern with any of His Highness's children, relations, subjects, or servants with respect to whom His Highness is absolute.

On the other hand, only forty States had treaties, and of them only twenty had definite treaty assurances that they were absolute as regards their subjects.

The content of the treaties varies greatly, but the meaning of a full-blooded document like that which we have quoted is clear. But what about gross misrule? Even the most diehard Prince would, in practice, agree that, when dissatisfied subjects rebelled and British Indian troops or police had to be sent to protect the Ruler, or when a grave, long-endured and gross case of misrule was proven, interference was justified. But, he would say, the political authorities interfered far too early, and in regard to the pettiest matters. They have, in the past, sometimes seemed to be mere agents for an unfriendly British India; the salt monopoly, the opium trade, sea customs, grabbing of excessively large areas round a Residency, closing mints, making difficulties over supplying arms and ammunition—these are some of the grievances on which the Princes or their inspired publicists dwelt.[34] They particularly complained of the use made of minority administrations to push through proposals which the Ruler, had he been of age, would not have allowed.

In relying on the treaties, the Princes were to some extent on the horns of a dilemma. If the treaties and the treaties alone had formed the basis of relations between them and the British Government, a great many States would have been left out in the cold. 'The enquirer of 1858 would have found that with seven-eighths of the 600-odd States with which the Company's government was in actual or potential contact, its relations were not and never had been defined.'[35] Only by coming under the umbrella of their big brothers could they claim any rights against the paramount power. But it was just this 'reading of the treaties as a whole' to which the apologists of the Princes objected. Comparatively few States had a treaty and of them some, for special reasons, had documents very different from that quoted above. Mysore, which for long years – from 1831 to 1881 – had been treated practically as British India, was tied down, when finally retroceded, by a treaty the terms of which were a model of severity and represent what the political authorities of the period considered ideal. Manipur, which, after a rising in 1891 in which high British officials were killed, had been declared to have forfeited its sovereignty, was recreated but similarly severely dealt with. While few States had very liberal treaties, fewer still had very stern ones. The fact remained that the great majority had none at all. And whatever the legalistic view, for practical purposes it was inevitable that the treaties be 'read as a whole'; that a corpus of political practice should be arrived at, and that cases as they arose should be decided on a mixture of precedent and commonsense.

Inevitable; but none the less unwelcome to the Princes. When, about the time of World War I, they began seriously to put forward claims, based on treaties, that the paramount power should leave them alone, what were their demands? We have seen how they succeeded in curtailing the introduction of reforms during minorities and, much earlier, securing the principle that their customary law should be followed in cases of disputed succession. The really vital problem which remained was that of gross misrule: the kind of situation which would lead to deposition of the Ruler. Proved murder or attempted murder, wholesale oppression of cultivators such as caused a rising which needed police or troops from outside the State to suppress it – these were the kind of things which constituted gross misrule. Now the Princes did not deny that in grave cases of this sort deposition might be the only solution. They were concerned, however, to see that the Paramount Power did not act purely on the reports of its own agents. Gross misrule must be carefully distinguished from lack of administrative efficiency. Such misrule has generally been held to justify deposition even by those who were the firmest advocates of strict recognition of internal Sovereignty. For example, in the Company period, Malcolm (1830) was reckoned a staunch supporter of the doctrine of non-intervention and signed a considerable number of treaties containing definite clauses guaranteeing non-interference in the internal affairs of States. In the treaty of Mandasor with Holkar he introduced the far-reaching term 'concern' in a clause reciting that the British authority would have no concern with the internal administration and affairs of the State of Indore; but in a minute recorded by him at the same time it was evident that there were reservations even in his mind to the limits to be set to unconcern. He wrote:

> We must alike avoid the minute and vexatious interference which lessens their (i.e. the Rulers') power and ability and that more baneful course, which, satisfied with their fulfilling the general conditions of their alliance, gives a blind support to their authority however ruinous its measures to the prosperity of the country and the happiness of its inhabitants.

In 1860 Canning–a most confident advocate of maintaining the rights and privileges of the Native States–wrote in his minute on the Canning Adoption *Sanads*:

> The proposed measure will not debar the Government of India from stepping in to set right such serious abuses in a native Government as may threaten any part of the country with anarchy or disturbance, nor from assuming temporary charge of a native State when there shall be sufficient reason to do so. This has long been our practice.

Whatever treaties might say or refrain from saying, the British Government took the view that under certain well-understood, but not defined, conditions, the British Government had a right of interference, and that the Princes and States were under obligation to the paramount power to conduct their administrations so as to render such intervention unnecessary. And most Princes agreed.

Gross misrule, during the administration of the Company, as has been noted already, had in some cases resulted in the annexation of a State, the deposition of its ruler and the extinction of his dynasty as a ruling house, as for example in Oudh and Coorg. During the Crown period, i.e. after 1857, the Princes remained deeply interested observers of the interpretation which would be placed on the phrase 'gross misrule' and the action which the paramount power would take in such situations.

The first case of importance which occurred was that of Malhar Rao, who succeeded as Gaekwar of Baroda in 1870. In the brief period of three years, his misrule produced widespread disorganization and confusion in the State; and in 1873 a Commission was appointed to enquire into the facts of the situation. As a result of the report of the Commission, the ruler was warned that he must mend his ways and carry out certain reforms; otherwise he would be deprived of his authority. He did not take the warning to heart; and three years later he was deposed from the sovereignty of Baroda on the grounds of notorious misconduct, gross mismanagement of the State, and incapacity to carry the suggested reforms into effect. A charge of attempting to poison the Resident was not proved to the satisfaction of all the Commission. A son, adopted by the Maharani, was placed on the throne.* No modification of the treaties with Baroda was made, and no fresh conditions of protection or recognition were imposed on the new ruler. Annexation was not even considered, and there was no suggestion of a regrant, upon new and more stringent terms, as in the Mysore case. The treatment of this case was reassuring to the Princes. Thereafter there were many cases where the tyrannical acts of a ruler, or gross and general maladministration, ended, after due enquiry, in his abdication or deposition. For example, the Maharaja Holkar of Indore was involved in 1926 in a murder committed in British India and abdicated; and the Maharaja of Nabha in 1925 violently trespassed on the rights of his neighbour, the Maharaja of Patiala, imprisoned and harassed his subjects, and after a judicial enquiry was deposed. In each of these cases the son succeeded, and no alteration took place in the relations of the Government of India with the State and its rulers. Other less heinous cases were met by rigid supervision by the Resident or Political Agent during a term while needed reforms were set on foot, or by the loan of an official to act as a Minister in order to rehabilitate branches of the administration which had been maladministered. As an outcome of discussions with the Chamber of Princes a procedure was evolved by which, in cases likely to involve some curtailment of a Ruler's powers or more serious results, the Government of India could seek the assistance of a panel of Ruling Princes in hearing the case and formulating conclusions of the facts. A tribunal of this nature was offered to the ruler in the Indore case, above referred to, but the ruler preferred voluntary abdication.[36]

* The story is told that a deputation of senior officials was sent to interview the three brothers in a family suitable from the point of view of relationship and caste but of humble status. They asked two of the three children whether they knew why they had come. Neither had anything to say. When they asked the third, he said: 'To make me Maharaja of Baroda.' And he was right.

Not only 'could the Government of India seek' assistance; they promised in a published Resolution to do so, and not to depose a Ruler without holding a judicial enquiry. Few such enquiries were in fact held, for the same reason as applied to the Indore case: the accused usually gave up resistance when formally offered an enquiry, and either abdicated or accepted whatever Government had been pressing for.

The number of cases of intervention was large, over the years. Not all were publicly known, through the press. Those that were based on some clear and scandalous crime (such as the 1926 Indore case) of course roused the greatest interest; but far more often a 'bad ruler' was the kind of man who would not dream of committing a murder but was a well-meaning muddler, surrounded by bad advisers. Again and again, the cause of intervention turned out to be finance. Few Rulers had a civil list (when such a thing existed) which satisfied their needs. The Sunday newspaper reader in the West who read in the gossip columns of 'fabulously rich Maharajas' (everything to do with them was 'fabulous') had no conception of the financial picture. If the gross income of the State were to be treated as the Ruler's exclusive property, he would in many cases have been very rich. But all but the worst-managed States had some kind of State budget, and even the most extravagant Ruler had to make a large allotment towards the administration of the State. Often prompt intervention in the nature of financial control could save a State and its Ruler. There were so few who were 'bad' rulers; there were many who meant well but were hopelessly extravagant and lived far too much away from their States. Even in such a notorious case as Alwar, where the large Muslim minority at last, in 1933, rose and had to be controlled by troops sent in by the Viceroy from British India, the trouble was largely due to the fact that the State was bankrupt. Notorious throughout India for his sadistic cruelty as was the Maharaja Jey Singh of Alwar, there were probably few who knew that his extravagance rather than his vices ruined the State and led to his removal.

The Political Department was handicapped by having to work in the dark: it had to save the face of the Rulers whom it was disciplining. But above all it was handicapped, in recent years, by the speech mentioned earlier–Minto's famous Udaipur speech. Udaipur, capital of the State properly known as Mewar, was a medium-sized Rajput State of incredible antiquity, its Ruler, in Indian eyes, being first by birth of all the highborn Rajputs. So long ago as 1833, Sutherland[37] wrote: 'Udaipur, when remonstrated with and recommended to be more prudent and circumspect in his transactions, replied: "Does the British Government not know that those are qualities which never belonged either to Rajas or to whores, who in those matters are always considered entitled to do as they like?'' And Udaipur was chosen as the venue for a speech which ham-strung the service for many years. In 1910, when Harcourt Butler was Foreign Secretary and Minto had succeeded Curzon as Viceroy (to say nothing of a Liberal ministry succeeding a Conservative one), Minto made a pronouncement which practically enforced a policy of non-interference on all Residents and Political Agents. So late as 1940, when Linlithgow, supported by Wylie, his Political Adviser, was pressing for reforms in State administration, political officers were saying 'Let the India Office formally cancel the Udaipur Speech and we shall be found very ready to go ahead.'

Lady Minto in *India: Minto and Morley 1905–1910* quotes the following essential parts of Minto's Udaipur speech:

It is sometimes asked by Ruling Chiefs, as well as by the public in India and Europe, what our policy towards Native States is? I can only tell you that the basis of that policy was laid down in Queen Victoria's Proclamation of 1858 and repeated in the Coronation message of His Majesty the King-Emperor. In 1858 Queen Victoria addressed the Princes of India as follows: 'We hereby announce to the Native Princes of India that all treaties and engagements made with them by, or under, the authority of the Hon'ble East India Company are by us accepted and will be scrupulously observed, and we look for the like observance on their part. We desire no extension of our present territorial possessions, and while we will admit no aggression on our dominions or our rights to be attempted with impunity, we shall sanction no encroachment on those of others. . . .' And 44 years later the King-Emperor wrote:

'To all my feudatories and subjects throughout India I renew the assurance of my regard for their liberties, of respect for their dignities and rights, of interest in their advancement, and of devotion to their welfare, which are the supreme aim and object of my rule, and which, under the blessing of Almighty God, will lead to the increasing prosperity of my Indian Empire and the greater happiness of its people.'

In pursuance of these pledges our policy is with rare exceptions one of non-interference in the internal affairs of Native States. But in guaranteeing their internal independence and in undertaking their protection against external aggression it naturally follows that the Imperial Government has assumed a certain degree of responsibility for the general soundness of their administration and could not consent to incur the reproach of being an indirect instrument of misrule. There are also certain matters in which it is necessary for the Government of India to safeguard the interests of the community as a whole, as well as those of the paramount power, such as railways, telegraphs and other services of an Imperial character. But the relationship of the Supreme Government to the States is one of suzerainty. Your Highness will, I know, recognize the difficulty that must exist in adhering to a uniform policy owing to the varying conditions of different States. It is this diversity of conditions which renders so dangerous any attempt at complete subservience to uniformity. I have therefore made it a rule to avoid as far as possible the issue of general instructions and have endeavoured to deal with questions as they arose with reference to existing treaties, the merits of each case, local conditions, antecedent circumstances and the particular stage of development, feudal and constitutional, of undivided principalities. . . .

The foundation-stone of the whole system is the recognition of identity of interests between the Imperial Government and the Durbars and the minimum of interference with the latter in their own affairs. I have always been opposed to anything like pressure on Durbars with a view to introducing British methods of administration. I have preferred that reforms should emanate from Durbars themselves and grow up in harmony with the traditions of the State. It is easy to overestimate the value of administrative efficiency. It is not the only object to aim at, though the encouragement of it must be attractive to keen and able Political Officers and it is not unnatural that the temptation to further it should, for example, appeal strongly to those who are temporarily in charge of the administration of a State during a minority. Whether they are in sole charge or associated with a State Council, their position is a difficult one. It is one of peculiar trust, and though abuses and corruption must, of course, as far as possible be corrected, I cannot but think that Political Officers will do wisely to accept the general system of administration to which the Chief and his people have been accustomed. The methods sanctioned by tradition in States are usually well adapted to the needs and relations of the ruler and his people. The loyalty of the latter to the former is generally a personal loyalty which administrative efficiency, if carried out on lines unsuited to local conditions, would lessen or impair.

'I can assure Political Officers I am speaking in no spirit of criticism. No one has a greater admiration of their services than I have. ... My aim and object will be, as it has always been, to assist them, but I would impress upon them that they are not only the mouthpiece of Government and the custodians of Imperial policy, but that I look to them also to interpret the sentiments and aspirations of the Durbars. It is upon the tactful fulfilment of their dual functions that the Supreme Government and the Chiefs must mutually rely. It is upon the harmonious co-operation of Indian Princes and Political Officers that so much depends, co-operation which must increase in value as communications develop and new ideas gain ground.

'We are at the commencement of a new era of thought in India. We shall have many new problems to face as years go on – problems surrounded with difficulties and anxieties in the solution of which I trust that the Ruling Chiefs will ever bear in mind that the interests of themselves and their people are identical with those of the Supreme Government.

'Your Highness, I shall always look back upon my visit to Udaipur with many recollections of your magnificent hospitality, the romantic traditions of Rajputana, and the enchantment of the palaces, lakes and islands of Mewar.'

# CHAPTER 14

## The Rise and Fall of the Federal Scheme

DURING the two decades between the two world wars, constitutional changes occurred which brought the problem of the Indian States into the limelight. The period opens with the coming into force of the Government of India Act, 1919, by which a system known as dyarchy was introduced in the provinces of British India, while there were only minor changes in the Government of India, at the centre. The details do not here concern us, but this Act, unlike previous constitutions, in effect committed the British Government to advance on democratic lines.

Whether progress was fast or slow, it seemed likely that a large degree of autonomy would before very long be conceded to British India. It was announced in 1919 that the whole question would be reviewed in ten years' time; and though it was not laid down that the review must lead to advance rather than retreat, few in England except a minority of die-hards seriously contemplated retreat. When the Simon Commission, appointed in 1928 and reporting in June 1930, recommended complete autonomy for the provinces (subject to reserved powers for the Governor) and minor but important advances at the centre, e.g. an enlarged bi-cameral legislature, events had already overtaken theory. A widespread and dangerous civil disobedience movement was, indeed, dying and shortly to be suppressed, but, like the more localized movement of 1919 and the more violent one of 1942, it marked the degrees on the political thermometer and showed that the temperature was always, in the end, rising. The rise was not steady: generally, in this period, there would be a period of peace and constitutional rule between two episodes of a sus-pended constitution and wholesale arrests of politicians. But always, to a watcher from the bastion of an Indian State, the British Government's forces were seen to be retreating, and the conflict to be approaching nearer him.

The problem was how the States—islands of complete autocracy scattered all over the map, and sometimes closely involved physically and economically with British India—were to be fitted into the contemplated changes. The Simon Commission report, in 1930, and the report of the Butler Committee which was published about the same time, saw the future as inevitably involving some sort of federal solution; but they did not regard it as practical to suggest any immediate step towards it. Not long after they reported, there was one of the moments of calm when, after a stiff fight, the political leaders were released from prison and appeasement was in the air, associated with the policies of Halifax.*

It was widely felt that some immediate gesture forward was needed. It was proposed to make an announcement about Dominion Status, and to hold a Round-Table Conference with Indian politicians (who had been excluded from the Simon Commission). Simon at first had doubts about both steps, but soon came round to supporting the idea of a Round-Table Conference, though not the Dominion status announcement. This announcement harked back to Montagu's declaration of 20 August 1917, which had read:

> The policy of His Majesty's Government with which the Government of India are in complete accord is that of the increasing association of Indians in every branch of the administration and the gradual development of self-governing institutions with a view to the progressive realisation of responsible government in India as an integral part of the British Empire.

The Dominion status announcement was made by the Viceroy on 31 October 1929, in an official communiqué in the *Gazette of India* reading:

> In view of the doubts which have been expressed both in Great Britain and in India regarding the interpretation to be placed on the intentions of the British Government in enacting the Statute of 1919, I am authorized on behalf of His Majesty's Government to state clearly that in their judgment it is implicit in the declaration of 1917 that the natural issue of India's constitutional progress as there contemplated is the attainment of Dominion Status.

This statement was the cause of much dissension among the Conservative right wing. But the proposal to hold a Round-Table Conference† including the States was generally popular, and Simon was put up to suggest it, in a letter to the Prime Minister at 16 October 1929, as though it were the Commission's idea.

Three Round-Table Conferences were held in London, beginning on

* 1st Earl of Halifax (1881–1959), at that time Lord Irwin. Viceroy of India, later Foreign Secretary and Ambassador to the U.S.A.

† This phrase dates back to the report of the 'Nehru Committee' appointed by the Congress, of which the chairman was Pandit Motilal Nehru, father of Pandit Jawaharlal Nehru.

12 November 1930. The first was boycotted by the Indian National Congress, as the overwhelmingly important political party at the Hindu Nationalists was called. This first Conference was composed of 89 delegates, 57 from British India, 16 from the Indian State, and 16 representatives of the Government and opposition in the Lords and the Commons.

A small group of moderate politicians now, as at other times in this century, played an important role as go-betweens from Government to the Congress. The most important were Sapru,* Jayakar† and Srinivasa Sastri,‡ and the first-named—like the Nehrus, a Kashmiri Brahman—was outstanding. His party, the small National Liberal Federation, was not of much consequence: but its leaders were. He personally, before the Conference, rallied a large number of politicians of different parties who favoured a Round-Table Conference; he also had many discussions with the Viceroy. (We shall see later that Lord Lothian played a somewhat similar role from the British side.)

D. A. Low, in a study of Sapru's activities,[38] writes that the crucial discussions on which everything hinged began before the conference met, in the ship, the *Viceroy of India*, on which the main body of Indian delegates—some of them from British India, some from the Princely States—travelled to London. 'Federation' began to be mooted. The Princes had become much concerned about their position *vis-à-vis* the Government of India in the aftermath of the Butler report (whose doctrine that 'paramountcy must remain paramount' was very distasteful to them); and under pressure from Haksar§—and his young associate, the irrepressible K. M. Panikkar‖—they began to discuss the establishment of an Indian Federation in which the Princely States could participate fully (and thus escape some of the leading strings of the Political Department). This had been mentioned as a possibility both by the Simon report and by the Government of India in their despatch upon the report, drafted by Fitze and described by him[39] as what he believed to have been the lengthiest despatch ever sent by the Government of India to the Secretary of

* Rt. Hon. Sir Tej Bahadur Sapru (1875–1949). Law Member of Governor General's Executive Council, 1920–3.

† Rt. Hon. Mukund R. Jayakar (1873–1959). Judge, Federal Court, India 1937–9, Member, Judicial Committee of the Privy Council, 1939–41.

‡ Rt. Hon. V. S. Srinivasa Sastri (1869–1946), C.H. Agent General for India in South Africa.

§ Sir Kailas Narain Haksar (1878–1953), C.I.E. In Gwalior State Service, 1903–1938; Prime Minister, 1927–9. Bikaner 1938–9; Prime Minister, Kashmir, 1943–1944.

‖ K. M. Panikkar (1895–1963). Held posts in Kashmir, Patiala and Bikaner. Noted historian. Ambassador for India in China, Egypt, France.

State. (It covers 72 printed foolscap pages and 31 pages of annexures.) But no one hitherto had thought of Federation as an immediate possibility.

The federal idea soon took firm root when the Conference delegates arrived in England and found how adamant Liberal and Conservative politicians were against any idea of Dominion Status. Sapru found Wedgwood Benn,* the Secretary of State, 'determined to help us', but 'he warned me against Lord Reading and Lloyd George'.† The opening speech at the first plenary session was made by Sapru. He demanded responsibility at the centre, and asked the Princes to support a federation. The Maharaja of Bikaner followed, and on behalf of the Princes promised to do so. Delegate after delegate rallied to their support. This was a decision of the greatest importance leading, as it did, to Prime Minister Ramsay MacDonald's announcement: 'With a legislature constituted on a federal basis, His Majesty's Government will be prepared to recognize the principle of the responsibility of the executive to the legislature.'[40]

This was an enormous advance, made at unprecedented speed. But at first there was consternation in Government circles in London over Bikaner's speech, according to Panikkar who was likely to know. The Labour Government had to make a very quick decision, and they did. A complete volte-face was adopted, and from then onwards, till war broke out in 1939, the questions on what terms the States would enter an All-India Federation and what the exact composition of the federal legislature would be, held the front of the political picture.

Bikaner's plea was for a federal constitution, subject to proper safeguards, and subject, on the other hand, to responsible government at the Centre being conceded. The Conference adjourned after a good deal of work had been done, and was followed by the second Round-Table conference late in 1931 at which the Congress agreed to be represented by Mahatma Gandhi 'with the addition of such delegates as the Working Committee may appoint to act under his leadership.' Though the Congress expressly dissented from the recommendations of the conference for a federal constitution, it was generally held that they would cooperate and see what they got out of it. Eventually they did, in the provinces, though the third session was again without Congress participation.

* W. Wedgwood Benn, first Viscount Stansgate (1877–1960). Secretary of State for India, 1929–31.
† David, first Earl Lloyd George of Dwyfor (1863–1945). Prime Minister, 1916–22.

This third session, in 1932, which no Princes attended, only States' Ministers, led to an agreed decision on the broad lines of constitutional advance. A White Paper was issued and had to be discussed and approved in both Houses of Parliament. Thereafter, a Joint Select Committee was set up to make recommendations for the draft bill, with Linlithgow* as chairman. The Committee was assisted in the consideration of the White Paper by a strong Indian delegation. The White Paper was approved in March 1933, but it was November 1934 before the Joint Select Committee reported after holding 159 meetings. Churchill and his small group of die-hards opposed the proposals clause by clause and caused two months delay by unsuccessfully charging Hoare of breaking parliamentary privilege.

Finally the bill reached Parliament, received its second reading in February 1935, and became law in July 1935, coming into effect in British India in April 1937 as the Government of India Act, 1935.

Hoare had the task of handling this formidable debate which he did in a masterly fashion–first, on the White Paper, then on the Bill. He was Secretary of State from August 1931 to June 1935. Another figure deserving mention–the holder of the normally obscure and uninfluential post of Parliamentary Under Secretary–was Lord Lothian.† He was a member of all three sessions of the Round-Table Conference, and of the Joint Select Committee. When the National Government was reshuffled after the 1931 elections, he accepted the post of Under Secretary, stipulating 'a status of somewhat more responsibility than that of an ordinary Under Secretary, and the right of access to the Prime Minister'. Hoare agreed.

Lord Lothian had previously worked on the problem of the Union of South Africa, and was in close touch with Curtis,‡ the inventor of Dyarchy.§ Replying to a letter of congratulation on his appointment from Smuts‖ of 14 December 1931, Lord Lothian[41] wrote, on 7 January

* 2nd Marquess of Linlithgow (1877–1951). Viceroy of India, 1936–43.

† Philip Kerr, 11th Marquess of Lothian (1882–1940), C.H. A well-known journalist; editor of the *Round Table*, 1916–21. Parliamentary Under-Secretary of State for India, Nov. 1931–Sept. 1932. Chairman, Indian Franchise Committee, Jan.–June 1932. Ambassador to Washington, 1939–40. (Not to be confused with Sir Arthur Lothian of the Indian Political Service, hereafter described as 'Lothian'.)

‡ Lionel Curtis (1872–1955), C.H., Barrister. Civil Servant in South Africa. Fellow of All Souls, Adviser on Irish Affairs, Colonial Office, 1921–4.

§ The name commonly given to the provincial constitution set up by the Montagu–Chelmsford reforms, embodied in the Government of India Act, 1919.

‖ Field-Marshal J. C. Smuts (1870–1950). Prime Minister of South Africa, 1919–24 and 1939–48.

1932: 'I do not see any prospect of our being able to solve the Indian problem on our present lines of creating a gigantic parliamentary federation.' But he felt that there were no other lines on which to proceed and that we could not go back. New forces would eventually emerge; a very liberal franchise would be needed. (Lord Lothian was shortly afterwards made chairman of a body, the Indian Franchise Committee, to settle this point; and their report, which increased voters from 7 to 36 million, was accepted and its conclusions included in the bill.)

He was on good personal terms with Gandhi, as whose guest he stayed when he visited India in 1937–8. Lord Lothian later went on to be an outstandingly successful ambassador to Washington. His activities in this, his Indian, period were a good example of the kind of background influence often exercised in England by men of good will, not primarily politicians. His pessimistic comment, so early as January 1932, to Smuts, corroborates the recollection of Hailey[42] that doubts whether federation would be successfully introduced arose so soon as the Conference was over.

The great debate in Britain on the principle of India's early advance to independence was settled with the 1935 Act. Whilst it lasted it was a close run thing. On three or four occasions in 1929–30 the decision might have gone the other way. During the ensuing four years, the die-hard opposition to it in Britain became increasingly formidable. It forced the Government to adopt an increasingly illiberal attitude towards Indian reform, and at a crucial Conservative Party conference in December 1934 the die-hards came within 23 votes – 543 to 520 – of upsetting the whole programme of reform. Had they succeeded, the consequences for India, and for British relations with India, would have been momentous.[43]

This long and elaborate document, the 1935 Act, contemplated two distinct periods. First was the immediate future, during which the provinces (less Burma, but including the North-West Frontier Province, and the two new provinces of Orissa and Sind) were to exercise autonomy while the Central Government was to continue with its general structure unchanged, i.e. rule by the Governor-General-in-Council. The members of the Executive Council were, as before, appointed at the discretion of the Viceroy. They were mostly British civil servants, though in recent times they always included a few Indian politicians. As time and the war went on, the offer was generally open to the Indian political parties to put forward candidates for membership. And eventually, in 1946, what was called the Interim Government was formed, consisting entirely of Indian politicians. But all this was done under the umbrella of this Government

of India Act, 1935. And stranger still, the same Act, with comparatively
few amendments, remained in force both in India and Pakistan for quite
a long period after Partition, until both of these countries (India in 1950
and Pakistan in 1956) placed a Constitution Act of their own on the
statute book. It was an excellent and most workable Constitution that
Pakistan had for some years, as a result of following this Act, slightly
amended.

Thus the 'immediate future' unexpectedly dragged out to ten years.
The second period contemplated by the Act was when its federal provisions should come into force. For this to happen, certain prerequisites
had to be fulfilled. Some of them, such as the setting up of a Reserve Bank,
do not concern us here. By far the most important and difficult was the
provision that required enough States to accede (a) to fill 52 out of the 104
seats allotted to the States in the legislature and (b) to cover half the total
population of all the States. Not only was this necessary, but—what is not
always remembered—the approval of both Houses of Parliament was
required. It was known that the Conservative right wing was still active
and had not bound themselves to rubber-stamp this last step necessary
before federation could be achieved. It was further known that they kept
a very keen eye on any suggestions of pressure by the Viceroy or his
political officers on States to agree to federate. In the *Morning Post* they
had a newspaper ready to denounce such action.

There was much bad feeling over this. A curious example is seen in a
letter of 25 January 1935 to his wife from Chetwode* (who as Commander-in-Chief, was a member of the Executive Council), in which an
echo of an anachronous clash from the duelling ground or crack of the
horse-whip seems to strike our ears. 'Rothermere,'† he wrote,

> has sent another cable to all the Princes saying that an increasing
> number of big people in England are determined to preserve the
> privileges and powers of the Princes. Will you tell Roger‡ to tell
> Adrian Crawley to tell Rothermere from me that he is a d——d liar,
> both about the Viceroy and officials bullying the Princes and about
> 'an increasing number of people at home' etc. If I was not in Employ-
> ment I would come home specially to tell him so and I shall have
> great pleasure in doing so publicly when I return at any place and

* Field-Marshal Sir Roger (later 1st Lord) Chetwode (1869–1950). Commander-in-Chief, India, 1930–5.
† 1st Viscount Rothermere (1868–1940). Newspaper proprietor, and brother
of Lord Northcliffe.
‡ Hon. Roger Chetwode (1906–40). Son of the Field-Marshal.

time convenient to him. I wish he could have heard the Princes who are here: Dholpur is the only one who is really die-hard.

Slow progress was made, since it was found that many of the States had particular claims and most of them engaged legal advisers who bargained hard regarding the exact terms to be accepted.

These layers included some of the most eminent in their profession such as Monckton,* as well as Judge Wadhams† of the U.S. bar. Their influence, as that of the *Dewans* (chief ministers) can hardly be over-estimated. It was largely negative: that is to say, it queried at every stage the federal proposals; and many of the Princes were timid by nature. Their advisers' influence acted on this tendency in a way wholly adverse to a decision to federate. A Reforms Office was set up in the Government of India; some political officers held that it acted rather as a fifth wheel in the coach. We have seen the enormous time that was required by the authorities in England to pass the Act. It has been widely suggested that the Political Department was guilty of dilatoriness, and controversy will long be carried on about this. Those who regarded – and indeed regard – federation as the ideal solution, and Partition as an evil one, naturally seek to affix responsibility for failure to implement the federal proposals.

The writer was and is a supporter of Partition, and does not agree with the federalists that the failure of federation, with its inevitable weak centre, was a bad thing. But why did it fail? It seems generally accepted that it failed largely owing to delay. Sir Arthur Lothian, indeed, felt very strongly about this and, in a note based on his experiences in the Political Department and as one of Linlithgow's emissaries, cites five other causes of failure, but places delay at the top. His causes are:

a. the time that elapsed;

b. the onset of the war in 1939;

c. after their experience of the inadequacy of the protection given them against internal subversion under the provisions of the 1935 Act, the apprehension felt by the Princes that protection under the Act would also prove inadequate in the federal field;

d. short-sightedness on the part of the Princes as to the advantages of federation;

e. the prohibition against bringing any pressure on them to accede;

---

* Lord Monckton of Brenchley (1891–1965), Q.C. Minister of Labour, 1951–5.
† Judge William Henderson Wadhams (1873–1952). Judge, New York, 1915–1921. Adviser to Indian States, 1935–47.

f. the nature of the 1935 Act, which gave scope for bargaining and consequent delay.

Hoare (Lord Templewood) in his *Nine Troubled Years*,[44] and Zetland, who succeeded him as Secretary of State for India in 1935, in *Essayez*,[45] have much to say about responsibility for delay. Briefly, Hoare asks whether we could have pushed the Princes harder and blames Churchill's opposition. He also suggests that greater efforts should have been made in Delhi. Zetland says that he was criticised in some quarters for a supposed lukewarmness towards the federal provisions of the Act. He explains at length the various foci of opposition to federation and says 'My predecessor as Secretary of State favoured a cautious approach, and was against any attempt to force the pace'.

Arthur Lothian, who was shown the first draft of Zetland's book, found that he had stated that Hoare had definitely advised delay when discussing the case in Cabinet, and that Zetland had only omitted this when reminded by the Cabinet Secretary that Cabinet discussions were not quotable. Instead, he curtailed his comment to the words just quoted about his predecessor. Lothian was firmly convinced that Hoare's criticism of 'Delhi's' lack of effort was disingenuous. The point is of minor interest now : the explanation would seem to be that, although Hoare may at one time have felt quite genuinely, and said in Cabinet, that a 'go slow' would get the best results, he later realised that this was not so : and tried to find an excuse for the delay, when writing his memoirs, in blaming 'Delhi'.

Though it is often repeated that no pressure was to be put on the Princes, Howe[46] has a curious story of intervention by King George V. He describes how he went to stay with the King, then convalescent at Eastbourne, at a time when a number of Princes, meeting at Bombay, had passed a resolution that appeared to repudiate the federal proposals.

> The King, who was intensely interested in everything that concerned India, and convinced that All-India federation was the right policy, was greatly incensed by the Princes' action. . . . 'I won't see them when they come to London. Why should they come to London at all and spend a lot of money ? Tell them to stay in their States and look after their own subjects.' It was clear that he regarded very seriously his responsibilities as King-Emperor . . . As to what he thought of the Princes' behaviour in Bombay, he left them in no doubt. The Viceroy was at once instructed to notify them of the

Imperial displeasure, while they on their side let it be known that they had not really repudiated Federation, and that their resolution had not meant what it said.

This seems a long way removed from the official policy to put no pressure on the Princes to accede. But apart from the merits or demerits of the policy of federation, and the tactics used to present it, there are strong grounds for supposing that it could never have come off. Even had the large number of major States necessary to implement federation agreed to it, and had the Conservative right wing in England given no trouble, still the Congress Party and the Muslim League remained to be persuaded.

Congress made heavy weather about accepting office in the provinces, and Nehru* in July 1937 spoke of the basic Congress policy of

> fighting the new constitution and ending it . . . we go to the assemblies or accept office . . . to try to prevent the federation from materialising, to stultify the constitution and prepare the ground for the constituent assembly and independence.

Though Congress accepted office in the provinces and enjoyed it and might well have overruled Nehru and his left wing had other factors allowed federation to be launched, the fact is that Nehru and his followers (and Muslim opponents) did 'stultify the constitution' and achieve a constituent assembly and independence.

Perhaps the greatest of all the forces that helped to kill federation was the Muslim League. While very many Muslims both in British India and the States, including Jinnah,† favoured federation in the early days before the 1935 Act came into force, the experiences of the Muslim minorities in those Hindu-majority provinces where Congress took office in 1937 came as a great shock to the Muslim community as a whole. The 'atrocities' which they condemned were doubtless exaggerated: when one considers the massacres of 1946 and 1947, the fuss about hymn singing in schools and so on in 1937 seems very small beer. But the great importance of the Congress provincial ministries' acts was that they brought home to India, particularly to Muslim India, for the first time, that the new constitution really had teeth in it: that the British raj really was on the way out; and that the theory that in Pakistan alone could a

---

* Jawaharlal Nehru (1889–1964). Prime Minister of India, 1947–64.

† Muhammad Ali Jinnah (1876–1948), Quaid-i-Azam; Governor-General, Pakistan, 1947–8.

Muslim lead a full and free Muslim life was more than a student's dream and was a practical political platform. And in Muslim reaction to these developments, great importance attaches to the attitude of the Nizam and the dominant Muslim community in Hyderabad State. When Linlithgow visited Hyderabad in the winter of 1937–38, the Hyderabad Executive Council led by Hydari* were still officially supporters of federation. But those who saw the Osmania University students demonstrate, however mildly, at such a time, in protest against federation, felt that behind the students' demonstration, was the Nizam's firm resolve—firmer still after some discussions during a visit by Jinnah—to keep out of federation.

To the far-seeing, then, there were early on fairly clear warnings that federation would not be implemented. The initial enthusiasm quickly waned. Every State of any size had to be approached and convinced individually; and since the queries and objections were most numerous, the Viceroy towards the end of 1936 adopted a method designed to accelerate negotiations which was really the last major diplomatic mission of the Indian Political Service. Our officers toured not, as once, to Shah Shuja or to Ranjit Singh to acquaint them that the British were coming, but to Hyderabad, Mysore, Gwalior, Kashmir and the rest, saying that the British were going. More particularly, their duty was to explain the Act and the draft Instrument of Accession to the Princes. To explain—not to persuade. They were in no sense plenipotentiaries.

The Viceroy's emissaries consisted of three experienced political officers, Latimer,† Lothian and Wylie, assisted by two technical advisers respectively concerned with finance and constitutional issues, Raisman‡ and Conran-Smith.§ All five were Indian Civil Service Officers. After a trial run in Western India, the technical advisers withdrew except when really complicated issues arose, when the emissary concerned was joined by one or both of the technical advisers.

The mission was not a success. Most States demanded far better terms than they were offered, and refused to accede unless granted them. The concessions asked varied from Hyderabad's request for a port at Masulipatnam to the two more guns in his salute which one Chief Minister said

* Sir Akbar Hydari (1869–1942). President, Hyderabad State Executive Council, 1937–41.

† Sir Courtenay Latimer (1880–1944), K.C.I.E., C.S.I.; I.C.S., Punjab, 1904; Resident for Western India, 1932–6.

‡ Sir Jeremy Raisman (b. 1892), G.C.I.E., K.C.S.I.; I.C.S., 1916, Bihar and Orissa. Finance Member, Government of India, 1939–45.

§ Sir Eric Conran-Smith (1890–1960), K.C.I.E., C.S.I.; I.C.S., Madras, 1915. Secretary and Member, various departments of the Government of India, 1939–1946.

would entirely satisfy his master. A surviving member, Wylie,* comments:

> The whole circus was of course a farce. We had no direction, no line to advocate, the big idea being that you leave that to the Princes, who were frightened out of their wits or clumsily clever with a whole litter of American lawyers in their way. . . . The 1935 Constitution was not in fact a practicable set-up for India, but if we had got it going the anomalies would have maybe ironed themselves out. Where we let the Princes down was in not giving them a lead.[47]

Others felt that the Act should have been amended to allow federation to be put into effect on the assent of a handful of Rulers. But this is speculation, and when war broke out negotiations with the States had practically failed. The Congress provincial Ministries resigned, and a promise was given that His Majesty's Government 'would be prepared to regard the scheme of the Act as open to modification in the light of Indian views'.

Thereafter, for the whole duration of the war, the situation remained static. Every so often some concession to British Indian politicians was proposed, from one source or another – the principal one being a set of proposals put forward by Cripps† in 1942 but not accepted by the Indian political parties.‡ Linlithgow, much and wrongly blamed, especially in the U.S.A., for refusing to give way on any vital point, undoubtedly took the correct line. The war and its conduct alone then mattered, and any tinkering with the administration of India would have adversely affected the war effort. There was never the slightest chance of the Congress co-operating on any terms which the Government could conceivably have offered; and if they had, their contribution would have been practically worthless. Their propagandists in England and in America, to say nothing of Chiang Kai-shek, who visited Delhi with his wife, and had to be warned off by Churchill when interfering in Indian affairs, were eloquent in picturing a united people, longing to step up the war effort if only this or that or the other concession were made. This picture, to which Bajpai§

* Sir Francis Wylie (b. 1891), G.C.I.E., K.C.S.I.; I.C.S., Punjab, 1914. Indian Political Service, 1919–38. Governor of Central Provinces, 1938–40. Political Adviser, 1940–1 and 1943–5, Minister to Afghanistan, 1941–3; Governor of United Provinces, 1945–7.

† Sir Stafford Cripps (1889–1952). Solicitor-General, 1930–1, Lord Privy Seal, 1942.

‡ Churchill is said[48] to have danced around the Cabinet room on learning of this failure of a mission.

§ Sir Girja Shanker Bajpai (1891–1955), K.C.S.I., K.B.E., C.I.E.; I.C.S. Among various posts he was Agent-General for India in the U.S.A., 1941.

and Halifax's attitude gave some support, had no link with reality. The Linlithwaite regime, so-called from the great influence exercised, and in a time of war rightly exercised, by Laithwaite,* Linlithgow's able private secretary, 'stood pat', as its American critics angrily observed. It was right to do so.

Extraordinary alternatives were proposed. In Washington on one wet Sunday afternoon in 1942, the author, then First Secretary of the Indian Agency General, was surprised to be rung up by Lady Halifax, wife of the British Ambassador, and asked to see her husband urgently, since Bajpai, the Agent-General, was absent on tour. He hurried round to the Embassy, and the Ambassador said: 'President Roosevelt sent for me this morning and suggested a solution of the Indian problem. He has always been much interested in the history of the American revolution, and is struck by the idea that one might, as was done in the U.S.A., give immediate independence separately to all the provinces in India and leave them, as in America, over a period of perhaps ten years, to decide whether to federate or not. What do you think of the idea?' 'If I may say so, Sir, it strikes me as complete nonsense.' 'So I thought; but I wanted to get a second opinion. Keep it under your hat.' Roosevelt persisted with this proposal, as we see in Vol. IV of Churchill's *Second World War*, in two important telegrams to which Churchill replied strongly.

The plain fact was that federation was killed in September 1939 when it was put into the cold storage from which it never emerged. Such moves as the creation on 22 July 1941 of a National Defence Council, composed of twenty-two members from British India and nine from the States, and the simultaneous expansion of the Governor-General's Executive Council to hold eight instead of four Indians, had no result of any consequence on the issue of the States. The Cripps Mission was indeed important in that it committed His Majesty's Government to setting up a Constituent Assembly after the war, with full Dominion status, i.e. including power to leave the Commonwealth, and that, for the first time, it seemed to contemplate the possibility of the creation of Pakistan. But nothing came of it, and it had little to say about the States.

A deputation of Rulers indeed saw Cripps on 2 April 1942.[49] The first point raised was whether, in the event of a number of States not finding it feasible to adhere to the Union, such States or groups of States would have the right to form a Union of their own with full sovereign status.

---

* Sir Gilbert Laithwaite (b. 1894), G.C.M.G., K.C.B., K.C.I.E., C.S.I. Private Secretary to the Viceroy, 1936–43. Permanent Under-Secretary of State for Commonwealth Relations, 1955–9.

Regarding this, Cripps said that personally he did not see any fundamental difficulty in the suggestion, but as that situation had not been considered in connection with the present scheme he was not able to give a
definite reply. Some searching questions were then asked regarding the
implications of adherence to the Union, such as whether the people of the
States would become subjects of the Union; whether the Union would
acquire Paramountcy over the States; and whether it would be possible
for a State to join the Union while reserving the dynastic and personal
affairs of the Ruler to the exclusive jurisdiction of the Crown. The replies
given were to the effect that everything would depend upon the nature of
the arrangements actually made. In any case, Cripps was definite that the
British Government did not contemplate transferring the Paramountcy
of the Crown to any other party. The adherence of a State to the Union
would have the effect of automatically dissolving the Crown's obligations
to it. On the other hand, Paramountcy would continue to be in force in
the case of States which did not join the Union.

Another point raised was whether in the case of non-adhering States
the Crown would continue to retain its obligations towards them and
would enforce them through the usual sanctions. Cripps replied that this
was so; the British Government would provide for everything necessary
to implement their treaty obligations to those States which did not join
the Union. This would include the use of force in the last resort, although
he was not willing to commit himself about the conditions under which
such sanctions would be operated.

Different proposals were discussed at length by the Cabinet Mission
which visited India after the war in 1946; and though they too were
rejected, they did lead up through a continuous debate to the final 1947
settlement which was accepted by the Hindu and Muslim politicians in
British India. The States were little affected by the intermittent negotiations between 1939 and 1945.

The Congress had all along taken a curiously stand-offish attitude
towards the States. In most large States there was usually a small, weak
party called by various names, such as *Praja Mandal* or *States Congress*.
But the British Indian Congress generally held aloof. They knew that
they had too much to do outside without getting involved in States'
affairs. They knew that most Rulers would retaliate sharply if Congress
interfered – they would perhaps use methods which the squeamish Political Department would shrink from using. They knew that there was a
certain nationalist leaning among many of the Princes, to say nothing of
their Ministers; and they felt it best not to offend this feeling.

But there was one vital point which came more and more to the fore as 1947 approached. This was the question whether the Rulers would nominate their representatives in the Constituent Assembly or would allow them to be elected by their subjects. On this a great deal depended. Had the Princes kept to their right to nominate–recognized in all the discussions which had taken place since 1942, at least, when the Constituent Assembly began to look a serious proposition–they could perhaps have formed an alliance with the Muslims and Depressed Classes and outvoted Congress. This was the point on which Congress were determined not to give way; and they were right.

We shall see that, soon after independence, the *Praja Mandals*–the State's people's organizations–were called in at Junagadh and Orissa, for example, to demand reforms. Elsewhere it was sufficient to threaten their use.

# CHAPTER 15

## Tidying Up: Too Little and Too Late

WE have seen that, in the years immediately preceding World War II, the States occupied the centre of the Indian political scene. An Act had been passed, the first part of which gave the British Indian Hindu politicians much to go on with; and if they did not like many aspects of the federal proposals, at least they seem to have been more or less prepared, while governing their provinces, to stand aside while His Majesty's Government attempted to settle with the States, so that the second part of the Act could be brought into force. During the war, the problem of the States was put aside, though the Chamber of Princes put its views forward at the time of the Cripps mission and later; but it was clear that, soon after the war ended, the problem would have to be faced again.

How did the Political Department view it? There cannot have been much hope that the federal provisions of the Act could, after all, be brought into effect. It seemed likely that British India would achieve something near to independence if not all at once, at least in a few years' time. What role were the States to play in this development? The separation from the Governor-General in Council of the paramount power, in the shape of the Crown Representative—the Viceroy's new title when he dealt with the States—had been in force since 1 April 1937; it had in practice meant less difference than had been expected. (Panikkar had stigmatized this change, advocated by Scott\* and accepted by the Butler Committee, as a 'plot'.) In the decade following 1937, there could be little planning of the future of the States, but there were two aims which, if achieved, would at least put the States in a better position to face the future. The first was a tidying up of certain anomalies, to be discussed below. The second was the announcement and acceptance by all parties that Paramountcy would lapse if British India became independent. This the States asked for, His Majesty's Government clearly promised and—though this is often forgotten—the Congress party accepted. It was embodied in the Indian Independence Act, 1947. Whether this was to the advantage of the States, as things turned out, is another matter; V. P. Menon in his book, *The Story of the Integration of the Indian States*,[50]

---

\* Sir Leslie Scott (1869–1950), P.C. Lord Justice of Appeal, 1935–48.

suggests that, had Paramountcy been transferred, the Congress Government might have been hampered in the execution of their policy of absorbing the States. As it was, they were 'writing on a clean slate, unhampered by treaties'. But once a decision had been taken that Paramountcy would lapse with independence – and taken at the highest level – it was the clear duty of the Political Department and its officers to see that this policy was carried out. Looking back, one can see that a case could have been made out for a different policy; but in 1946 and 1947, no one seriously challenged its rightness; and in any case it was a binding, Cabinet ruling. Events moved so fast in 1947 that it is doubtful whether the States could have been placed in such a position that they could have stood up united and faced the future as colleagues of the new governments instead of their vassals. Once a lead towards surrender was given by Baroda, quickly followed by Cochin, Udaipur, Jodhpur, Jaipur, Bikaner, Rewa and Patiala, who took their seats in the Constituent Assembly on 28 April 1947, there was no longer any possibility of States forming a confederation or regional grouping of any kind. But at least the lapse of Paramountcy which was promised took place.

Earlier the question of 'tidying up' of certain anomalies occupied the time and thoughts of many political officers. When, in 1939, federation was put aside, a conscious effort – little known and less appreciated – was made to bring the States into a position where they could present a more respectable front to the post-war world. Linlithgow decided that authoritative advice should be given to all but the largest States to improve their administration. It was indeed made clear by the Secretary of State* that we should not interfere to advise particular forms of, or indeed any, *constitutional* advance, as Linlithgow would have preferred. That was for the Rulers to decide; and though a few organized embryo assemblies and cabinets, most did not. But a serious effort was made to induce States to improve their *administrative* machines. Those States which did not publish their budget or issue an annual Administration Report were strongly urged to do so. In collaboration with the Standing Committee of the Chamber of Princes, successful attempts were made to fix many Rulers' civil lists by agreement, at a reasonable percentage of the State budget. Small States which could not individually afford a well-qualified departmental head or judiciary were pressed to combine and set up a joint High

* Later, when the Labour Government was in power, this ban was lifted. In the Cabinet Missions' memorandum of 12 May 1946, on Paramountcy and in Attlee's letter of instructions of March 1947 to Mountbatten there was clear authority for pressure for constitutional reforms. But this came too late.

Court or a Joint Police or Forestry Adviser for all the States in the Agency.* A Political Agent in 1935 encouraged a number of very small States in Kathiawar, whose territory was hopelessly mixed up owing to the Kathi custom which excluded primogeniture, to exchange a village here, a share in a village there, so that the map was to some extent tidied up. If that process had been forced through by the use of Paramountcy, at any time between 1860 and 1900, and extended to even large States like Gwalior and Indore, whose territories were scattered up and down Central India, the States would, especially if British Indian territory had been allowed to take part, have presented a very different and more defensible picture. Again, if all States below a reasonable level had been forced to amalgamate with their neighbours or with British India, the 562 States would have been reduced to about the 108 whose Rulers sat in the Chamber of Princes in their own right.

Such were the dreams of some political officers; but with Lord Minto's 1909 Udaipur speech still echoing in their ears, few would have considered such wide extension of the exercise of Paramountcy conceivable. And yet a cautious scheme was actually devised and put into effect by the exercise of Paramountcy, and that during World War II. It was known as the Attachment Scheme or, after its author, the Shattock† scheme, and applied to the small States and Estates of the Western India and Gujarat Agencies, where the problem was most acute.

For some time the future of these States under federation had been a recognized problem. Some of them, in Western India and Gujarat called Estates, were so small, we have seen, as to be grouped in *thanas* and not to be allowed to exercise any jurisdiction: not even the three months' imprisonment which some of their slightly larger brothers were allowed to award.

The problem was not confined to Western India and Gujarat. There were, indeed, States in Central India, the Deccan, the Eastern States and the Punjab Hill States which were so small that they had been excluded from division XVII of the first schedule to the Government of India Act, 1935. They were left over for later consideration. The small States presented a constitutional problem and they were the first to be tackled by the post-independence Government of India, which took up first of all the States in the Eastern and Western India States Agencies. Meanwhile the Attachment Scheme was introduced in Western India and Gujarat in

---

* Some progress on these lines was made, particularly in the Eastern States. Elsewhere the Rulers showed the greatest reluctance to accept this advice.

† J. S. H. Shattock (b. 1907), C.M.G., O.B.E.; I.C.S., Bengal, 1931; Political, 1939. H.M. Diplomatic Service, 1947.

1943, on the ground that such States could not stand by themselves in the brave, federal new world that was still, during the war, expected to emerge. Indeed, in the world which did emerge in 1947, with Paramountcy lapsing, there would logically have been complete chaos–no police, no courts, no legislature–had the problem not been tackled in good time. They could of course–though it would have been a reversion to pre-Mutiny days simply to annexe them–have been annexed and given to major neighbouring States or to Bombay, as convenient. This could, perhaps, have been done without any great outcry if the Attachment Scheme had been applied only to the non-jurisdictional *thana*-confined Rulers. But it was decided to go further, and attach not only all *thanas* but many States which had perhaps as many as a dozen villages and an annual income of £10,000 or more. (These figures may raise a smile, but they were not considered ridiculous in Western India. Nor were these States necessarily unhappy or badly ruled.) Complete annexation without warning, without charges of miṣrule, would have been extremely harsh. Their face was saved–though they greatly resented the whole business–by attaching them instead of annexing them. This attachment was not to British India but to neighbouring Salute States, often ruled by a member of the same clan and sometimes the actual State from which they had been given in appanage.

Baroda, Junagadh, Nawanagar, Gondal–these rich and well-governed States, and half a dozen more, were chosen as attaching States on grounds mostly of geographical propinquity to the attached State. In theory, the attached State continued to exist, somewhat like a German mediatized State, but its subjects had access to a higher standard of administration– much was made of the existence in these larger States of better schools and so on. This scheme was announced in April 1943 and put into effect in August 1943, in spite of protests; had this been done fifty years earlier, the map of Kathiawar and Gujarat would indeed have been tidier in 1947. The formula was that the police and courts of the attaching States exercised the powers inherent in the attached States on behalf of the Crown Representative whose officers had previously filled this role. The attachment scheme was, of course, popular with the attaching States, who doubtless intended, in due course, to absorb them completely, and would have done so had they not been anticipated by the post-independence Government of India. What was done is explained by V. P. Menon[51] as follows:

As soon as the States Ministry came into existence, we saw that we had no alternative but to take over the residuary jurisdiction in semi-jurisdictional and non-jurisdictional States.* The Instrument of Accession, which had been evolved after discussion with these rulers, laid down that in these areas the Government of India would exercise all such powers, authorities and jurisdiction in respect of civil and criminal justice as had formerly been exercised by the Crown Representative. To begin with, we appointed an officer on special duty at Rajkot.

This must have been the very first act in seizure of Paramountcy of the post-independence Government of India.

What had the Political Department expected to happen at Partition? Corfield[52] records that Rau† alarmed the Viceroy by stressing the theoretical lacuna that yawned, but Corfield felt that the attaching States had got their claws so firmly in that any attempt by these States to break away would have been quashed at once, had Paramountcy not been so unexpectedly revived.

Western India is a litigious place; and in August 1943, shortly after the scheme came into force, the Talukdar of Bhadwa (pop. 1,401), a former railway guard but a Jadeja Rajput who had been attached to the State of the Maharaja of Gondal (a remarkable man who was a doctor of medicine of Edinburgh as well as a Jadeja Rajput and had done so well on the Bombay Stock Exchange that he abolished all direct taxation in his State), undazzled by these advantages, filed a revision application in the court of Davies, the Judicial Commissioner,‡ claiming that the order of attachment was *ultra vires* of the Government of India Act, 1935 (and for good measure, of several other documents). The Judicial Commissioner held that it was *ultra vires* of the proviso to section 1 (2) of the Act which read: 'Provided that any powers connected with the exercise of the functions of the Crown in its relation with Indian States shall, in India, if not exercised by His Majesty, be exercised only by, or by persons acting under the authority of, His Majesty's Representative for the exercise of these functions of the Crown.' As a result, the whole scheme collapsed.

The Talukdar of Bhadwa (who really was a railway subordinate before he succeeded to his State, the annual income of which was Rs. 17,000 –

* i.e. they smashed the attachment scheme and reverted to the old *thana* system.

† Sir B. N. Rau (1887–1953), C.I.E.; I.C.S., Bengal ,1910. Judge, Calcutta High Court, 1938–44. Officer on special duty, Reforms Office 1935–8.

‡ R. W. H. Davies (b. 1896). I.C.S., Bombay, 1922. Judicial Commissioner, Western India States Agency. A member of the Bombay judicial cadre who, while seconded to this post, exercised all the powers of a High Court judge.

or £1,275) must have got a good lawyer to smell out this point of law. The proviso was, of course, meant to exclude the Governor-General in Council or any other British Indian authority and never contemplated this Attachment Scheme. However good or bad the point of law was (and the Attorney-General told the Commons that, in his view, an appeal would have succeeded), Government were not inclined to file an appeal to the Judicial Committee of the Privy Council owing, they said, to the delay involved. Instead, they introduced a bill in the House of Lords[53] which, read a first time on 2 February 1944, and debated at length, reached the Commons in March, and produced two fairly lengthy debates there, and an amendment which the Lords and Government accepted. Members of both Houses had been bombarded by cables from interested parties in India (complaining, *inter alia*, that the text of the bill was not available in India)—doubtless mostly the petty Chiefs concerned in the attachment. They quoted freely from these cables, though few except Hailey seem to have quite understood what it was all about. Strabolgi* opposed the measure in a long speech during which he said that he had lived in Indian States and the people seemed happier and better dressed; sound Socialist sentiments. Altogether, and considering that the war was raging outside and that the bill had to be rushed through if the scheme were to be kept going, the debates make remarkable reading.

This episode is mentioned not because it affected more than minutely the main development of States' affairs as they approached their *Fürstendämmerung*, but as an example of the ceaseless activity of political officers in advising and encouraging all that made for better rule in States, when they were allowed to do so.

* 10th Baron Strabolgi (1886–1953). Chief Opposition Whip, 1937–45.

## CHAPTER 16

## The Lapse of Paramountcy

So long back as 1929, when the Butler Committee reported, the question of Paramountcy *vis-à-vis* a democratic Centre had been raised. Referring to what happened to the States in post-partition India, Fitze[54] speaks of the tragic accuracy of the Butler Committee's warning that

> On paramountcy and paramountcy alone can the States rely for their preservation through the generations that are to come. Through paramountcy is pushed aside the danger of destruction or annexation.

The Committee had recorded the 'strong opinion' that

> In view of the historical nature of the relationship between the paramount power and the Princes, the latter should not be transferred without their own agreement to a relationship with a new government in British India responsible to an Indian legislature.

This recommendation was accepted by the British Government, who never gave way on this point; indeed, so late as 17 July 1947, Listowel, the Secretary of State for India in the Labour Government, repeated this pledge in a speech on the second reading of the Indian Independence Bill in the following terms:

> Your Lordships will remember that the Cabinet Mission in their Memorandum of May 12, 1946, informed the States that His Majesty's Government would in no circumstances transfer paramountcy to an Indian Government. To that pledge we firmly adhere . . . from the date when the new Dominions are set up the treaties and agreements which gave us suzerainty over the States will become void. From that moment the appointments and functions of the Crown Representative and his officers will terminate and the States will be the masters of their own fate. They will be entirely free to choose whether to associate with one another of the Dominion Governments or to stand alone, and His Majesty's Government will not use the slightest pressure to influence their momentous and

voluntary decision. . . . Whatever the future relationship between the new Dominions and the States may be, it will require prolonged consideration and discussion before the final adjustment can be made.

There was a moment in 1945 when the Princes doubted this promise, and the Standing Committee of the Chamber of Princes resigned *en bloc*. Corfield, on taking over from Wylie as Political Adviser–head of the Political Department–was faced with a situation which he thus describes :[55]

My first interest on returning to India was to find out exactly why the Standing Committee had resigned and how they had been persuaded to withdraw their resignation. After long talks with the Nawab of Bhopal, who was Chancellor of the Chamber of Princes and Chairman of its Standing Committee, it became clear that the Rulers had at last realised that the British Government intended to transfer power over British India as soon as possible and they were afraid that in so doing the British Government might also transfer power over the States. To obviate this danger, the Rulers wanted every form of interference by the British Government in their internal self government to be eliminated before power was transferred : they considered this to be a just claim in view of their treaty rights, and that unless it was conceded they could not bargain successfully with the British Indian politicians over their place in the future set up. The reply which they received from my predecessor to this claim had been so unsympathetic that they had resigned. Lord Wavell had then taken a hand in the negotiations, and had assured them that the paramount power would not hand over its control to any other authority without their consent, on the understanding that their consent to any negotiated changes would not be unreasonably withheld. Their resignation had then been withdrawn.

The Chancellor, however, still had to be persuaded that the existing control of the paramount power would be suitably relaxed before any transfer of power. Provided the interests of the country and its people as a whole were not jeopardised, it seemed to me that the Rulers had every right to expect from the paramount power all the freedom to which they were entitled under their treaties. As soon as the Chancellor and his colleagues were persuaded that this would be the future attitude peace was restored, and arrangements could be made for the Chamber of Princes to meet. This proved to be their last formal meeting and in fact their most historic (though few of them realised it at the time), because they passed a resolution saying that they fully shared the general desire of the country for the immediate attainment by India of her full stature. From this resolution the logic of subsequent events proceeded inexorably: the British Government had already declared that if British India desired independence no obstacle should be placed in its way: the Rulers had now declared their wish to be no obstacle and that their consent to any necessary changes would not be unreasonably withheld.

In 1946, soon after the Chamber had dispersed, the Labour Government despatched three Ministers (Lord Pethick-Lawrence, Sir Stafford Cripps and A. V. Alexander) to settle with the Indian leaders the new constitution for an independent India. Lord Wavell summoned me to an early meeting with them, at which I stressed the importance of maintaining the balance between the complete freedom of each State to make its future choice and the Rulers' express wish (as expressed in the Chamber of Princes' Resolution) to remain part of a future independent India.

The Cabinet Mission then held detailed talks with the Rulers and some of their leading Ministers, and in due course Sir Stafford Cripps produced a draft memorandum on States' Treaties and Paramountcy, which after some amendment was approved and issued. It made four main points crystal clear:

(a) the British Government could not and would not in any circumstances transfer paramountcy to an Indian Government;

(b) the States would be required to negotiate the terms on which they should join an Indian Government;

(c) all the rights surrendered by the States to the paramount power would return to them, leaving them free to negotiate and

(d) during any interval after paramountcy had lapsed and before negotiated terms had been settled 'standstill' arrangements would be required, especially in the economic and financial sphere.

Nothing could have been fairer from the Rulers' point of view, though not all the implications were appreciated. It took some time before the Rulers realised that the lapse of paramountcy meant that there would be no power left in India to protect them, other than their own forces and the loyalty of their subjects. It took the British Indian politicians even longer to realise that each Ruler would have complete freedom of choice, if these promises were fulfilled.

Meanwhile, the Cabinet Mission had failed to secure agreement between the Congress and the Muslim League, and as the three Ministers were unwilling to return to England without some result they produced their own plan. This provided for a loose federation which would be prepared by a Constitutional Assembly and in which each member would represent approximately one million inhabitants. No one knew how long it would take for this Assembly to be convened and even more how long before a new constitution would emerge. Whatever the length of time, the government of the country still had to be carried on; and this was becoming increasingly difficult owing to the communal disputes which the prospect of future power based on the counting of heads had encouraged. The Services were discouraged and the maintenance of law and order was daily becoming more difficult. So the Viceroy was instructed to replace his existing Cabinet with one composed of the Congress and Muslim League leaders and other politicians, in the hope that communal feeling would thereby be allayed. This hope was not fulfilled; and it took Lord Wavell nearly three months to negotiate an agreed distribution of portfolios. . . .

But there was still no constitutional link with the States: and this seemed to me essential if their legitimate interests were to be protected during this interim period. So I drafted proposals for a Joint Consultation Council, on which the new Cabinet Ministers and the Chief Ministers of the States would share representation and which would meet at regular intervals to discuss matters of common concern. The Secretary of State approved and the proposal was included as the first item on the agenda of the first meeting of the new Cabinet. I was in attendance as usual to represent the States' point of view. Except for the Viceroy himself and his private secretary (George Abell), I was the only Britisher present, and it fell to me to explain the proposal and stress its importance as a clearing house for future developments. It was greeted with stony silence. Though the Congress members had agreed with reluctance to share portfolios with the Muslim League, it was clear that neither side was prepared to share with the States' representatives any of its prospective power to influence future events. . . . I had to concentrate on other measures to provide the essential administrative link between the States and the Centre. The ground for a link had already been prepared during the war, principally over the distribution of food grains. It had been found quite feasible to allow the Central Government departments to correspond direct with the larger States and through political officers with groups of smaller States. Since political officers would disappear with the lapse of paramountcy, it was necessary to group the smaller States by other means. The Central Departments could then deal direct with the whole body of States over matters of common concern. Detailed arrangements were worked out and communicated to the Central departments.

A more difficult problem was the preparation of a Standstill Agreement, which would ensure that the existing arrangements between the States and British India, relating to customs, roads, railways, ports and telegraphs, currency and other like matters would continue after the transfer of power until the new constitution emerged from the Constituent Assembly. A draft was prepared and subsequently used by the new Government of India without acknowledgement of its source.* Its provisions remain on record in the Indian Independence Act as proof that the very last thing that the Political Department can be accused of was working for the balkanisation of India.

On the other hand I was determined that to the best of my ability the promises included in the Cabinet Mission Memorandum of States' Treaties and Paramountcy should be fulfilled. The most urgent task to this end was to bring into being the States Negotiating Committee which that memorandum contemplated. This would not be easy, because the Committee must not be too large, yet large enough to give every State the confidence that its interests would be protected. Eventually, after I had met the Rulers and their Ministers for two days in Bombay, a representative Committee of sixteen was agreed upon, (a feat which had never previously been achieved), and negotiations with the Constituent Assembly representatives began. The Committee was more successful than its members had hoped and much more than the Congress leaders liked. Mr. Nehru even had to concede that the monarchical form of government in the States was not being questioned and that negotiations for the representation of the States in the Constituent Assembly would be on this

---

* But V. P. Menon in *The Story of the Integration of the Indian States*, p. 108, writes: '... we had ... revised the original draft of the Standstill Agreement prepared by the Political Department.'

basis, though some weeks before he had said that it would be difficult to negotiate unless the States Committee contained representatives of the people of the States. It was clear that if the Rulers continued to stand by their Negotiating Committee, they would be in a strong bargaining position to secure the terms they considered essential for joining the Constituent Assembly. Unfortunately for them, disintegration had already begun. The Dewan of Baroda had not been included in the Committee and the Maharaja seemed to think this was an insult to his State, so he decided that he would deal direct with the Constituent Assembly. Perhaps he thought also that he could obtain a better bargain by direct negotiation.

Meanwhile, open dissension between the Congress and the Muslim League members of the Central Government had come to a head: and it was being whispered into the ears of Hindu Rulers that they might be ill-advised to continue negotiations through the States' Committee of which the Chairman and spokesman, the Nawab of Bhopal, was a Muslim. Soon, one by one, helped at times by the advice of Dewans whose future might depend on the good will of the Congress leaders, and led by the Maharajas of Bikaner\* and Patiala, the Rulers followed the example of Baroda and decided to join the Constituent Assembly without conditions. The States' Negotiating Committee soon ceased to exist.

This was a great disappointment to those of us who hoped that if the States' representatives could have entered the Constituent Assembly as a bloc, the Muslim League might have agreed to partake in the work of the Assembly, since their joint representation would have been nearly half the total and a compromise constitution could perhaps have emerged, which would have made it unnecessary to partition India. There was obviously no hope of this now. All I could do was to make preparations for the lapse of paramountcy, in such a way that the day to day administration of the country was not endangered and the individual bargaining power of the Rulers

\* Guy Wint, in *The Third Killer*, p. 156, writes of Panikkar, the Chief Minister of Bikaner: 'They [*sc.* the Princes] might have refused to go quietly and might have complicated very greatly the transition to the new national India. But they acquiesced in their own liquidation, and the credit for this goes primarily to Panikkar's diplomacy, persuasion, skill in drafting difficult State documents, and Machiavellianism; other advisers of the princes were there to share the credit, but he, indubitably, supplied the principal ideas on strategy, and spun from his own brain the silken thread with which the princes were induced to bind themselves, and led them without their protesting violently up the precipice from which they hurled themselves.'

maintained in accordance with our undertakings.

In order to prepare the ground for these fundamental changes I had already called two conferences of all the Residents and now that the final stages were being reached I summoned the third, which proved to be the last.

On 22 March 1947, a few hours before this conference met, Mountbatten had succeeded Wavell with orders to transfer power by June 1948. After much talk and drafting, a man was imported to perform clear and simplified acts. He attended the opening meeting, but then turned to British Indian politics (which were enough to occupy any Viceroy's time, it is true) and had few contacts with his own Department, the Political.* He had, for instance, no time to study the recommendations of this conference. The Political Adviser and his staff had to do their best, e.g. by getting decision by higher authority. There was nothing new or improper in this, as a recent book[56] has suggested.

Mountbatten in a letter of instructions dated March 1947, from Prime Minister Attlee, quoted by Edwardes,[57] by Connell,[58] and H. V. Hodson, was told:

> It is, of course, important that the Indian States should adjust their relations with the authorities to whom it is intended to hand over power in British India; but as was explicitly stated by the Cabinet Mission, His Majesty's Government do not intend to hand over their powers and obligations under paramountcy to any successor Government. It is not intended to bring paramountcy as a system to a conclusion earlier than the date of the final transfer of power, but you are authorized, at such time as you think appropriate, to enter into negotiations with individual States for adjusting their relations with the Crown.
>
> You will do your best to persuade the rulers of any Indian States in which political progress has been slow to progress rapidly towards some form of more democratic government. You will also aid and assist the States in coming to fair and just arrangements with the leaders of British India as to their future relationships.

The instruction concluded

* Not, indeed, that Wavell had very many. Not long before he left, a golf partner dropped out, and a junior political officer was laid on to replace him at short notice. 'You're in the political, aren't you? Isn't that the service which they say is staffed with civilians who don't want to work, and soldiers who don't want to fight?' It was a well-known and harmless quip; but it was hardly for Wavell to quote it.

You will no doubt inform Provincial Governors of the substance of this letter.

It said nothing about Corfield, the Political Adviser, who has no recollection of seeing any letter from Attlee to Mountbatten.* He presumes that Mountbatten interpreted the instructions 'to aid and assist the States in coming to fair and just arrangements with the leaders of British India as to their future relationships' as authorizing him to see that arrangements were sealed, signed and delivered before Paramountcy lapsed. Corfield, however, would not have accepted this without definite instructions from the Secretary of State, who, he feels, would have supported the view that aid and assistance should not include pressure.[59]

Here we perhaps face a misunderstanding which history will clear up, when all the documents are available. Fitze blames Mountbatten for a line of action broadly describable as 'pressure on the Princes', while Edwardes blames Corfield for a course which may be described as 'failure to cooperate with his chief, the Crown Representative'. May it not have been that the source of the trouble was – understandably, in a period of rush – Mountbatten's failure to follow correctly the bureaucratic machinery? Attlee's instructions – traceable only from books† which do not explain their source, and give no date – are of major importance, and if regarded as binding would seem to clear Mountbatten of the charge of improper pressure. Corfield, however, seems right in suggesting that such a document as Attlee's letter was not binding and could not overrule the orders of Government conveyed officially through the Secretary of State. This is not the first time that we have seen private and personal correspondence between Whitehall and India playing a curious role. Mountbatten cannot be blamed for failing to foresee that the successor Government of India would break the promises clearly made to the States before Partition, though the role he played over Kashmir and Hyderabad after Partition, when he rashly stayed on as a constitutional Governor-General, seems hard to defend. And he was responsible for the rush, and for frequent by-passing of the Political Department.‡ The rush, it must be explained, was due to the decision of the British

* 'This document Lord Mountbatten took with him to India and he sent a copy of it to Auchinleck about a month after his arrival.' Connell, *op. cit.* p. 866.

† Except Hodson's recent *The Great Divide.*

‡ Note particularly the Nizam's most important letter of 9 July 1947, which never received a reply beyond an acknowledgment. The excuse was made that this was due to an oversight in the Political Department. This was not true; it was dealt with in Mountbatten's private office (*vide* Sir Herbert Thompson's letter in the *Evening Standard* of 14 January 1955).

Government, on Mountbatten's advice, announced on 3 June 1947, to transfer power in India on 15 August 1947, not in June 1948, and to accept the Muslim demand for Pakistan.

The Cabinet decision that Paramountcy was to lapse clearly required the issue of the necessary notifications restoring cantonments in good time, so that there should be no British Indian troops on State territory on 15 August 1947. But here the Political Department, who had brought in Thompson* as Resident on Special Duty to supervise the process, ran into a difficulty. The Defence Department fell within the portfolio of a Sikh member of the Executive Council who (or more probably whose advisers) hit on a clever method of sabotaging rendition of cantonments. The system long prevailing in the Government of India for obtaining the concurrence of another department when, as often happened, more than one department was concerned with a problem, was as follows. Instead of drafting a self-contained letter, with perhaps lengthy enclosures, asking for the other department's concurrence, the whole original file was sent 'unofficially', as it was called, and the consulted department then read all the relevant past history and, if they agreed, said so in a minute on the file, and returned the file in original.

The system had its faults and its advantages, but was never designed for a situation where the head of one department was out to sabotage, for political reasons, the work of another. The Defence Department, having no reply to urge against the proposal to retrocede administered areas, simply held on to the files and failed to reply. The Political Department had then to seek the Crown Representative's personal sanction without the approval of the Defence Department: which was not readily forthcoming.

But all this was a side-show to the great central problem of the State's future. Once the great mass of them decided to come into the Constituent Assembly, there lay open to two very able men, Sardar Vallabhai Patel, Member, and V. P. Menon, Secretary, of the newly formed States Department (India), a course of action which no one had thought possible. (The States Department [Pakistan] had as its Member, Sardar Abdur Rab Nishtar,† its part-time Secretary, M. Ikramullah,‡ and its Deputy

* Sir Herbert Thompson (b. 1898), K.C.I.E.; I.C.S., Madras, 1923. Political, 1926. Resident for the Punjab States, 1945–7.

† Sardar Abdur Rab Nishtar (1899–1958). Muslim League politician from Baluchistan. Held various posts in the Pakistan Cabinet.

‡ Mohammad Ikramullah (1903–63). I.C.S., C.P. 1927. Secretary, Ministry of Foreign Affairs and Commonwealth Relations, Government of Pakistan with responsibility for States Affairs as well, 1947–51. Later High Commissioner in Ottawa and London and Ambassador to France.

Secretary, Akhtar Hussain,* I.C.S. It played no important role till after partition.)

We have already seen that a standstill agreement had been drafted by the Political Department which was quite sufficient to enable the transfer of power to be carried out smoothly without any breakdown of administration, while the two new governments negotiated a permanent relationship with the States at their leisure. There was no reason to suppose that the States would have bitten their own noses off by declining to sign it. But Patel and Menon, by a brilliant concept, went further. Patel, on Menon's advice, decided to ask States which had joined the Constituent Assembly to accede to India, but on three subjects only – defence, foreign affairs, and communications, and to refuse them a Standstill Agreement unless they acceded. These were the three subjects which the Cabinet Mission, in their plan of 16 May 1946, had proposed that the States should cede to the 'Union'. This plan, Nehru had told the Princes on 9 February 1947, had been accepted by Congress 'with all its implications' – which, of course, included the lapse of paramountcy. Later the Congress seem to have regretted this acceptance. The spring of 1947 saw numerous but inconclusive discussions between the States and British Indian politicians; but after 28 April, when seven important States joined the Constituent Assembly, the united front of the Princes collapsed. A month later, on 3 June, Mountbatten announced the plan for a much earlier devolution of powers, but emphasized that there was to be no change in the policy towards the States announced by the Cabinet Mission.

Time was now very short. On 3 June, the Viceroy and the Political Adviser discussed the latest plan with a number of representatives of the States. Again, on 13 June, the Viceroy called a meeting of party leaders at which the whole question of the lapse of Paramountcy was thrashed out. Nehru wished the Political Department and Residents to continue after the transfer of power. The Viceroy instead suggested the setting up of a new department, to be called the States Department, which was agreed to. V. P. Menon took over and, as we have seen, obtained the approval of Patel and Nehru to his plan for accession on three subjects (he had already devised a plan for accession on two only in 1942, but Linlithgow had not accepted it). These three subjects covered a great deal more than appeared at first sight.

> If [wrote Menon] the rulers acceded on 'defence', the Government of India obtained right of entry into any State where internal

* Akhtar Hussain (b. 1907). I.C.S., U.P., 1932. Pakistan Ambassador to Italy, U.S.S.R., Iran, Algeria, etc.

stability was threatened. 'Defence' covered not only external aggression but internal security as well.

Nehru and Patel both had doubts whether the scheme would go through, but agreed to try it.

> Incidentally, [adds Menon], I proposed that the active cooperation of Lord Mountbatten should be secured. Apart from his position, his grace and his gifts, his relationship to the Royal Family was bound to influence the rulers. Sardar [Patel] whole-heartedly agreed and asked me to approach him without delay. . . . I should add that Nehru, with the approval of the Cabinet, readily entrusted Lord Mountbatten with the task of negotiating with the rulers on the question of accession and also with the task of dealing with Hyderabad.[60]

Acting with extreme speed and efficiency, the newly constituted States Department drafted the necessary documents and by 31 July organized the necessary propaganda to persuade all Rulers to accede by 15 August. Apart from States which were enclaves in Pakistan, only six States did not accede: Hyderabad, Jammu and Kashmir, Junagadh, Manavadar, Sardargarh and Bantwa (the last three were small Muslim States in Kathiawar adjoining Junagadh). Menon, in his detailed account of these transactions, pays tribute to the great assistance given him by the Viceroy in persuading States to accede. He adds:

> Jinnah, of course, objected to the policy of accession. He told Lord Mountbatten that it was utterly wrong and he publicly announced that he would guarantee the independence of the States in Pakistan.[61]

Thus the last vital steps leading up to the lapse of Paramountcy saw the Political Department fade out of the picture. Most of the Hindu staff moved over to the States Department, which of course gained greatly from the knowledge and experience which they took with them. The Political Adviser went on leave preparatory to retirement; the author, one of the two deputy Secretaries, joined the Government of Pakistan. The other joined the British Foreign Service in the High Commission in Karachi. The few remaining officers arranged for the transfer to the States Department of the headquarters office and its contents, and of the Residencies and other such buildings, on 14 August.

The Indian Political Service was wound up from midnight of that day, and those of its members who were serving under the Crown Representative (with the exception of Hopkinson,* the Political Officer in Sikkim and Daubeny,† who was on the Viceroy's staff, who were retained for a time by the Government of India) retired or moved over to service in Pakistan. In the circumstances of the transfer of power, there was no formality about their departure. They left with neither a bang nor a whimper.

* A. J. Hopkinson (1894–1953), C.I.E.; I.C.S., U.P., 1920; Political 1924.
† R. A. Daubeny (b. 1907), O.B.E. Indian Police, 1926. Political, 1936. Comptroller, Viceregal household, 1947–8.

# CHAPTER 17

## Partition and After: Indian States

I APOLOGIZE for going slightly outside my role, in discussing what happened after August 1947; but to omit some mention of the striking developments in the States would leave the story half told.

The trains that took the political officers home had scarcely steamed out of the States, in mid-August 1947, when a process began which was entirely unexpected and entirely successful. The Princes, who had loomed very large in the future of India, dramatically ceased to be. The newly created Ministry of States, with Sardar Vallabhai Patel as Minister and V. P. Menon as Secretary, proceeded to function in a manner never contemplated by pre-Partition politicians. Patel was the most powerful personality in the Indian Cabinet; his early death in December, 1950, had a profound effect on Indian history; but he lived long enough to give Menon, his executive arm, the support which he needed for the mediatization of the States. (Menon lived on till 1966 but did not play any important role after the death of his patron.)

V. P. Menon, from being a viceregal *éminence grise*, influential but very much behind the scenes, blossomed out in 1947 into a figure feared but respected by the Princes and whose gifts for negotiation were exceptional. They were ably assisted by a small scratch team of Hindu I.C.S. officers, such as N. M. Buch–very few of them former politicals–and a large number of promoted subordinates who were, from their experience, walking record-rooms of political practice. Patel was also Minister of the Interior and was determined to preserve law and order and to do this by supporting the old I.C.S. system of rule. Incidentally, he supported the civil servants as individuals in a way that they never could have hoped for.

These two men formed an extraordinary partnership; they were working at extreme pressure, largely improvising, and Patel had many other problems (e.g. refugees) besides the States. They took decisions of far-reaching importance quickly and surely; and what they did was nothing less than the complete mediatization of the States, in a year or two after Partition. They were not concerned with the second campaign, described in the report of the States Reorganization Commission of 1955, which finally integrated state territory and what was formerly provincial territory, and settled the vexed question of boundaries and linguistic regions – in many ways, an achievement as surprising as theirs. But they had laid the foundations for it.

Menon thus describes the situation which Patel and he found awaiting them:

> The accession of the rulers on three subjects and the participation of their representatives in the Constituent Assembly should, as was hoped, have given the States Ministry some breathing time to evolve a scheme of permanent relationship between the States and the Government of India. But after the transfer of power, one crisis after another in quick succession supervened and engrossed the attention of the Government of India. Firstly, we had to tackle the situation in Kathiawar created by the action of the Nawab of Junagadh in acceding to Pakistan. Then, there was the two-way exodus of refugees, which threatened to engulf both Dominions in one big calamity. There followed the tribal invasion of Kashmir. Lastly, the situation in South India resulting from the non-accession of Hyderabad was causing us no little anxiety.[62]

But it was not against such major issues that Menon took the field. Of all States, he chose the Eastern States for the extraordinary experiment of 'integration' which shortly moved across India, and up and down even the most important States, like a forest fire. The Eastern States were small to medium in size, well-governed on the whole, *pace* Menon, but vulnerable in one direction. For many of them had large aboriginal populations with whom (e.g. at the time of Bazalgette's murder) there had already been serious trouble.* While the paramount power remained, the Rulers could always be given protection by the Crown Representative's Police or the Army. After its departure, the Rulers had to look after themselves. It is Menon's theme that, pretty well everywhere in India, the subjects would have risen to force the Rulers to curtail their powers, if the Ministry of States (i.e. Menon himself in person, usually) had not intervened to make a settlement. This seems doubtful. How far these minor risings which did, in fact, occur in a few States, were spontaneous and how far instigated by the Congress, it is hard to say. What is certain is that, whether or not the Congress Government could have called off the activities of the States' peoples' organization (which with different titles,

---

* Later, in 1966, the Maharaja of Bastar, who had been deposed by the Government of India, was believed to be dreaming of restoration and his Gond aboriginals to be on the verge of revolt. He was killed by the police.

the most popular being *Praja Mandal*, had long operated, usually with slight success, as an opposition in most States), it could certainly call them on. The bath plug had gone, but the taps were still there. And even where *Praja Mandals* were not active, Menon could use the threat of rousing them as a strong argument to recalcitrant Rulers.

Menon gives a vivid account, in Chapter VII of his book, of how, between August 1947 and the end of the year, all the Eastern States Rulers (excepting Mayurbhanj who was allowed to stand out from complete merger till 1 January 1949), were induced to sign away their sovereignty. It is not clear how far it was his and Patel's fully thought out intention, from the start, to take over all States and merge them into what was formerly British India. They would not seem to have had a cut and dried plan for anything so extreme. But *l'appétit vient en mangeant*; and it so happened that the Eastern States were the first to be examined and became a test case.

Menon writes so well, and his case is so persuasively put, that the iron beneath the velvet is not always apparent. Desai,* his assistant, is less tactful. He quotes himself as saying to a small Central Indian Ruler who pleaded for time to consider what he should do: 'Either you sign what we have got now or you do not sign at all, and you take the consequences of your action. Our Crown Reserve Police [*sic*] would walk into the State and you are free to take such steps as may be open to you.' He adds, truly: 'They were friendless, and one could have dealt with them even more harshly than Sardar Patel in his moment of victory and authority did.'[63]

It is worth examining in some detail what was done in this the first of Menon's campaigns. Can a case be made out for him?

The case against him is well set out in Arthur Lothian's review in the Royal Central Asian Society's *Journal*, Vol. XLIV, Part 1, 1957 (pp. 58–62), and his article 'A neglected aspect of recent modern history' in the *Quarterly Review* for October 1962 (pp. 392–402). These constitute an eloquent indictment of the Governor-General, Minister of State and Secretary of that Ministry. Briefly, the charge is that States which, with the lapse of Paramountcy, had resumed their independence were dragooned into accepting complete integration into the new India.

There are, however, important arguments the other way. Many political officers would have agreed, before Partition, that for these small States to be judged 'viable'–the ruling 1947 cliché–several things were essential. Merger with neighbours for at least some subjects, and com-

---

* C. C. Desai (b. 1900) 1923; I.C.S., Central Provinces, 1947. Joint Secretary, Ministry of States.

pulsory budgetary control by some central authority–or at the very least, a fixed privy purse–seemed essential to survival. But these would be minimal requirements. Much more radical steps would be needed to achieve good rule. Were then the Indian politicians into whose hands the States had dropped like ripe fruit not to seize the opportunity? It meant breaking promises–but had our earlier administrators from Clive and Warren Hastings onwards always been so meticulous as Minto? Had the Political Department adhered to every word of all the treaties? There is much to be said for the Congress view that it was their duty as much as their chance to 'take up the white man's burden': to seize the paramountcy which had lapsed. A continent-wide piece of *Machtpolitik* on this stupendous scale, involving the absorption of one third of the area and two fifths of the population of pre-Partition India in a few months, cannot be judged by the standards of humdrum administration. Lothian's charges are unanswered and perhaps unanswerable. But the end can perhaps be said to justify the means if one considers the enormous difficulty of unifying India and the speed, ease and mildness with which it was done.

This, however, assumes that this unification turns out to have been a good thing. At the mid-century, few people familiar with India would have denied that it was a very great achievement, perhaps worth all the broken promises and broken hearts which it entailed. Fifteen years later, doubts arise. Has the total disappearance of the Indian States been so unmixed a blessing? Though the second stage of unification in the 1955 Blue Book which we shall shortly examine appears at first sight a magnificent achievement, second thoughts make one wonder whether the patient was really fit to face such a series of radical operations, followed by wars with China and Pakistan, not to mention fighting in the Naga country and Kashmir. This wholesale redistribution of States mostly on linguistic lines must have led to a degree of friction and disruption that staggers the imagination. The transfer of even one district from one province (now called State) to another, with many different laws and a different land revenue system must have led, one would think, to a mass of problems, including much litigation. The serious linguistic riots of 1956 in Bombay will be remembered. The changes were so radical that one is hardly surprised to see Hyderabad, blotted off the roll of State capitals earlier, returning to some pale reflection of its earlier glory as once more, in 1966, capital of a State, although a very different kind of State.

Let us now revert to 1947 and see first what happened in the Eastern States. Menon's account makes it clear that the unexpected accession of

Junagadh to Pakistan alarmed the Ministry of States considerably. They crushed it by wholly illegal methods as, rather later, Pakistan just failed to crush a similar accession of the minority ruler of Kashmir. But no firm standard had been laid down for tackling the smaller States. Menon says –and in his chapter vii we have a detailed blow by blow account of this fight–that the neighbouring provincial governments of Orissa and the Central Provinces had been pestering the Government of India to intervene as there was 'trouble' in some of these States. The ministry revived paramountcy by appointing officials to Sambalpur and Raipur–the headquarters of the former Political Agents–to 'look after' these States. The Rulers of most of them had formed a Union–the Eastern States Union–which began to function from 1 August 1947. But it did not suffice to prevent the demand for responsible government which, in some States, led to serious trouble. In Dhenkanal, Menon tells us, only the presence of a tame leopard in the *zenana* of the palace held off the insurgents.

However serious it may have been, there was clearly, as Menon states, a fairly grave aboriginal rising, probably pro-Raja in nature and opposed to *Praja Mandal* agitation for responsible government, in the small State of Nilgiri. Aboriginals, well armed with bows and arrows, were not to be taken lightly in these parts; and on 20 November 1947, Menon held a meeting in Delhi, attended by the Premier of Orissa, which reached these tentative conclusions:

a. the Government of India would not recognize the Eastern States Union.

b. The smaller States should be required to agree to the local Provincial Government administering certain subjects. This was the proposal of the Congress-elected Premier of Orissa.

c. The Ministry of States should shortly call a meeting of the smaller States.

Next day, Menon had a long discussion with Patel. After discussing many alternative solutions, they decided to turn down the Premier of Orissa's compromise scheme, and to merge the Orissa States in Orissa and the Chattisgarh States in the Central provinces. Patel 'was prepared to go all out to secure the merger of all three classes of Orissa States with the provinces of Orissa'. But Patel very cunningly directed that the smaller States known as B and C class, should first be tackled, and later the A class States. This was the tactic adopted by the Ministry of States everywhere, and it was very successful. At first, Menon had qualms.

I pointed out to Sardar [Patel] that the proposed merger of the States was contrary to the assurances held out in his own Statement of 5 July [1947] and in Lord Mountbatten's address to the Chamber of Princes on 25 July 1947. . . . While admitting the force of my arguments, Sardar felt he could not be a party to an attempt to perpetuate something that was inherently incapable of survival.

The Ministry thus got orders to proceed with the merger. The first problem was the Rulers' privy purse.

Menon examined two precedents. The first was a formula produced by the Political Department in 1945 in consultation with a sub-committee of the Chamber of Princes: a purely advisory document. The second was one devised by a sub-committee of Congress for the Deccan States Union. Both erred, in his view, on the side of generosity, especially the former. In the formula which Menon suggested, the Rulers were to get fifteen per cent on the first *lakh* of the annual revenue; ten per cent on the next 4 *lakhs*, and seven and a half per cent on all revenues above 5 *lakhs*, subject to a maximum of 10 *lakhs*. (A *lakh* is 100,000, a *crore* 10 million. A rupee was then worth 1s. 6d., so Rs. 10 *lakhs* meant £75,000.)

This formula is important, as it formed the basis of negotiations everywhere. Only in Kathiawar was it exceeded wholesale. Kathiawar was tackled next after the Eastern States, before the success of the merger-policy was an assured thing. The Kathiawar Rulers were mostly advanced, well-educated men, popular with their subjects and on not too bad terms with the Congress party. They had valuable customs incomes from their ports, and altogether would have been hard nuts to crack had they stood out against merger. Their privy purses were thus fixed at a higher level, 'though', comments Menon, 'I was hard put to it to explain this differentiation'.

Other exceptions to the Eastern States formula were certain large states, such as Gwalior, where the Ruler was to be head of the unit about to be formed, under the newly-coined title of Rajpramukh. Frankly, those who made enough trouble and put up a stiff enough resistance seem to have got away with an extra allowance.

All the privy purses were guaranteed for all time free from taxation, whether State or Central. In view of the high level of direct taxation in India, this was an important concession. Whether this promise was fully carried out is doubtful, however. Not only was a good deal of pressure applied later on for voluntary reduction; new taxes such as a Wealth Tax were later introduced; and though the formula should have covered them, there seems to have been some trouble in getting full exemption.*

In the Eastern States, once the scale of privy purses was settled, it remained to get this decision across. The B and C class States were addressed by Patel and Menon, and given a draft merger agreement to study. In a matter of hours they gave way and accepted it, leaving their two masters to handle the larger, A class States. Here the difficulty was to decide whether all powers should be taken over by the neighbouring provinces or whether some rump confederation of the States should remain autonomous. Hesitant Rulers were told clearly–and, at their request, by Menon in writing–that the Government of India would take over their States 'rather than allow the peace of the province to be endangered'. Opposition then collapsed.

When the news of this reached the press, something of a sensation was caused, particularly by Menon's letter just mentioned. Patel sent Menon to explain the whole business to Gandhi and Nehru, who accepted his explanation, as did the Cabinet. A precedent was now formed; and though some months elapsed before all the States in India received similar treatment, this precedent was substantially followed in all cases.

There were important differences of detail. In areas like Rajputana and Central India, Unions of a few States were at first formed, to be followed later by Unions comparable in size to pre-Partition provinces. There was, in many instances, a process of experiment, with some change in set-up or boundaries made before the final picture took shape. But nearly everywhere the *modus operandi* was the same. Menon, occasionally accompanied by Patel, would descend on an area and, working usually to some extremely close programme, would put pressure on a group of Rulers to agree to a complete surrender of their sovereignty by some date-line, such as the time fixed for Patel's departure. In the first instance, the two arrived at Cuttack on 13 December 1947, and left after holding up their train for some hours on 15 December. Discussions went on all night and never perhaps had such skilful use of the time factor been made in the history of these States. Later, in Gujarat, we read, 'The rulers complained that they were being rushed:' well they might! In some cases (e.g. in the Orissa and Chattisgarh States) the surrender was followed by merger into a province; in others, as in Kathiawar and Rajputana, by merger into a United State–the Kathiawar covenant being taken as a model for all later Unions.

Unions had in some cases been formed voluntarily before Partition– we have seen that one existed in the Eastern States, and a flourishing one

* The privy purses have been unilaterally abolished (1969).

was formed and hoped to survive in the largely Mahratta area of the Deccan. The Deccan rulers tried early on to get some guarantee out of Patel, but Menon advised him not to commit himself until the Eastern States were done with. When they were, the Deccan Union collapsed like a pack of cards, and its component parts joined Bombay province.

This wholesale and unexpected process of surrender was not accepted quite without protests. Early on, on 7 January 1948, shortly after the merger of the Eastern States, there was a conference of major Princes at Delhi with Mountbatten, now a constitutional Governor-General and no longer the Crown Representative. According to Menon, Mountbatten 'emphasized that there was no intention of applying the merger system to the larger States'; and Menon himself added that 'the principle of merger would not be applied to those States which had individual representation in the Constituent Assembly'. There may, at that time, have been no intention of forcing mergers on large States; but later they were, in fact forced.

An important change that was introduced gradually was a clause, at first permissive, in later negotiations (e.g. the Madhya Bharat Union) mandatory, enabling the Union 'to concede to the Dominion legislature the same power of legislation which it exercised *vis-à-vis* the provinces in regard to all federal and concurrent subjects'. This was introduced, in permissive form, in the case of the Second Rajasthan Union. The intention was unification and avoiding the demand for separate constitutions for each Union.

Thus gradually the whole political map of India was transformed, and a degree of unity achieved which no one, politician or civil servant, Indian or Englishman, would have dreamed possible before August 1947. Some areas took rather longer than others to come in; some were rushed, others charmed into total accession.

Only three areas stand out as exceptions: Kashmir, the Muslim Kathiawar States, and Hyderabad. Their story is a long and controversial one, and so far as Kashmir is concerned pertains to current politics and not to history. But in all these three areas the position existed that a Ruler of one faith ruled over subjects of whom a large majority belonged to another – as was, indeed, also the case in Goa. The legal position was very clear: the Ruler had absolute choice which Dominion to accede to. The whole trend of post-war politics, however, was to grant the ruled the right of self-government, which would undoubtedly mean following the faith of the majority. You could not have it both ways: follow legality in Kashmir and public opinion in Junagadh and Goa.

Jinnah's acceptance of the accession of Junagadh seemed, at the time, foolish, but presumably was based on a desire for a *quid pro quo*, Junagadh to be exchanged for Kashmir. The case was taken to the United Nations, which decided that the case of Junagadh should stand over until Kashmir was settled: which of course, it has not yet been. Juridically, Junagadh's case is still pending and it is still claimed by Pakistan. The Nawab escaped to Pakistan as did the Ruler of the small, formerly 'attached' State of Sardargarh; the Chief of Manavadar was not so fortunate. Both these States had Muslim rulers and a large majority of Hindu subjects. The Indians killed the sentry on duty at Manavadar's house, and arrested the Chief. He was kept in custody under very harsh conditions for many long months. Menon's footnote, 'Both the Sheikh of Mangrol and the Khan of Manavadar subsequently went away to Pakistan', is a remarkable understatement. The Chief of Manavadar was in fact 're-leased' and allowed to go only after his prolonged imprisonment had become a crying scandal. Sardargarh and Mangrol got away to Pakistan.

The case of Mangrol was peculiar. Mangrol was a feudatory of Juna-gadh and had never been recognized by the paramount power as a State. In some of its villages, a group named Babariawad, Mangrol exercised no jurisdiction save in revenue matters. In other words, Mangrol was merely a jagirdar there. In the rest of Mangrol's villages, Mangrol exercised criminal and civil jurisdiction and, what was most important, managed the small but useful port of Mangrol with its customs. Mangrol's powers were not more extensive than those of some of the big landlords in, e.g., Hyderabad or Gwalior. Mangrol had always claimed independence of Junagadh, but her claim had been turned down flatly by the Secretary of State. He had, however, strangely ruled that Mangrol's consent would be necessary for Junagadh to secure Mangrol's accession to the proposed Federation. Menon encouraged the Sheikh of Mangrol to revive this claim and accepted it, in return for a document in which this feudatory purported to accede to India. So soon as the Sheikh returned to his home, he was persuaded by his family and officials to revoke his 'accession'; but India naturally did not recognize his change of mind. The Mangrol docu-ment gave India some excuse, which would otherwise have been entirely lacking, for interfering in Junagadh affairs.

The accession of Junagadh to Pakistan was ridiculous; as ridiculous as the accession of Kashmir to India. Kashmir, like Junagadh and Hydera-bad, had an immense majority of members of the opposite creed to that of the Ruler. It is true that the Hindu minority was mostly situated in

Jammu province, the south-eastern portion of Kashmir State, but even there the Muslims were in a majority of about 60 per cent to the Hindu 40 per cent. (This census-proved fact is often suppressed or denied.) It is true that the Muslims there were massacred wholesale–this was probably the worst of all the 1947 massacres–and the remainder fled to Pakistan, so that at present there are practically no Muslims left in Jammu. It has been obvious for years now that the only practical solution of the Kashmir problem is one that could be settled in five minutes to the great advantage of both sides: the partition of the State along the line of the river Chenab, giving Kashmir to Pakistan and Jammu to India. This was discreetly put forward, for example, by representatives of the Commonwealth countries, in 1948 and later, but at that time Pakistan demanded a plebiscite which would undoubtedly have given her the whole state. Years of failure would now force her to welcome such a solution; but there is no evidence that India would agree to it.

Hyderabad is distinguishable from the case of these northern States because there was never any question of her acceding to Pakistan. She wished to be independent of both India and Pakistan; had she been allowed to retain this status–which was clearly juridically hers, as discussion at the United Nations made clear–she would almost certainly have proved a good neighbour, like Nepal, to India. But India determined to force the issue. Not merely before Partition, but right until his departure on 21 June 1948, Mountbatten played an active role in negotiations with Hyderabad which, as we have already noted, has been much criticized. Before Partition, Hyderabad says, he failed to lay her case correctly before the British Government–he certainly blamed the Political Department for ignoring a letter which he never passed to it from his private office. After Partition, the role which he played seemed inconsistent with the status of a constitutional Governor-General. His intentions were, of course, admirable; and if anyone could have achieved a settlement it was he. But he failed, after long negotiations; and on 7 September 1948, Menon wrote to the Prime Minister of Hyderabad asking to be allowed to send Indian troops back to Secunderabad 'in such strength as might be deemed necessary for the prompt and effective restoration of law and order' (one hears the echo of the Sudetenland claims against Czechoslovakia). Permission was of course refused. On 13 September 1948, Indian troops with a heavy armoured force marched in. Four days later, the Hyderabad forces surrendered. 'The number of dead was a little over 800': we have Menon's confession on p. 376 of his *Story of the Integration of the Indian States*. By a strange coincidence, 376 is a figure well known in India. It is the number of the section of the Indian Penal Code which punishes rape.

The endless discussions that took place over Hyderabad's status must not detain us. It was perhaps inevitable that Hyderabad would eventually become an integral part of India. But that figure of 800 killed (and Hyderabadis claim a much higher figure: the surrender of their army did not end the Indian repressive action) sticks in the throat. It is astonishing that a country with such claims to neutrality and a peace-loving policy should, through the words of one of its leading civil servants, confess so calmly to this wholesale murder.

For that is how the Hyderabad affair ended: murder (Section 302) with rape (Section 376). Except for Kashmir, the outside world is unlikely to hear or to want to hear more of the Indian States as such. The tragedy of Hyderabad is that it could and should have been avoided.

Hyderabad is now the capital of the State of Andhra, composed of the largest part of the Telegu-speaking population of south India. The unique meeting place of Hindu, Muslim and European culture which that fascinating court offered to the political officer posted there is no more. Gone is its extraordinary Hindu Prime Minister,* who had both Hindu and Muslim wives and used to scatter coins to the children as he drove in his car; gone is Nawab Salar Jung, last of three generations of Prime Ministers, most unskilful of collectors;† but Lieutenant-General His Exalted Highness Asaf Jah Muzzafar-ul-Mulk wal Mamalik, Nizam-ul-Mulk Nizam ud-Daula, Nawab Sir Mir Osman Ali Khan, Bahadur, Fateh Jang, Faithful Ally of the British Government, G.C.S.I., G.B.E., Nizam of Hyderabad, lived on in his eighties, until 1967, in his modest house, King Kothi. He used to sign his official letters M.O.A.K., and sometimes wrote them on the backs of old envelopes. A strange figure to end a strange line; in some ways rather like Queen Victoria: often wrong-headed but experienced and shrewd. 'He has retired from public life', is how he summed up his position, in *Who's Who*. When, earlier, Corfield was authorized to tell him that the British Raj was ending and that Paramountcy would lapse, the Nizam bounced up in his seat and with a gleeful grin said: 'You mean I can then do as I like?' Corfield suggested that perhaps his ministers and people would have something to say about that; and reminded him that, when we left, he could no longer rely on our

* Maharaja Sir Kishen Pershad (1864–1940), descendant of Chandu Lal and hereditary Peshkar; Prime Minister, 1901–12. President of Executive Council, 1926–37.

† His servants used to steal from his huge collection of celadon plates and put them up in the weekly auction; he would then enjoy buying these 'finds'.

support to maintain his rule. But he remained quite unconcerned.

To complete the picture, let us see how, in 1956 (note the date) the States (i.e. the former Princely States plus Provinces) were 'reorganized'. There had long been a plank in the Congress platform demanding a re-grouping of units on linguistic lines. And the Montagu–Chelmsford and Simon reports had seen the force of this claim. So early as 1948, a commission presided over by S. K. Dar, a retired High Court judge, reported on this problem: adversely, since it took the view that any changes in the *status quo* would weaken the unity of India. Not satisfied with this, Congress set up a committee of three–Nehru, Patel and Pattabhi Sitara-mayya–covering the same ground. They, too, unexpectedly recommended no action, though adding that if there were an insistent demand, there should be further enquiry. There was such a demand, particularly from the Telegu speakers (who live in what was northern Madras and eastern Hyderabad); and a Telegu State called Andhra was created, after much dispute, in December 1952. Later, in 1953, a three-man States Reorganization Commission was appointed, with Sayeed Fazl Ali, Governor of Orissa, as chairman, and with Pandit H. N. Kunzru, a parliamentarian, and K. M. Panikkar, the former Chief Minister of several States, as members. There can be little doubt that the report owes most to Panikkar, whose last appearance in State policy is dramatic.

They reported in 1955, and recommended the reduction of States from 27 to 15 (plus three 'Territories' formerly called Chief Commissioners' provinces), the abolition of Rajpramukhs and of the classification (A, B and C) which had retained still some distinction between former provinces and former states. They advised the creation of three new linguistic states–Kerala, Karnataka and Vidarbha; and of two bilingual states, Bombay and the Punjab. Kerala was the Malayalam-speaking part of Madras, added to Cochin and Travancore; Karnataka was Mysore, plus the Canarese-speaking districts of Hyderabad and Bombay; Vidarbha was the Marathi districts of the old Central Provinces. All the rest of the Mahrattas–from Hyderabad and Bombay–were dumped in with the Gujarati-speaking part of Bombay; and the Punjab was to be enlarged by the addition of what were formerly the Punjab States.

This last proposal infuriated the Sikhs and was dropped; that concerning Bombay infuriated the Mahrattas, who rioted violently in Bombay (80 killed, 450 wounded). Eventually they won, and got Bombay as an exclusively Mahratta capital of an at last united Maharashtra, Ahmada-bad becoming the capital of Gujarat and Kathiawar. (So late as 1966 there was still friction between Mysore and Maharashtra over Belgaum district.) The Commission advised the union of Telegu-speaking Hyderabad with Andhra in due course; in due course it was carried out. Lastly Panikkar, in a minority report, recommended splitting Uttar Pradesh, the old United Provinces, into two because its disproportionate size (and, one might add, proportion of Cabinet Ministers) upset the balance of the whole picture. Nehru is said to have resented this proposal, which was not carried out. After great wrangling, a bill was passed in November 1956; 14 states and 7 'territories' replaced the 27 states and 3 territories, and there they now stand. Brecher, writing in 1959, says: 'There was comparatively little violence, though enough to cause concern. And communal passions and regional loyalties had been aroused as by no other act since Independence. It is too early to know how this will affect loyalty to India as a whole. But it is certain that the bitter feelings in Bombay and the Punjab will die more slowly than they came to life.'

# CHAPTER 18

# Partition and After: Pakistan States

WHEN it was decided to partition the country, the Departments (after Partition called Ministries) of the Central Government in Delhi were reorganized for the remaining few weeks before Partition, each having two wings – the Indian and the Pakistani. Thus a sort of Provisional Government of Pakistan existed in the bosom of the Government of India, sharing stationery and office fixtures, but with its own officers and clerks. Those of us who 'opted' for Pakistan – this was the official phrase – felt, like Hamlet, that we were attending a funeral and a wedding (or rather baptism) more or less simultaneously.

In the case of the Ministry of States, Pakistan had a skeleton organization under Sardar Abdur Rab Nishtar as Minister and an Indian Civil Service officer, Akhtar Hussain, as Deputy Secretary. After Partition, the Ministry was for a time merged in the Ministry of Foreign Affairs and Commonwealth Relations, of which Mohammad Ikramullah, also an Indian Civil Service officer, was Secretary – States' affairs occupying the time of one branch only of the Ministry. Not long afterwards, a new Ministry of 'States and Frontier Regions' was constituted. After some time, Qaid-i-Azam Jinnah, now Governor-General, personally held the portfolio for this Ministry till his death – a very strange arrangement and, as he was a dying man, not a wise one. Major A. S. B. Shah,* of the former Political Service, was Joint Secretary and later Secretary of this Ministry until, on his appointment as Ambassador to Kabul, Lieut.-Colonel Abdur Rahim Khan,† of the same service, succeeded him.

As we have seen, Jinnah did not approve of the Indian methods of dragooning the States. The problem in Pakistan was quite different. There were far fewer States, and they varied greatly in their characteristics. But all were a force for stability, and there was little to be said for rushing them into a final settlement and much to be said for patient

---

* Major Agha Saiyid Bad Shah (1903–66), O.B.E. Indian army, 1923. Political, 1930. Secretary, Ministry of States and Frontier Regions, Pakistan. Ambassador, Kabul and Cairo.

† Lt.-Col. Abdur Rahim Khan (b. 1898). Commissioned, 1920. Political, 1925.

evolution. Rulers and subjects were nearly all enthusiastic supporters of Pakistan.

The States fell into three groups:

a. Bahawalpur and Khairpur, the Indus valley States, organized before Partition on the same lines as other Indian States and then part of the Punjab States Agency.

b. The North-West Frontier States: Dir, Swat and Chitral in the Malakand Agency, and the small States of Amb and Phulra, which were in political relations with the Deputy Commissioner, Hazara. (Phulra, a tiny State, with a population of about 7,000 only, was in 1949 amalgamated with the North-West Province.)

c. The Baluchistan States: Kalat, by far the most important, and Las Bela, an enclave in Kalat. They were in political relations with the Agent to the Governor-General.

To group c. the Ministry added two new States, Kharan and Makran, which were an invention of theirs. This was done to put pressure on Kalat of which they had always been, in fact, an integral part. (Similarly, as we have seen, the Indian Ministry of States invented as a State Mangrol, a feudatory of Junagadh which, though it had long sought independence, never had it under British rule and only got it from Menon for a few days as it enabled him to put pressure on Junagadh.)

The long discussions which led up to the passing of a constitution for Pakistan and the establishment of the One Unit scheme in West Pakistan involved the Frontier States as well as the others. Three relationships were, under the new constitution, possible for the States. Bahawalpur, Khairpur and the Baluchistan States were completely merged. The Frontier States were constituted a 'Special Area' under article 104 of the constitution. The third status was reserved for Kashmir.

a. Group a., important because the States were large, and more advanced than groups b. and c., gave little trouble. In Bahawalpur, there was some tendency in the early amorphous days towards independence. Moon,* the revenue minister, writes of this period:

> If we went cap in hand to Pakistan, we should put ourselves at their mercy and enable them to assert the Paramountcy of the old British-Indian Government. The Nawab and Gurmani† [the Chief

* Sir Penderel Moon (b. 1905), O.B.E.; I.C.S., Punjab, 1929. Retired, 1944. *Divide and Quit*, p. 157.

† Mushtaq Ahmed Gurmani (b. 1905). Member, Punjab Legislative Assembly, 1937–45. Chief Minister, Bahawalpur, 1947–8. Minister, Government of Pakistan, 1949 and 1950–4. Governor of Punjab, 1954 and 1955–7.

Minister] were anxious to avoid this and considered it both possible and desirable that Bahawalpur should maintain a quasi-independent existence.

There was, indeed, some little delay in accession, but so early as 3 October 1947, the Ruler signed a deed of accession, followed by supplementary deeds on 1 October 1948, on 19 January 1949, 29 April 1951 and 11 April 1952. He obtained a privy purse of a little under Rs. 30 *lakhs* p.a. (more generous than the Indian formula) and by the end of this process the State was as fully merged in Pakistan as any of the Indian States in India. There was much intrigue and wrangling in the process during which the Ruler became first a constitutional monarch and later a mediatized Prince.

Khairpur presented fewer problems. The former Ruler was insane, and was so declared by the Crown Representative on 20 July 1947. He was succeeded by his minor son, who was educated in Europe, and a Council of Regency approved accession on 5 September 1947. On 1 February 1949, a supplementary instrument was signed; and the minor Ruler, then eighteen, was invested with full powers on 16 September 1951. The State followed broadly the course set by Bahawalpur to merger in West Pakistan.

b. The States on the North-West Frontier were a case somewhat apart. They had long been regarded as islands of quiet in a stormy sea, and for long years before 1947 had given the British Government little or no trouble. Their one wish was to retain such semi-independence as they had long exercised; and whatever theoretical ambitions for full merger the Ministry of States may have had – and they were very apt to interfere factiously and unnecessarily in frontier affairs, to the annoyance of the frontier Governor and Government – in practice it was obvious that these States were best left alone, provided that they were well ruled. Swat, a model State, developed into a popular tourist resort, and its ruling family intermarried with the President's. Dir at last advanced from a long record of bad rule and isolation. Chitral's communications improved and, thanks to the Kashmir imbroglio, it achieved freedom from a vague suzerainty formerly exercised by Kashmir. All the Frontier States acceded in 1947.

c. Baluchistan States, before Partition, bore many resemblances to the tribal area of which most of the rest of Baluchistan consisted. After Partition, the story of Baluchistan until recent times centred round the position of Kalat, much the largest State. It begins with a demand, back in June, 1946, for the retrocession of Quetta, the Bolan Pass and certain other leased territories. This was turned down flat by Nehru, then member for External Affairs. After Partition, there was delay on the Khan of Kalat's part in acceding to Pakistan, and curious manœuvres took place, made none the less odd by the fact that the Khan's Foreign Minister was Fell,* a former member of the political service.

A standstill agreement between Kalat and the Government of Pakistan was reached three days before Partition; between this date and the final accession of Kalat to Pakistan there were strange goings-on. Wilcox[64] describes them, but his account is in many ways incorrect, and he has promised Fell to correct it in a later edition.

The Chief Minister of Kalat at Pakistan was Aslam,† a Muslim officer of great ability. The Khan (Ruler) of Kalat wanted a British adviser and offered the post to Hickinbotham. He refused it and suggested Fell, who consulted the A.G.G. who advised acceptance, as did Colville, the Governor of his province of origin. The Secretary of State was approached and gave his approval in September 1947. Fell became Foreign Minister. In late September 1947, Aslam and Fell went to Karachi to negotiate for a treaty with Pakistan. Ikramullah, the Pakistan Foreign Secretary, said that he had no authority to negotiate a treaty–only to get the Khan to sign an instrument of accession.

Fell and Aslam returned to Kalat and discussed the case with the Khan. They felt that they must consider all possible lines of action. It seemed to them that there were five possibilities and five only:

1. To join the United Kingdom as a Crown Colony;
2. To join Persia in some undefined relationship;
3. To join Afghanistan in some undefined relationship;
4. To accede to Pakistan;
5. To accede to India.

Fell advised that there was no chance of 1.–the British Government, he felt sure, would not agree. (He checked with Clauson,‡ of the Commonwealth Relations Office that this suggested solution was impracticable when he went to England in December 1947, primarily on family business.)

As regards 2.: relations with Persia were not particularly friendly. The

* D. Y. Fell (b. 1910). I.C.S., Bombay, 1934. Political, 1938. In Kalat State service, 1947–8.

† Nawabzada Muhammad Aslam Khan, of Amb (b. 1905). Bar-at-law, Provincial Civil Service. Political Service, 1944. On deputation to Kalat, 1945.

‡ Miles Clauson (1902–49), C.I.E. Official at the India Office, 1927. Transferred to the Commonwealth Relations Office, 1947.

addition of a lot of Baluchis to Persia, who already had enough of their own to constitute a problem,* would not be welcome to Persia. There was nothing to be said for 2.

Solution 3. was favoured by some members of the Khan's family. Fell advised strongly against it on the ground that Russian influence was strong and would be stronger in Afghanistan. The temptation to Russia to overrun a poor and backward country like Afghanistan was slight; but if it included Kalat with some 200 miles of coast and ports on the Indian Ocean, the temptation might be very great. The Khan was very anti-Communist and turned down this solution firmly.

There remained 4. and 5. To accede to India was impossible geographically and would be very provocative to Pakistan. It had no support among the people or anywhere else.

Thus they came back to 4.–Pakistan. This seemed by far the best course to adopt. The Khan decided that Aslam should try to settle this, while Fell had better keep out of the limelight; he should go to England, get legal advice from J. H. Morgan, K.C., about the States' constitutional position and its oil rights, and should also carry out some negotiations with an oil company. He also recruited General Purves to train the State Forces, and took steps to see whether second-hand equipment for them could be obtained, under licence from the Pakistan Government, from the British Army Disposals Authorities.

Meanwhile, negotiations over accession had been going on, at a Jinnah-Khan of Kalat level. Though they were old friends, there seems to have been some mutual misunderstanding. Jinnah did not like discussions in Urdu, and the Khan's English was not very good. It is doubtful whether Jinnah always understood the Khan. At all events, when Jinnah paid a formal visit in the early spring of 1946 to the annual Sibi *Jirga* and Horse Show, it was widely expected that the Khan would announce his decision to accede. He was not, however, an absolute monarch. Under the Kalat constitution, the Sardars (nobles) had a good deal to say; and Bhai Khan Gichki, supported by the rest of the Sardars, asked the Khan not to sign a deed of accession. Aslam was trying to get agreement to accede on almost any terms. The Khan was hesitant, and playing for time; and he decided to summon and consult the 'State Assembly'–quite a large elected body. A number of outside journalists were present, and all felt that no pressure was being put on the Assembly. However that may be, the Assembly unanimously turned down the proposal to accede.

* There are Baluchis all over Persia; and even a few Russian-speaking ones near Merv. No one would want another Kurdistan.

Events then moved fast. Aslam reported to Jinnah, now back in Karachi; and almost at once the Government of Pakistan approved the accession of Las Bela and Kharan, both, Fell claims, feudatories which Pakistan now treated as full-powered States, and of Makran–a province of Kalat, not even a feudatory, which had never been recognized as a State by the Government of India, but now became one, with Bhai Khan Gichki, as ruler.

At this stage, Shah, the Secretary of the Ministry of States and Frontier Regions, came to Quetta, and said to Fell that he would only discuss accession. Fell told Shah that, if the Government of Pakistan intended him to remain in Kalat, he would have no hesitation in pressing the Khan to accede, though he reminded Shah that the Baluchis were opposed to accession and he would need active Pakistan support. Shah asked Fell to remain on; Fell did so, and pressed the Khan to accede. Meanwhile, Shah on his own approached two other chiefs, the Banghalzai and the Sanjrani, with a view to their, too, acceding as independent States; and the Khan, seeing the State falling to pieces round him, reluctantly signed.

Later, there was continual trouble over the Baluchistan States. A Baluchistan Reforms Committee, set up late in 1950, reported in November 1951 and recommended a unified Governor's Province with 'protection of the rights of any Pakistan State'. Its report was not accepted. Instead, in March 1952, it was proposed to set up a Union of Baluchistan States with the Khan of Kalat as life-president. It was a failure, and in 1954 it was instead proposed that the Union be broken up and put into the One Unit plan. Under this the Khan was to sign away all his sovereignty, his privy purse being at the same time increased from Rs. $4\frac{1}{4}$ lakhs to Rs. $6\frac{1}{2}$ lakhs.

So things went on till 1958, when a rebellion broke out in Kalat in which three of the Khan's retainers were killed and the Khan was arrested and deposed, but reinstated by a later regime.

We have come a long way from Sandeman, to whom, with Lawrence, Nicholson, Edwardes and other mighty names, we shall now return, as we examine the affairs of one of the most turbulent and difficult areas in the world: the North-West Frontier.

*The map opposite is based on a map by George Philip & Son Ltd.*

# CHAPTER 19

# Baluchistan: Policy

THE long north-west frontier of Pakistan, running down from 'where three empires met'–China, Russia and India–to the point on the Indian Ocean where Pakistan and Persia now meet, was and is divided into two areas. First, in the north-east, the North-West Frontier Province (usually called the N.W.F.P.), a comparatively small but excessively tough region between Afghanistan and the river Indus; and second, in the south-west, Baluchistan, a large but very thinly inhabited territory, facing on to Persia, Afghanistan and the sea, and backing on to Sind and the Dera Ghazi Khan district of the Punjab. Both these areas were administered by the Indian Political Service, Baluchistan since 1877 and the Frontier Province since 1901.

Why this division into two? Logically, one might say, because the N.W.F.P. was inhabited almost exclusively by democratic Pathan tribes, while in Baluchistan, though there were a few Pathan tribes, power mostly rested in the hands of the Baluch and a few Brahui chiefs. But history is seldom planned like that: they grew up apart because the N.W.F.P. adjoined, and was soon taken over by, the Punjab province, while Baluchistan lay alongside the Sind division of Bombay and, when annexed by the British, remained separate from its Pathan neighbour. We will deal first with Baluchistan, by far the less important of the two. Baluchistan is about equal in area to Italy, though its population is little over a million. Its boundaries have varied but little, and their northern end still is roughly the Gumal river, running from the Afghan border to Dera Ismail Khan. The north-eastern part of Baluchistan is inhabited by Pathans, and the rest by Baluchis and Brahuis. There are no Baluchis in the North-West Frontier Province, but the Punjab district of Dera Ghazi Khan contains a tribal area exclusively Baluchi in population, and there are many Baluchis in Sind. 'The Frontier Problem' is so much centred in the North-West Frontier Province that, by comparison, Baluchistan may seem of slight importance; but it is by no means to be ignored.

For 100 years from the 1840s, the eastern border of what is now Baluchistan adjoined two provinces: the Punjab and Bombay (of which

Sind was till 1937 a part). The Punjab Government were concerned with the northern part, bordering on the district of Dera Ghazi Khan. South of that, relations were conducted by the Bombay Government, acting through the Commissioner in Sind and the Political Superintendent, Upper Sind Frontier. But whereas the Punjab Government were concerned solely to protect their border from raids, the Sind authorities had actual political relations with the Khan of Kalat. There were Political Agents, Kalat, from 1856 to 1867 (H. Green, Macaulay, M. Green) and from 1869 to 1872 (Harrison) when the agent was removed because the Khan insulted him. All were subordinated to the Bombay Government through the Commissioner in Sind. Kalat was a confederacy and, while the Khan had some control over the weaker and more accessible tribes, his suzerainty over two important tribes, the Marris and Bugtis, was nominal. So in practice, the Sind authorities (which for many years meant Jacob*) had to deal direct with any tribesmen who were foolish enough to raid. Few did, once Jacob got into the saddle; and, all along, the Sind officials preserved the theory that political relations must be with the Khan alone. The area opposite Sind consisted of the large State of Kalat, the small State of Las Bela, some loosely administered Afghan territory, and some wholly tribal independent territory. The area opposite the Punjab district of Dera Ghazi Khan comprised the large Baluch tribe of the Bugtis and, behind them, the Marris; and the Khetrans and a number of smaller Pathan tribes.

The officials in Sind (conquered in 1843 by Napier†) had a way of controlling their neighbours which had met with much success. In fact, the extreme supporters of the Punjab school and of Sandeman (*v. infra*) have been less than fair to Sind, whose officers have been called hard-hitting soldiers who had no ideas beyond killing raiders. Sind produced officers of great personality, skill and gallantry–of whom Jacob was the greatest–who spent the best part of their lives in the climatic inferno known as the Upper Sind Frontier. So far from sitting back and ignoring trans-border Baluchis until they arrived as raiders, they constantly crossed the border and indeed, as we have seen, had Political Agents accredited to Kalat State at an early date. Green,‡ Jacob's successor, set

* Brigadier-General John Jacob (1812–58). Political Superintendent, Upper Sind Frontier.

† General Sir Charles Napier (1782–1853), G.C.B. Commander-in-Chief, India. Resigned, 1847.

‡ Major-Gen. Sir Henry Green (1823–1912), K.C.S.I.; I.C.S. Acted as Commissioner in Sind and was Political Superintendent and Commandant on the N.W. Frontier of Sind, 1860–8. Retired, 1874. As stated in *Who Was Who*, after

up advanced posts in the Baluch hills to protect the newly cultivated areas developed by Jacob's irrigation. Nor were they 'purely military'. Jacob, who was in charge of the Upper Sind Frontier from 1847 till his death in 1858, had political powers as well as two mounted regiments, whom he used to hit hard with when necessary. He was, it is true, brought in by Napier, the arch anti-civilian, and did not get on with Pringle, the former Chief Secretary, Bombay, who was his chief as Commissioner in Sind, and was the only I.C.S. officer in Sind; but his methods were 'political'.

And these men took over a problem little less tough than their colleagues further north, While it is true that the Sikhs left, in the Frontier Province, a shocking tradition of cruelty–their General Avitabile demanded a regular toll of Afridi heads–the Mirs of Sind were little less cruel and stupid. And Sind is, to this day, full of Baluchis–tamed, now, it is true – but who were originally a grave problem.

So early as the winter of 1866–7, the Bugtis welcomed the Commander-in-Chief, Bombay, who toured in their country. Sind officers constantly urged the occupation of Quetta; first, Jacob, in 1866, in letters to Canning, followed by Mereweather, in 1857, at the request of Nasir Khan, Khan of Kalat, and, again, in 1866 when Green and Frere revived the proposal. (Lawrence was then Viceroy and vetoed it.)

Results, too, were good. The whole of Baluchistan enjoyed profound peace for some years before 1868, when Green retired. But in the period which we are about to discuss, Kalat affairs were in a sorry state; the tribes were in a state of rebellion; and though Sind's policy of supporting the Khan exclusively was theoretically correct, it ran into practical difficulties. For Kalat was not a unitary state but a confederation of tribes, over some of which the Khan exercised only a vague suzerainty.

In 1835 there was born in Scotland–from where so many of our political officers came–Robert Sandeman,* who was destined to achieve perhaps more, with less expenditure of lives and rupees, than any other political officer on the frontier. He arrived in India as a subaltern in 1856, took part in the suppression of the Mutiny, joined the Punjab Commission as an Assistant Commissioner in 1859, and was posted to the North-West Frontier. (Quite apart from the procedure in the political

---

much campaigning in the Sikh wars, he was 'employed on special duty under H.M. Foreign Office from the opening of [the] Russo-Turkish war to the close of [the] Crimean as a colonel in the Turkish Army'. Political Agent in Baluchistan, 1859; 'conducted expedition of tribes of Khan of Kalat against the Marri tribe and recovered British guns captured in 1839 and 1859'.

* Colonel Sir Robert Sandeman (1835–92), K.C.S.I.; Military political. A.G.G. in Baluchistan, 1877–92.

service, the Punjab, as well as Burma, Sind and some other territories, in the nineteenth century borrowed freely from the Indian Army to staff its posts. These officers were known as 'military civilians'. Officers of the Indian Army serving on the frontier before 1901 were, therefore, not strictly speaking political officers, any more than Indian Civil Service officers were.) Still a junior officer, Sandeman was posted in 1866 as Deputy Commissioner, Dera Ghazi Khan, and served there for ten long years. During this time, he established warm relations with the nine Baluch *tumandars*, or chiefs of tribes, of his district, all save one of whom had their headquarters in the plains, though also extending their sway into tribal territory in the hills. Of them the most important was the Mazari, the chief of whom, the blind Nawab Sir Imam Bakhsh Khan, played a most important part in Sandeman's life work. (He and his son, Nawab Sir Bahram Khan, who lived till 1928, were two of the greatest of all frontier chiefs.)

In 1867, tribesmen from the Marri, Bugti and Khetran tribes (nominally subordinate to Kalat) raided Harrand Fort in Dera Ghazi Khan and were successfully repulsed by Sandeman, who captured 200 prisoners. When he addressed Green, his Sind colleague in Jacobabad, and asked him to obtain redress from the Khan, Green replied that, though the Marris were nominally the Khan's subjects, he had no control over them.[65] Sandeman thereupon took the law into his own hands, and sent messages across the border through his own tribes–who are racially and socially extremely close to their Baluchistan cousins–saying that if they wanted the prisoners back they must come in and negotiate. This they did, at an important meeting at Rajanpur. At it they agreed to abstain rigidly from raiding in Dera Ghazi Khan, and to protect the routes into their hills, while Sandeman agreed to 'give service' to a small number of tribal horsemen, their principal duty being to take communications to and from their chiefs and the British authorities. A little later he secured the return of the Deputy Commissioner of Dera Ismail Khan, who had been kidnapped by the Qaisranis, a tribe further north.

Here we see the small beginning in the Punjab of a very big process, the payment of tribesmen to carry out certain obligations. But here again, Sind has been refused credit for much earlier action; Eastwick, Political Agent, Upper Sind, introduced tribal service so early as 1839, and Jacob, from 1842 onwards, employed many more tribesmen. The earliest example outside Sind, as it is one of the most efficient, is the Border Military Police in Dera Ghazi Khan. The tribal 'levies' in Baluchistan are less closely linked to Government and somewhat more closely to their chiefs; the *khassadars* in Waziristan are further again from regular police.

This system, known as the 'tribal service system' has been wrongly described as the payment of blackmail. It was certainly nothing of the kind; there was very much a *quid pro quo*, and a great deal of hard work— to say nothing of the provision of a horse and arms, in some cases—was paid for, and that cheaply.

> Seldom has better value been received for outlay than that received from the tribal levies of Baluchistan. They guard roads, lines of communication and traffic, protect posts, trace, discover and sur- render criminals, recover stolen property, bring in witnesses and accused persons, carry out *jirga* decrees, bring information, make independent inquiries, carry letters all over the country in places where there is no imperial post, produce fodder, grain, and com- missariat supplies, escort prisoners, protect survey parties, and assist in the collection of revenue, without difficulty or friction, and all this at the mere fraction of the cost of regular establishments.[66]

(This would have been an equally good description of the Dera Ghazi Khan Border Military Police in 1947.)

Sandeman's action horrified the Sind authorities and the Khan of Kalat; and from now on for some years the gravest friction took place over the question whether Sandeman should be allowed to deal direct with these trans-border people. It is a long story, mixed with politics and a change of Viceroys; but briefly, Sandeman was so successful that the protests of the Bombay–Sind authorities were overruled, and in 1876 he was made Agent to the Governor-General, a newly-created post with headquarters at Quetta, where he continued to serve until his death in 1892.

In Baluchistan, Sandeman introduced the 'system' called after his name: the Forward Policy in its fullest sense. Right from the date in 1867 when he called in the Marri, Bugti and Khetran chiefs, Sandeman worked for this. And the Punjab Government supported him. After the affair at Harrand, they wrote to his Commissioner, 'His Honour regards with even greater satisfaction the *policy* which has been kept in view throughout by yourself, Lieut. Sandeman and Brigadier-General Wilde, of seeking, as far as possible, without condoning offences or compromising the position of the British Government, the promotion of friendly rela- tions with the chiefs of border tribes.'[67]

There was the crux of the matter. Before Sandeman's time, there was a clear understanding all along the Punjab border that British officers were not to cross it into tribal territory. Sandeman set the fashion for doing just this, therein following the practice earlier introduced by Sind officers.[68]

In 1868, Sandeman crossed the border on a tour of twenty days, risking his life and his career, accompanied by a contingent of his own and of the Baluchistan *tumandars*. The tour was a success; and the irregularity was condoned by the Punjab Government. But the Sind authorities were bitterly opposed to this interference in their charge. All this time, the Khan of Kalat's tribesmen were in rebellion, and Bombay's policy was to help him to suppress them. It did not work, and Sandeman's policy of peaceful penetration, eventually adopted, did. Before long, things had reached a pitch which necessitated a ruling from the Government of India. They ordered a conference which was held in 1871 after some delay since Durand,* the Lieutenant-Governor of the Punjab, was crushed against an archway and killed through his elephant panicking while going through Tank bazaar on the way to the conference. At the conference, an unsatisfactory compromise was reached, by which Sandeman was to handle the tribes and continue to employ tribal horsemen, but under the control of the Sind authorities.

Conditions across the border now reached the scale of civil war. An appalling state of confusion existed till 1875, when Sandeman was authorized to cross the border. He took a small escort of Punjab troops and over 1,000 horsemen from his Dera Ghazi Khan tribes. He reached Quetta and defied two orders of his Sind superior to return. The Government of India backed him, and transferred him to the control of the Commissioner of Multan (i.e. a Punjab officer). At this stage, when Sandeman seemed at last to have won his private war, the picture was further confused by the resignation of the Viceroy, Northbrook, who was succeeded by Lytton.† The latter came out intending to replace Sandeman by Pelly, a much senior political officer; but on arrival he changed his mind to the extent of not moving Sandeman, though he gave him no encouragement. Sandeman, who had returned to British India after a short stay in Quetta, now went back on his second mission with a much enlarged escort, including two mountain guns and a strong force of

---

* Sir Henry Durand (1812–71). Father of Sir Mortimer Durand of the 'Durand line' and of two other sons who served in India. Sir Henry had a varied career: Commissioner, Tennaserim, 1844–6; Political Agent, Gwalior and Bhopal, and later A.G.G. in Central India in 1857. He was Foreign Secretary in 1861.

† 1st Earl of Lytton. *See* p. 50.

infantry and cavalry. He started in April 1876, and the Mastung Convention which he drew up remained the Magna Carta of Baluchistan, defining, as it did, the rights of Khan and chiefs. He seems to have received scant support from Government, probably owing to the change in Viceroys, till on 3 June 1876, he was formally congratulated, though warned on no account to commit the Government of India on policy. They finally reached a conclusion, favourable to Sandeman, which they reported to the Secretary of State, in a despatch dated 23 March 1877, which Lytton personally worked on in such detail that it was reprinted in draft some seventeen times before it was finally approved. Before this, Lytton, though inclined to accept Sandeman's proposals, felt doubt of his reliability and fitness (he was not at his best on paper) and sent his Military Secretary to Kalat to sum him up.

So continuous intervention was at last decided on, and the Viceroy met the Khan at Jacobabad in December 1876 and signed a treaty with him in which, unlike the 1854 treaty, his feudatory chiefs were mentioned. Sandeman was made a C.S.I., and gazetted Agent to the Governor-General in February, 1877, a post which he held until his death in 1892. (It was raised to a first-class Residency in 1887.) He was also made Chief Commissioner for Pishin and Sibi. By this treaty, Quetta was leased by the Khan to the British Government on a perpetual quit-rent, with the right to lay a railway and telegraph line linking Quetta with India.

Remarkable personality as Sandeman was, he might never have been able to secure the Government of India's consent to his entering Baluchistan had not their attention been fixed on the steady advance of the Russian Asian empire towards their borders. In 1865 Russia had annexed Tashkent, and begun the struggle which ended in the conquest of Bokhara. Ten years later Khiva fell, and the conquest of Merv was clearly only a matter of time. It looked as if sooner or later the two great empires were going to meet, and soldiers and statesmen began to argue where our frontier could most advantageously run, if India was ever to be defended against attack by a European power.

Friction with Russia in Europe was at this time intense, and the favourable reception of a Russian mission by Amir Sher Ali resulted in the Afghan War of 1878–80. But while Anglo-Indian soldiers and statesmen were arguing whether our frontier should be permanently extended to a line running west of Kabul, Ghazni and Kandahar, a general election took place in Great Britain, and Mr. Gladstone came into power. So far as Frontier history is concerned the enquiry, 'What did Mr. Gladstone say in 1880?' is no rhetorical question. He said, 'Clear out of Kandahar and quit Quetta.' Lord Lytton was replaced as Viceroy by Lord Ripon, who came out with instructions to withdraw from Baluchistan with all speed. The railway line was at once torn up and preparations for the retirement made. But in 1884 the Russians occupied Merv; we decided to hold Baluchistan; and the railway line was once more laid at great expense, and extended to Chaman.

Previously, in 1879, we had obtained Pishin, Sibi and Loralai by the treaty of Gandamak. Their retention or surrender, as we have seen, became an issue in home politics; had they not been held, the Baluchistan that we know could not have existed.

So Sandeman had his way; and what was it? The famous 'Sandeman system', followed with but rare and faint deviation all along in Baluchistan; sought, unsuccessfully, to be applied in Waziristan after Sandeman's death; and in fact applied, without much change, in parts of the Kurram and Malakand Agencies of the North-West Frontier Province and in the Dera Ghazi Khan district of the Punjab, copied by Lyautey[69] in Morocco, and relevant to all the areas where indirect rule was the ruler's method.

Sandeman's system may be summed up as follows:

1. Know your tribes and make friends with them.

2. Deal with them through their Chief; if, like the Wazirs, they seem too democratic for this to be possible, build up small leaders into big leaders.

3. Pay much attention to tribal service – it is no use relying on the Chief if payments do not percolate down to the tribesmen. And so should punishments: the guilty individual should be found and punished, not a whole tribe.

4. Always prefer peaceful methods, and reserve military force for the rare occasions when it cannot be avoided. But it must always be there in reserve: an overwhelming force ready to be used if unavoidable.

5. Adhere to tribal *riwaj* (custom); no westernized laws and law courts should be set up save for cases arising inside municipal boundaries, offences by Europeans and so on. All other cases should be tried by *jirga*, a system to be explained below.*

'Intense human sympathy' for individuals is quoted by those who knew Sandeman as his great characteristic. Thirty years ago the writer asked Sardar Drehan Khan, the aged Drishak *tumandar*, who had known Sandeman, whether he was a really great man or lucky in his timing – for many said that no one in his position could have gone wrong: the Balu-

* *See* p. 162.

chis were just waiting to be taken over. 'Yes,' said the old man, 'we certainly were; but Sandeman Sahib was much more than an opportunist. He had a star in his forehead!' There seems no doubt that sympathy was the element in the true Sandeman policy which made it work. Bruce* had it too. Those who write – and convincingly – of the impossibility of taming the Mahsud, write of him as a man you can respect as an enemy: but as a grim enemy, none the less, not as a potential friend. And the so-called forward policy as applied in parts of the N.W.F.P. seems, perhaps, to lack that touch of sympathy.

This, then, was the full, genuine Forward Policy for which so strong a plea is put forward in Bruce's *Forward policy and its results*. It was tried, it may be said, in Waziristan and failed – in exceptionally difficult circumstances. This is how Caroe tells the tale.[70]

> The signing of the Durand Agreement with Amir Abdurrahman in 1893 coincided in time with the arrival of Bruce as Political Agent, bright with ideas for the conduct of relations on the Baluchistan model. A loyal disciple of Sandeman, Bruce believed that the principles applied from Quetta with great success – and applied by the way to the Pathans of Pishin, Zhob and Loralai as well as to the Baluch tribes – would be of equal efficacy in the conditions of Waziristan. The principle seemed simple and sage enough; if you want to get anything done in dealings with tribes, work through the tribal organization; let the tribal leaders produce the goods in their own way. In other words, it was the principle of indirect rule. So, 'Let there be maliks,' said Bruce, and maliks there were.
>
> Since by the Durand Agreement the Mahsuds were clearly acknowledged as a tribe within the British sphere of influence, it was decided to make efforts to introduce among them this system of indirect rule. At this time a Public Works Department officer named Kelly was murdered in Zhob, and a sowar and four sepoys were murdered near the Gwaleri Kotal in the Gumal Pass, and both crimes were traced to a gang of five Mahsuds, two Abdurrahman Khels and

---

* R. I. Bruce (1840–1924), C.I.E. Provincial Civil Service, 1863. With Sandeman in Dera Ghazi Khan, 1864–75 and in Baluchistan, 1876–88, as his right-hand man. Author of the gazetteer of Dera Ghazi Khan. D.C., Dera Ismail Khan and Commissioner, Derajat, 1888–94. Though his family were in Burke's *Irish Landed Gentry*, he always felt (probably rightly) that the fact that he began his career in the 'uncovenanted' or Provincial Civil Service stood in his way, and prevented him succeeding Sandeman. This throws light on the question how far even in those days, the political service was treated as a 'service', with definite rights to promotion, etc.

three Abdullais. By prolonged negotiation . . . Bruce succeeded in securing surrender for trial by jirga of the five men actually wanted – a most remarkable achievement in dealing with Mahsuds. After surrender they were duly tried and convicted, receiving sentences up to seven years' imprisonment. The success was illusory. The opposition among the Mahsuds saw that to bow the knee to the rule of law meant the beginning of the end of their licensed freedom and were determined such things should not be. Their leaders were Jaggar as executive, and as counsellor the Mulla Powinda, a Shabi Khel Mahsud who now became prominent for the first time and was undoubtedly the brain behind the resistance. Jaggar had been concerned in Kelly's murder in Zhob, and under his leadership the maliks who had effected the surrender of the five wanted men were made to feel the full weight of the tribal resentment. Three were killed, two were hounded out of the country, the rest went in peril of their lives.

Indirect rule does not work in the absence of support, and if necessary protection, which must be afforded to the tribal authority expected to obtain the results desired by the government. The fiat that there should be maliks was not enough. In Baluchistan the Sandeman system had been accompanied by the construction of cantonments, forts and roads, making force available at tactical points for the support of the tribal authority. Baluchistan had been penetrated; Waziristan at that time was an almost pathless tangle of hills. Faced with Jaggar's action, the Panjab Government, with a glimpse of insight into the essentials of the Sandeman system, recommended a punitive expedition to deal with the offenders. But the Government of India, more interested in the immediate aim of frontier demarcation arising out of the Durand Agreement, turned a deaf ear. Bruce was instructed 'to continue his communications with the jirgas with the object of procuring the punishment of the murderers of the maliks by the tribes themselves'. Nothing came of that. So perished the endeavour to apply the Sandeman system to the Mahsuds.

The 'forward policy' of Sandeman was confused, often, with a policy of moving forward to the Durand line and wholesale disarmament of the tribes – a policy popular with subalterns, but totally impracticable if only because, once at the Durand line, you have all Afghanistan before you. And behind Afghanistan, Russia.

We have already seen that Sandeman's system was followed, by and large, in most of the Malakand Agency and in the Kurram. The test, however, was Waziristan. More lives have been lost, more rupees poured out in Waziristan than in all the rest of the Frontier combined.* Could it not have been avoided? Of course, as we shall see later, Waziristan was a fiendish problem, and by far the most difficult proposition on the whole frontier. And it had perhaps become insoluble owing to the enormous increase of the arms traffic by, say, 1910. But one still wonders. Supposing the army had been pulled out (and real economies made: normally when a garrison was cut on the Frontier, it was used somewhere else, and no real saving was made). Supposing someone with the personality of Sandeman or Lyautey or Roos-Keppel† had been told: Here is half the normal army budget spent on this area: you have full authority to spend it. Go ahead and see what you can do. Your pay is doubled and you have ten years to get results. No questions will be asked. You are in sole charge of an adequate force of army and air force in the plains if you need them. You can be ruthless, you can be lavish. (Roos-Keppel kept the Afridis quiet as mice during World War I by doubling all their allow-ances.‡ Lyautey in the same war, kept Morocco quiet by making his officers celebrate French defeats with garden parties and taking up new archaeological excavations.)

It was never tried. Many variants of the two main N.W.F.P. policies – the so-called Forward Policy of complete occupation and the Close Border policy – were tried: but curiously, very seldom after R. I. Bruce was a Baluchistan officer of sufficient seniority to put new policies into effect transferred to the N.W.F.P. or vice versa. The one notable excep-tion in this century was the transfer of Parsons,§ an outstandingly

* In 1922 the expenditure was so vast that all the civilian members of the Executive Council of the Governor-General formally demanded economy and had to be overruled by the Home Government. In 1945, two senior officers of the Indian Army and Royal Air Force wrote (in the Tuker report) that the expendi-ture of 48 battalions and ancillary troops, together with 10,000 militia and 500 Frontier Constabulary then committed to Watch and Ward duties, directed at tribesmen armed only with rifles, restricted by poor communications, low food-stocks and limited ammunition to keeping the field for very short periods, and who rarely mustered more than a few thousand, was quite intolerable.

† Lt.-Col. Sir George Roos-Keppel (1866–1921), G.C.I.E., K.C.S.I. Political Agent, Khyber, 1899–1908; Chief Commissioner, N.W.F.P. 1908–19. Member, Council of India, 1920.

‡ This was well remembered. Once Cunningham, when signing some docu-ment, said to an Afridi *malik*, 'This was Roos-Keppel's pen.' 'Then use it as he did!' was the reply.

§ Major-Gen. Sir Arthur Parsons (1882–1966), K.C.I.E., C.B.E., D.S.O. Served exclusively in N.W.F.P. and Kabul until transferred to Baluchistan in 1935: A.G.G. Baluchistan, 1936.

distinguished Frontier Officer, to the post of A.G.G. Baluchistan in 1936. He reacted heavily to certain mild abuses over easements – Baluchistan was the sort of place where ramps flourish like green bay trees – and rather confirmed the general view that Baluchistan was best left alone.

But was it? Did we follow fully in Sandeman's footsteps? Was there not rather a tendency to freeze things and would not Sandeman himself have done more to civilize the people? It is a curious thing that in so few of the numerous extant reports and minutes on Frontier and Baluchistan affairs does one come across any adequate recognition that there were other neighbouring areas whose methods were slightly different and at least worth examining. We refer to Upper Sind and the Dera Ghazi Khan district of the Punjab. Both made full, though different, use of the Frontier Crimes Regulation[71] – the Bible of Baluchistan, which we shall shortly expound. But whereas, in Baluchistan, tribal custom was considered the only test for deciding a case, e.g. of the killing of an adulterous wife, in Dera Ghazi Khan, very gradually and with less severity in the hills near the Baluchistan border than in the Indus valley, punishments were added and attempts, often successful, made to induce enraged husbands to accept monetary compensation in lieu of killing – which so often led to a blood feud. Again, in Dera, we did not deal exclusively through the *tumandars* or chiefs. The *muqaddams*, as the tribal sub-chieftains were called (*maliks* in N.W.F.P. terminology) were, especially if the chief were incompetent, dealt with to some extent direct; they or their sons were often N.C.O.s in the Border Military Police, and the best of them were very good indeed. This force was more and more becoming a Government-controlled body, the *tumandars* having little to do with it save for the right to nominate a few recruits. The Baluchistan levies fell far behind it in efficiency and loyalty. Dera, with a population comparable to Baluchistan, was governed far more cheaply, and with a handful of staff.

We have spoken above of the *jirga* system and the Frontier Crimes Regulation or F.C.R. The *jirga*, or Council of Elders, could mean several things. In the N.W.F.P. it often meant the complete gathering of a tribe or at least a clan, especially in Waziristan where every man was as good as his neighbour – 'and a damned sight better', he would claim. It had also a more restricted meaning, very close to that of a juror in Anglo-Saxon usage. Fully to understand this use of the word, we must examine the F.C.R. This short Regulation (equivalent for all purposes, to an Act of the Legislature, but for reasons into which we need not enter, classified as a regulation) was in force with slight variants all over the N.W.F.P.,

Dera Ghazi Khan district, Baluchistan and – with the title Sind Frontier
Crimes Regulation – in Upper Sind. The sections which concern us were
as follows:

8. The Deputy Commissioner (Government had power by notification
to delegate all his powers under the Regulation to other senior magistrates
as well) if satisfied that this was called for, could withdraw any civil case
from a civil court (he had to act quickly, before it got fully started) and
refer it to a Council of Elders. They were bound by no formal law of evidence and were expected to supplement the evidence of witnesses by
local enquiry. On receipt and consideration of their report, he passed a
decree which was unappealable, though revision lay to the Commissioner
or Chief Commissioner.

11. The Deputy Commissioner could take similar action in a criminal
case, in which event he had powers to acquit, whether or not the *jirga* so
advised, or (if, and only if, the *jirga* held the accused guilty) to convict
and impose sentences up to 14 years rigorous imprisonment. (A death
sentence could in no case be imposed in a *jirga* trial.)

36. The Deputy Commissioner could banish from the district or from
any part of it anyone not resident there, or with the Commissioner's
sanction, a person resident there.

40. This gave rather more stringent and summary poweis than the
usual law to bind down to keep the peace anyone expected to commit a
crime. (Much used, and very successfully, upon the relatives of a murdered man who were likely to seek revenge.) If they could not produce
the necessary sureties, they went to gaol for a time.

41. This allowed one to demand similar sureties from someone not
personally suspect but in a position to control the suspect, e.g. the father
of an absconding potential killer, or his *muqaddam*. This power, totally
unknown to the normal law, shocked the lawyers (who, incidentally,
were not allowed to appear in F.C.R. proceedings), but saved thousands
of lives and often stopped blood feuds starting.

Another section of the F.C.R. permitted whipping as an addition or
substitution for imprisonment in all cases in which the accused was a
juvenile, and in many cases where he was an adult. Whipping is highly
out of fashion, these days; but as a means of avoiding a sentence of imprisonment – surely the thing to be avoided above all, in any scheme of
penal reform – it had its advantages. The writer remembers when the D.C.,
Dera Ghazi Khan, trying a Baluch of eighteen who had killed his wife
and her lover a few hundred yards from the Baluchistan border. Had the

crime been committed a mile to the west, he would have gone scot free. Had it been committed, say, in Lahore, the High Court would have sentenced him to about four years' imprisonment. Had it been committed in the plains area of Dera Ghazi Khan, he would have been tried by *jirga*, since the parties were Baluchis and Baluch tribal custom was involved, and would have received perhaps 6 months' or 1 year's imprisonment. As it was, after the *jirga* had held him guilty, the writer sentenced him to a whipping and no imprisonment. This illustrates the adaptability of the F.C.R. procedure.

We referred just now to Baluch custom being invoked. In this respect, Dera Ghazi Khan differed strongly from the N.W.F.P. As Caroe clearly brings out, the Regulation was only too often used in the N.W.F.P. as an easy means of getting a conviction in a weak case. In Dera Ghazi Khan, the sole test was, were the parties Baluchis, and was Baluchi custom involved? If so, the case, whether civil or criminal, whether the parties were plainsmen or hillmen, went to *jirga*: otherwise, all cases arising in the plains, i.e. British India, went to the regular courts. There were no Government orders to this effect; it was simply the local policy, followed by one D.C. after another with some variance of strictness.

In Baluchistan and Dera Ghazi Khan there were two kinds of *jirga*: the ordinary *ad hoc jirga* which the Deputy Commissioner convened for a straightforward case, civil or criminal, and the Chiefs' *jirga*. The latter, convened twice a year, dealt with cases where men of more than one tribe were concerned, or even men of more than one province. The members were tribal chiefs, and their decisions, like decisions of a High Court, formed precedents and were treated with great respect. The F.C.R. was one of the most valuable pieces of legislation ever to be enforced. It is sad that the political parties – largely under the influence of the bar – consistently attacked it and have, since Partition, secured at least curtailment of its use.* No political officer who was familiar with *jirga* procedure could ever feel quite happy again in trying a regular case, where there was seldom any convincing reason for believing that a witness was speaking the truth.

* *The Times* of 3 February 1965 reported that a High Court had declared the F.C.R. unconstitutional, and that the Government of Pakistan was framing a new law which, inter alia, allowed for appeals while retaining *jirgas*.

# CHAPTER 20

# Baluchistan: Administration

CAROE rightly says that the name Baluchistan is a misnomer. While all the tribes south of a line drawn roughly east-west through Quetta, in that area which runs down to Sind and the sea, are Baluchis or Brahuis, all those north of it are Pathans; of whom, he comments, only the Achakzais are in any way formidable. This huge but largely empty area was divided early on into six Agencies: Zhob, Loralai, Sibi, Quetta, Chagai, and of course Kalat, which was a full-blown State and, with its smaller neighbour, Las Bela, constitutionally, at least, akin to the States we have written of earlier.

The Zhob Agency had its headquarters at Apozai, later to be called Fort Sandeman. This Agency alone touched the N.W.F.P. and occasionally shared tribal problems with Waziristan. It had a long frontier with Afghanistan which provided much excitement. That could not be said of Loralai, a very pleasant and remote place on the road between Quetta and Lahore, where the tribes–all Pathans save the Kharsins–were mostly small and well-behaved. Further south and west, the Political Agent of Sibi–perhaps the hottest place in the sub-continent in summer–was in charge of the two most important and occasionally troublesome Baluch tribes: the Bugtis and the Marris, whom we have met before. Very poor and backward in barren hills, their *tumandars* or chiefs were men of considerable wealth thanks to Government's generous land-grants. The Extra Assistant Commissioner (E.A.C.), Bugtis and Marris, was an officer of the Baluchistan Provincial Civil Service, and handled these two tribes for the Political Agent. Indeed, powerful as these E.A.C.s were in all Agencies (petitioners were usually not allowed to see the P.A. unless the interview were approved by the E.A.C.), this particular officer probably exercised greater powers, for good or evil, than any others. Few P.A.s ever spoke fluent Baluchi, the only language known to these tribesmen, and the E.A.C. was clearly of primary importance. Since Partition, in 1952, gas has been discovered in large quantities in the Bugti country.

Loralai district contains a hill station of great beauty and considerable height, Ziarat, marred only by a water supply inadequate for more than a handful of officials. Its juniper forest is unique in that part of the world.

The Political Agents of Loralai and Sibi summered there, as did the A.G.G. and his Revenue Commissioner. After Partition, Quaid-i-Azam Jinnah who loved Ziarat spent some time there; already a dying man, he was moved from Ziarat to Karachi, his last resting place.

Quetta, perhaps the most important charge in the Province, was totally destroyed, save for the outlying cantonment area, one summer's night in 1933, by a devastating earthquake at a time when the town was full to far beyond its winter population with tourists from Sind. It has since been rebuilt. Besides a large garrison, it was always the headquarters of the local Government, from Sandeman's time onwards. It took a few years for the effects of occupation to give results. There is a vivid account[72] of the earthquake by Wakefield,* a political officer who was in it; and Wingate† brings out excellently the atmosphere of Baluchistan generally and Quetta in particular.[73]

But Quetta's chief importance was its position between the Bolan and the Khojak passes as the door between India and Afghanistan: on a route much more used in history than the better-known ones through the Tochi Kurram and Khyber, further north. Chaman, the last outpost on the wide-open route to Kandahar, did not bristle as did the Khyber with guns; but the rails for a complete line to Kandahar were stored at the terminus, and it was well recognized that, in the lamentable event of yet another war with Afghanistan, this would be the invasion route. The P.A. was *ex officio* Deputy Commissioner as well, since part of his charge was classified as British India.

Kalat was an Agency *sui generis*. It takes up two thirds of Baluchistan, and Mekran, a district of Kalat to the far south-west, was supervised by an Assistant Political Agent who was *ex officio* Commandant of the Mekran Levy Corps. He normally had an Indian Army officer as adjutant, who was in charge of the day-to-day management of this force. Conditions in Mekran were such that only by maintaining a fleet of good cars, turned in each year for replacement, could the problems of transport be faced.

For an account of life in Kalat, there is nothing so recent and authentic as Wakefield's memoirs, already referred to. He was Chief Minister in three Indian States—a Hindu (Rewa), a Sikh (Nabha) and a Muslim (Kalat): a record surely unequalled.

Lastly, there was Chagai—an Agency which lay between Afghanistan and Kalat, with its headquarters at a God-forsaken place called Nushki. It ran right down to the triple Persian–Afghan–Indian frontier, at Koh-i-

* Sir E. Wakefield, Bt. (1903–69), C.I.E.; I.C.S. Punjab, 1927. Political, 1930.
† Sir R. Wingate, Bt. (b. 1889), C.B., C.M.G., C.I.E., O.B.E.

Malik-Siah. During both world wars, this route became one of import-ance; Skrine's* and Gould's† memoirs are revealing on the conditions over the border, as is Haig's‡ account of life in Meshed in World War I. Nothing much happened in Chagai in peacetime. Thrice weekly a rather ghastly train dragged its way into Nokkundi, the last station before Persia. On one blazing hot summer's day, in 1930, two New Zealand journalists turned up in Dera Ghazi Khan: they had motored from Europe to Persia and Chagai, and called on the writer. They described their first sight of India at Nohkundi – entering very much by the back door, after a grim drive over Persian roads – and it was, to their surprise, an elaborately decorated railway station. 'Why,' they asked, 'all this bunting? In honour of whom?' 'The P.A.,' they were told. When they had discovered what the reader doubtless remembers – that P.A. is the usual abbreviation for Political Agent – they followed up with the query: 'Why is he coming?' 'To make T.A.' was the reply. When this phrase was interpreted (it means 'travelling allowance'), one felt that they were well on the way to master-ing Indian administration.

We have left to the end the king-pin of these Agencies: the A.G.G who, as we have seen, was Sandeman till his death in 1892. He was fol-lowed by St. John, Barnes, Browne, Yate, Tucker and then a name well known to history – McMahon.‖ At Partition, Prior¶ was A.G.G. and stayed on for some weeks thereafter – a difficult period. But he was not the last of the British political officers to hold this post under the new regime of Pakistan. He was succeeded in 1947 by Dundas** who, when Cunning-ham had to resign from the post of Governor, N.W.F.P., owing to ill-health, followed him in Peshawar, and was succeeded by Savidge†† in Quetta. He too resigned on health grounds. Later, Saker,‡‡ the last British

---

* *See* p. 274.        † *See* p. 271.        ‡ *See* p. 227.

§ Lt.-Col. Sir Henry McMahon (1862–1949), G.C.M.G., G.C.V.O., K.C.I.E., C.S.I. Indian Army, 1885; Assistant Commissioner, Punjab, 1887; demarcated Baluchi–Afghan frontier, 1903–5; British representative on Tibet–China–U.K. treaty, 1913–14. High Commissioner, Egypt, 1914–16. In this last post he was the author of the famous *McMahon Letters*, to King Hussein, the inconsistency between which and the later Balfour Declaration caused so much trouble in Palestine. While Foreign Secretary, he was responsible for the 'McMahon Line' – the frontier with Tibet.

¶ Lt.-Col. Sir Geoffrey Prior. *See* p. 45.

** Sir Ambrose Dundas (b. 1899), K.C.I.E., C.S.I.; I.C.S., U.P., 1922. Political, 1925. Served almost entirely in N.W.F.P., A.G.G., Baluchistan, 1947–8. Gover-nor N.W.F.P. 1948–9. Lt.-Gov., Isle of Man, 1952–9.

†† C. A. V. Savidge (b. 1905), M.B.E.; I.C.S., C.P., 1929. Political, 1934.

‡‡ Major R. K. N. Saker (b. 1908), C.B.E. Indian Army, 1932. Political, 1933.

Revenue and Judicial Commissioner, several times acted as A.G.G. in the mid-50s.

Though both Baluchistan and the N.W.F.P. came under the (Indian) Foreign Office, as opposed to the Political Department, which controlled the States, the work was sufficiently different to cause a certain specialization. Few officers served exclusively in one only of these areas; but most tended to stay most of their service in one or the other. Taking leave of Baluchistan with its generally admirable climate and comparatively easy problems, we now turn to the stern and never fully solved problem of the N.W.F.P.

# CHAPTER 21

## The North-West Frontier Province: Early History and Terrain

IN 1901, Curzon set up the North-West Frontier Province, whose frontiers remained unchanged for the rest of the British period. It consisted of the Hazara district east of the Indus, and all the former Punjab districts and agencies west of the Indus and up to the Afghan frontier except Dera Ghazi Khan which, because of its Baluch character, was retained in the Punjab, together with a very small part of Dera Ismail Khan and the Isa Khel *tahsil* of Mianwali. The new Province was made up of five districts (later six) and five agencies (again, a sixth was added by the Government of Pakistan after Partition). With few exceptions, the districts were all in the plains, the agencies were all in the hills. All of the districts, under Deputy Commissioners – the term used in the Punjab and N.W.F.P. for what, down-country, was called a Collector – had a portion of tribal territory attached to them. In early British days, such contacts as there were with the tribes were made by the Deputy Commissioners of adjoining districts. Later, but before 1901, the five agencies were at intervals created.*

The province ran on an arc over 400 miles long from the north of Chitral to an extreme west point near Wana in Waziristan (an area the size of Yorkshire, in the south-west of the province, of which we shall have much more to say). Its western, international frontier was and is the Durand Line, negotiated by Durand† with Abdul Rahman‡ in 1893. There was, however, also an inner line, which we may call the border as opposed to the frontier, which ran broadly along the foot of the Suleiman range and which constituted the division between the districts (administered more or less as other parts of the then British India) and the agencies where the King's writ did not run.

This border was the outer frontier of India when the British

* Khyber, 1878. Kurram, 1892. Malakand, Tochi and Wana: 1895–6.
† Sir Mortimer Durand (1850–1924). I.C.S., Bengal, 1873. Foreign Secretary, 1884–94 'Durand Line', 1893. Minister, Teheran, 1894–1900. Ambassador, Madrid, 1900–3; Washington, 1903–6.
‡ Amir Abdul Rahman (1844–1901). Ruler of Afghanistan.

arrived and took it over unchanged, in the sense that their predecessors had not occupied the mountainous area. Let us see very briefly who these predecessors were, noting forthwith that, whatever else they had been, they had *not*, except briefly around the beginning of the Christian era, been Indians, until the short period (1823–49) of Sikh rule. For a full history of this area, Caroe's *The Pathans*[74] is outstanding.

When Alexander the Great invaded the Frontier in 327 B.C. it was part of the Persian empire. He was followed by a Greek dynasty which ruled for some centuries in what is now Afghanistan. Meanwhile, the Indian dynasties which introduced Buddhism, of which the great king Asoka (285 B.C.) was the chief ornament, ruled over the plains – a country highly civilized which contained walled cities and a famous tradition of art and sculpture. Early in the Christian era, the Kushans came down from the Central Asian highlands; for some 600 years these nomads and their successors held sway. The next great change came with the Muslims; after earlier raids, the Ghaznavid dynasty, towards the end of the tenth century A.D., saw the beginning of Muslim rule which was to last till 1823. There were several Muslim dynasties, of which the Moghuls were the chief; with their decline came the invasion of the Turkoman Nadir Shah in the seventeenth century who, after winning the Persian throne and reaching Delhi, was assassinated on his way home, and followed by Ahmad Shah, the first Afghan to rule in these parts, and the founder of the Durrani empire. In its heyday, it covered all our area, as well as most of the Punjab, Afghanistan and Kashmir; but it did not last. The Sikh conquest was at hand; but the occupation, though for a brief period only, of Peshawar and most of the plains of the Frontier by the Durrani Afghans, had an important result. It left the Kabul dynasty with a certain feeling of irredentism for Peshawar which expressed itself in two ways. First, during all the British period, there was a tendency on the part of the Afghan rulers to intrigue with the tribes and make as much trouble for the British as possible; and second, after British rule ceased in 1947, there was a move for the actual transfer of the whole Frontier to Afghanistan, in the shape of propaganda for what was known as the Pakhtunistan or Pathanistan movement. This movement, Cunningham records, started about May 1947, with few supporters in the tribes save among the Wazirs and Daurs. Even in the Afghan cabinet, the elder members were reported to be opposed to it. Though it never had more than nuisance-value, and was almost entirely without popular support, this movement – inspired by these historical memories and financed by Indian money paid through their Kabul embassy*–had the disappointing result that the close friendship between the new state of Pakistan and its Muslim neighbour, Afghanistan, which was expected to follow Partition, did not materialize. Only in the last few years have relations between them become even correct, to say nothing of friendly.

This is no place to recount once more the lamentable story of the three Afghan wars. But as background to what we shall have to say of the Frontier in these chapters, it must never be forgotten that twice in the nineteenth century the British invaded Afghanistan, each time for fear of Russian influence in that country, leaving behind a legacy of hatred. It is true that the three most important Afghan rulers†–Dost Mohammad, Abdul Rahman and Habibullah Khan–stuck with great fidelity to their promises. Dost Mohammad did not take advantage of the Mutiny crisis in 1857; Abdul Rahman abode faithfully by his settlement with Griffin‡ and Durand; and finally, in spite of great temptation from Germany and Turkey, Habibullah remained strictly neutral during World War I–and paid for it with his life. His successor, the foolish Amanullah Khan, mounted an unprovoked invasion against the Frontier in 1919. Though he was defeated in a few days, and was lucky to have offered him a very lenient peace treaty, his forces did have a temporary success in one theatre of the war which had disastrous results for our policy in Waziristan, as will be recounted later.

The first Afghan war dismissed for ever the notion that it would be possible to make another Hyderabad of Afghanistan, and it taught the Indian authorities to be very shy in future of involving themselves in that country. Thus when the conquest of the Punjab brought our border to the slopes of the foothills, our officers were expressly forbidden, from about 1848 to 1887, to concern themselves with what went on across the administrative border. Their preoccupation was almost exclusively with the minor objective–the defence of the Indian plains from raids.

Thereafter, frontier policy went through different phases, which we shall examine in more detail in a later chapter. It varied with period, and with terrain–sometimes, in opposite ways. For instance, it can be broadly

* The Government of India deny this. The authority for the statement is intelligence reports received by the Government of Pakistan and seen by the author at the time.

† Dost Mohammad (1793–1863). Abdul Rahman (1844–1901). Habibullah Khan (1860?–1919).

‡ Sir Lepel Griffin (1840–1908), K.C.S.I.; I.C.S., 1860. Chief Secretary, Punjab, 1878. A.G.G., Central India, 1881–8. Chief political officer with the forces in the 2nd Afghan War. Father of Sir Cecil Griffin.

said that, till 1887, the close-border policy was followed, to be succeeded by a more forward policy up to 1899 when Curzon took over; to be succeeded by the 'Curzon policy', a modified form of close border policy, which lasted up to about 1922, when a modified forward policy was introduced and followed until 1947. Yet it could equally truly be said that policy depended less on time than on place. During the most emphatically close-border periods, we find, once the 1897 campaign was over, regimes in the Malakand and Kurram agencies which can in a sense be called 'forward', right up to 1947; in the Khyber, even in the most 'forward' periods, we find that the Afridis were left severely alone; even when the Khajuri Plain was occupied in 1930, the policy towards them remained 'close border'. Unlike the Mahsuds, the Afridis – every bit as powerful and potentially menacing a tribe – were dependent on nearby plains for their grazing and indeed their shopping. It was therefore never necessary to build roads in their mountain home, the Tirah. They had agreed, in 1881, to have no dealings with foreign powers, accepted allowances (in lieu of tolls formerly levied by them in the Khyber), furnished tribal levies and took full responsibility for the Khyber Pass. That was considered sufficient; British officers were still not allowed into their tribal territory; right up to the end, with the exception of the military invasion during the 1897 campaign, the Tirah remained inviolate. Roos-Keppel in 1902 when P.A. Khyber, openly visited the Tirah as the guest of an Afridi *malik*. He was the first European to do so; if there were others, they were very rare.

What were the factors which made up the Frontier problem? The terrain, the people, Russia, Afghanistan, Islam, the tribes, the instrument (i.e. first the Punjab and later the N.W.F.P. Government), the district administration, the Punjab Frontier Force, the Regulars, the Scouts, the Border Military Police, the *Khassadars*, the levies – these are the factors put forward by Howell, the doyen of surviving frontier officers. He adds, very truly:

> An administration the majority of whose subjects – if they can be so called – had (and have) their international status determined not according to the authority to whom they pay taxes – for they pay none – but according to the authority from whom they receive allowances surely deserves detailed description and informed comment.

The terrain was perhaps as important as the people – geology vying with ethnology as the explanation of this strange problem. Nearly all generalizations about the Frontier – which we here use in the sense of the

North-West Frontier Province including its tribal territories–run into the difficulty that what was true in Kohat was not true in Waziristan; that what was true in Swat was not true in Dera Ismail Khan. The people were mostly Pathans and Sunni Muslims–though, in the plains, there were numerous non-Pathan Muslims, to say nothing of the small but rich and very influential Hindu community which, after Partition, fled completely to India. And in the Kurram Valley there was a pocket of Shia Muslims whom we shall discuss later.

The word 'Pathan' was what Europeans and Indians of other provinces called the race. They called themselves Pashtuns or Pakhtuns, and spoke Pashtu, which has a northern and a southern dialect, a language with no very close relations, spoken only in the Frontier Province, in the southern part of Afghanistan, and, as we have seen, in north-eastern Baluchistan. It is a curious fact that the boundary of the northern and southern dialect (which runs east-west, approximately, through Kohat, half way up the map) is also the boundary of the hair-do and the dance. Tribes south of this odd frontier wear their hair bobbed,* so that it covers the ears, and on slight provocation break into a dance–generally known down-country as the Khattak dance, though they are by no means the only tribe who dance it. They also speak the soft variety of Pashtu. North of this line, you have hard consonants, short hair and no dancing, and the language is called Pakhtu. Non-Pathans mostly speak a kind of Western Punjabi known as Hindko–akin to the western Punjabi known in Dera Kghazi Khan as Jatki or further east as Multani.

But leaving aside a linguistic minority, and a difference in hair and dance fashions, we had on the Frontier a homogeneous people, of one faith and one language, who yet reacted most differently in different areas. Here we come back to terrain. Plains and hills; that is the broad distinction. The higher and remoter the hills, the more devoted were the tribes to independence and apt to raid in the plains.

Thus we find a Muslim, Pakhtu or Pashtu-speaking society, infused with an intense loyalty to an abstruse body of customary law (known as Pakhtunwali), which includes the blood feud and the duty to grant asylum and hospitality to strangers; a frontier, never very far away, beyond which lay and lies Afghanistan, beyond which lay and lies Russia; and 100 years of British rule, the last half of which (1901–47) was the rule of the political service. British rule has been an experience seen near by if not personally felt by all the tribes: 100 years of history, quite

---

* The Baluch tribes wear their hair uncut altogether, in ringlets, and also–traditionally–wear exclusively white clothes.

different from the history of Baluchistan, with which area all contacts – marriage, political, and the rest – seem to have been rare.

These 100 years have seen different systems, inspired by differences of terrain and different approaches by individual officers, and by some differences in pre-1847 history (the Mahsuds and Wazirs had always been independent: the cultivator of the Peshawar plain had, latterly, under the Sikhs, earlier under the Durrani Afghans and still earlier under the Moghuls, been accustomed to be ruled). But allowing for all these differences, the fact of British rule – almost exactly 1847–1947 – was of primary importance. We may have been hated more in one area than another; we may have altered the overall culture of the Pathans less than we altered that of many other provinces of pre-Partition India; our system of administration may even itself have been more altered than altering. The fact remains that the British Raj was a tremendous thing. It entered into every hole and corner of the country and of the Pathan consciousness. Unlike some powers who, by the introduction of numerous colonists and a mass bureaucracy, changed the country they conquered by the direct influence of their nationals, there were very few British at any time on the Frontier – the vast majority of them private soldiers, who had but the slightest contact with the Pathans.

But look what the Pathan saw, from birth to death. The food he ate (what Pathan drank tea before the arrival of the British?), the cloth he wore, the schooling and medical attention which he got in however small doses, the roads, trains and buses, the changed breed of cattle or horses, the changed tactics when he fought, the wireless that he listened to, the gun which perhaps finally killed him – all, or nearly all these things were either British or adaptations of British ideas. He was no admirer of our legal system: but the courts to this day administer British law. Of course, the coming of Pakistan has changed many things: in particular, the, removal of the irritant of the presence of the British and Hindu troops and the removal of the temptation to raid and kidnap the Hindu merchant or British officer (there are none of either left) have astonishingly changed for the better the apparently insoluble problem of Waziristan.

The 'uneducated' tribesman was passionately interested in world politics, and was an avid wireless fan. Curtis* when P.A., South Waziristan, was camping in the back of beyond among the Mahsuds in the summer of 1943. 'What is going to happen next in the war, Sahib?' 'I'm no expert, and your guess is as good as mine. But the whole enemy army in Tunisia has just surrendered, and we shall have to take some new step. As I say,

* G. C. S. Curtis (b. 1904), O.B.E.; I.C.S. Punjab, 1929. Political, 1933.

I am merely speculating, but I think we may attack a small but strategically important island. . . .' 'Ah, you mean Pantelleria!' The author, on one of his very few visits to the Frontier, was dining with some maliks in the Malakand agency in 1946. They surprised him by starting the conversation with the question: 'What, in your opinion, are the prospects of a restoration of the Italian royal family?'

Not all tribesmen were so well-informed. A Pakistani friend of the author, not long after Partition, was patrolling with a body of constabulary in a remote and barren tract, and halted at midday in some slight shade. A young Pathan shepherd was there, watching his flock; and they passed the time of day. 'How are things?' asked the policeman. 'So-so,' said the Pathan. 'What change do you find the new Government has brought?' 'Change? All I know is that there used to be a king called Jarj;* now there's a king called Pakistan; and cloth has got scarcer.'

We find great differences between the N.W.F.P. and the Hindu provinces; but there is always this unifying factor, the British. Certainly, as so many writers rightly emphasize, there was a marked feeling of change as you crossed the Indus from the Punjab: a breath of Central Asia in the air; but let us not forget how much greater it would have been had the Frontier been handed over to the Afghan Government 100 years ago (as Lawrence† in 1857 contemplated) and it had remained non-British. Lawrence has been blamed for proposing to evacuate Peshawar during the Mutiny and for only being restrained from so doing by Herbert Edwardes.‡ Actually, what he wrote on 9 June 1857, was:

> I think we must look ahead and consider what should be done *in the event of disaster at Delhi.* [Author's italics.] My decided opinion is that in that case we must concentrate. All our safety depends on this. If we attempt to hold the whole country, we shall be cut up in detail. . . . We could easily retire from Peshawar *early in the day*, but at the eleventh hour it would be difficult, perhaps impossible. . . . Consult Brigadier Sydney Cotton and Nicholson, but no one else.

He proposed to hand over Peshawar and Kohat to the Amir, retaining

* His late Majesty, King George VI, was meant.

† John, first Lord Lawrence (1811–79). Assistant Commissioner, Delhi, 1830–1834. A.C. and D.C. 1834–48. Member of Board of Administration, Punjab, 1848–52. Chief Commissioner, Punjab, 1853–7. In India Office, 1859–62. Viceroy, 1983–9.

‡ General Sir Herbert Edwardes (1819–68), K.C.B., K.C.S.I. Gazetted in Indian Army, 1841. On political duties from 1846–7. Settled Bannu, 1848–9. Siege of Multan. Commissioner, Peshawar, 1853. Refused governorship of the Punjab owing to ill-health.

the Derjat, but only if there was a disaster at Delhi. He was rightly over-ruled by Canning, the Governor-General; and Edwardes, Sydney Cotton and Nicholson all agreed in opposing this proposal. But it was no more unreasonable to plan for the worst than, in 1940, to consider moving the fleet and the Royal Family to Canada, if Britain were invaded.

Curiously, though strongly against abandoning Peshawar, Edwardes in his reply suggested handing over Multan to the Nawab of Bahawalpur, and made the odd comment: 'Europeans cannot retreat. Without rum, without beef, without success, they would soon be without hope and without organization.' This transfer was not needed, since, unasked, Bartle Frere,* the Commissioner in Sind, sent up troops to Multan.

This is no place for re-telling the story of the Indian Mutiny (1857) and the Frontier's role in it. Suffice it to say that an area taken over from the Sikhs only eight years before remained quiet and even reinforced the main force which was besieging Delhi, largely owing to the outstanding characters in the Punjab Commission–mostly soldiers turned civilians–who then ruled the Frontier, and of whom Caroe writes.

* Sir Bartle Frere (1815–84), Bart.; I.C.S., Bombay, 1834. Commissioner in Sind; Governor of Bombay, 1862–7.

# CHAPTER 22

# The Punjab Period

AFTER the conquest of the Punjab in 1849, a period of about fifty years (1849–1901) followed during which the Punjab Government ruled the Frontier. Our forces were gradually built up; the tribes were not till the end of the period rearmed with modern weapons from the Persian Gulf; and though the close-border system held the field till 1887, it was tempered from time to time with very real intervention. These punitive expeditions–nicknamed Tip and Run, Butcher and Bolt, Harry and Hurry, and other rude names–were also known to the army as 'columns'. After a tribe had misbehaved too badly and too often, a column would be sent out. The only other weapon to hand, until the arrival in 1916 of the Royal Flying Corps (later R.A.F.), was the blockade; there were major ones, from 1879 to 1881 and from 1900 to 1902, against the Mahsuds. The success of the second one was very limited.

But the column was another thing. It is true that it usually ended with attacks on its retreat, comparatively little damage to the tribes and a huge bill for the Indian taxpayer to meet. But it could not be ignored; and during those early years it was used again and again, especially in Waziristan, as a penalty for raiding.

The first thirty years after the Mutiny were a period of comparatively quiet development, though there were eleven punitive expeditions, and both 1863 (Ambela) and 1868 (Black Mountain) saw major campaigns with heavy casualties. (15,000 troops were used in the latter.) After 1877, things hotted up. There were twelve expeditions between 1877 and 1881; 1878–80 saw the second Afghan war. Between 1890 and 1897 there were further departures from the policy of non-interference in Waziristan and Orakzai country.

Later, in 1897, there was what would have been a mass rising of all the tribes of any importance had not the Mahsuds stood out as an important exception. There were several reasons for this. For one thing, the Mahsuds were licking their wounds after a column had been sent against them in 1894; the Afghans had been intervening in their affairs in a way they disliked, and so they were temporarily not so anti-British as usual; and they had learnt to fear blockades.

The 1897 campaign may be taken to illustrate how trouble could blow up, sometimes at a moment's notice and often in the face of repeated announcements by Government of a policy of non-intervention. There had been peace in the land since the end of the second Afghan war. Apart from the occupation of the Samana ridge in 1891 to control the Orakzais and to protect the Miranzai valley, and peaceful occupation (at the tribes' request and surprisingly with the encouragement of the Amir of Afghanistan) of the Kurram valley in 1892, there had been little to report. 1893 had seen a most important and unexpectedly easy solution of a very difficult problem: Mortimer Durand had visited Kabul and agreed with the Amir Abdul Rahman upon the eastern boundary of Afghanistan. It is fascinating to read in the Amir's own words[75] how this agreement was reached; Durand's excellent knowledge of Persian seems to have helped. (He had no such assistance when, in 1906, President Roosevelt intrigued successfully for his removal from the post of British Ambassador to Washington.) The agreement was followed by demarcation on the ground which, not surprisingly, in Waziristan led to fighting. On 10 June 1897, a party under a political officer was attacked by Wazirs in the Upper Tochi valley. All the British officers were killed or wounded and the escort under their Indian officers only made good their retreat with great difficulty and courage.

However, this premature attack was a blessing in disguise. Immediate steps were taken to punish the offenders, and so Waziristan was cut off from the north, well before the next outbreak in this uniquely co-ordinated rising in which every major tribe, we recall, joined in but the Mahsuds.

The scene shifts to the Malakand. The isolated non-Pathan mountain state of Chitral, at spitting distance from Russia and little more from China, had been visited in 1885 by Sir William Lockhart from Gilgit* and friendly relations established. Later, dynastic fighting broke out, and in 1895 Robertson, the Gilgit P.A. who had come to investigate, was besieged in Chitral fort. He and his men had to be rescued; and by far the quicker and easier route was not via Gilgit but from Peshawar and Mardan over the Malakand Pass. The only difficulty was that this was virgin land: no British officer had ever crossed the Malakand nor the long stretch of Swat and Dir† which lies on the way to Chitral. There was tough fighting when we forced this pass; but thereafter things soon settled down. The

* *See* p. 242 (Durand's *Making of a Frontier*).

† Peter Mayne describes Dir as a state where 'practically every hawk has a man's wrist under it'.

Nawab of Dir—unique among Pathans as a real ruling prince with no nonsense about democracy, and a dynasty nine generations old—soon submitted and entered into an agreement to retain levies paid by Government. Chitral was relieved; a Political Agent was posted—directly under the Government of India, it will be remembered—at the Malakand pass, with an assistant at Chitral; and a small garrison moved in to the Malakand and the fort of Chakdara, at the crossing of the Swat river, a few miles on, and appropriately* laid out a polo ground.

But first the question of future policy came before the Government of India. Two alternatives presented themselves: either they must abandon the attempt to keep up any effective control over Chitral, or they must put a sufficient garrison there. In pursuance of their recognized policy, the Executive Council decided unanimously that to maintain British influence in Chitral was 'a matter of first importance'. In a despatch to the Home Government they set forth all their reasons, and at the same time declared that it was impossible to garrison Chitral without keeping up the road from Peshawar, by which the relief force had advanced.

On 13 June, Lord Rosebery's Cabinet replied decisively, with courage if not with wisdom, that 'no military force or European agent should be kept at Chitral, that Chitral should not be fortified, and that no road should be made between Peshawar and Chitral'. By this they definitely repudiated the policy which had been consistently followed since 1876. They left Chitral to stew in its own juice. They overruled the Government of India. It was a bold and desperate attempt to return to the old frontier line. The Indian Government replied: 'We deeply regret but loyally accept decision', and began to gather up the severed strings of their policy and weave another web.

But in the nick of time the Liberal administration fell, and Lord Salisbury's cabinet reversed their decision. During the two years that the British flag had floated over Chakdara and Malakand, 'the trade of the Swat valley had nearly doubled. As the sun of civilization rose above the hills, the fair flowers of commerce unfolded, and the streams of supply and demand, hitherto congealed by the frost of barbarism, were thawed.' So writes the chronicler of this campaign: a subaltern in the 4th Queen's Own Hussars who, bored at Bangalore, managed to get leave and visit the front as a war correspondent: Lieut. Winston Spencer Churchill, in *The Story of the Malakand Field Force*. It abounds in similar purple patches,

---

* Appropriately, because Chitral, round the corner, was the home of polo which, with variations which include handling the ball and an orchestra, is still its national game.

but is a clear and fascinating account of this campaign.

In spite of the charms of commerce and polo, a local religious leader known as the Mad Mullah had been preaching a crusade against the infidel. A recent victory of the Turks over the Greeks, and the circulation of a provocative book by the Amir of Afghanistan on *jehad*, etc., fired the mine, according to Churchill. Anyhow, the whole frontier went up in flames–the Mahsuds always excepted. On the afternoon of 26 July 1897, the usual game of polo at Khar, a mile or two from the fort, ended and the grooms were putting the rugs on the ponies, when the tribesmen who had been watching the game warned them 'to be off home at once, for there was going to be a fight'.

Later that afternoon, the P.A., Deane* (who had been markedly successful in the two years that he had held this post), warned the Brigadier-General commanding the garrison that a great armed gathering had collected round the Mad Mullah's standard and that an attack was probable. (He had given several warnings earlier, and by 23 July all concerned knew of the danger.) He decided that the Guides be called out (from Mardan, down in the plains). A telegram was sent to the Guides at 8.30 p.m.; they started off at 1.30 a.m. on 27 July, and their cavalry arrived that same morning. Their infantry arrived at 7.30 p.m. on 27 July, having covered thirty-two miles in seventeen and a half hours in intense heat and choking dust, and were sent into action immediately they arrived.

On 29 July in the evening there arrived at Dargai, at the foot of the pass, the 35th Sikhs and 38th Dogras. They had marched all day in the most intense heat. 'In the 35th Sikhs, twenty-one men actually died on the road of heat apoplexy. The fact that these men marched till they dropped dead is another proof of the soldierly eagerness displayed by all ranks to get to the front.'[76]

To revert to the evening of 26 July. The General interviewed his C.O.s at 7 p.m. and ordered a movable column of nearly two battalions of infantry, one squadron of cavalry, and two guns to start at midnight for the Amandara pass, four miles away. After preparing for action, the officers sat down to dine at 9.30, still in polo kit from which they had not had time to change. At 9.45 p.m. the alarm sounded–the enemy were making a surprise attack. An officer collected some twenty men and rushed out to a narrow defile where the most intense fighting went on. The enemy, about 1,000 strong, came within an ace of rushing the camp.

* Lt.-Col. Sir Harold Deane (1854–1908), c.s.i. Indian Army, 1877. Superintendent of Police, Andaman Islands, 1880–5. P.A., Malakand, 1895–7. Resident in Kashmir, 1900–1. 1901–8, first Chief Commissioner, N.W.F.P.

But somehow this tiny force held out till, after about twenty minutes of desperate fighting, a lieutenant and thirty more men arrived, followed by the rest of the battalion. About 2 a.m. on 27 July, the tribesmen retired.

Action comparable in severity and difficulty went on for six days – or rather nights, which the enemy preferred – ending in the relief of Chakdara fort by cavalry after seven days' and seven nights' close siege. This was an astonishing feat of arms, made possible largely because the enemy were so sure of victory that they did not fire at the horses of which they hoped to make prizes. The enemy all along vastly outnumbered the garrison; but after reinforcements arrived from the plains – of ammunition as well as men – the situation round the Malakand and Chakdara forts became reasonably secure and, in mid-August, an advance was made up the Swat river. The 'Gate of Swat' was forced on 17 August and the Upper Swat valley people then made their submission.

Churchill, who arrived at the Malakand on 2 September, soon ceased to be solely a journalist and was employed in a military capacity as he had hoped would be the case. Meanwhile, the flags of a holy war were being raised elsewhere on the Frontier. By 17 August, the blaze had spread to Mohmand country; a fortnight later, Afridi and Orakzai Tirah were alight. The Mohmands, inspired by a priest called the Hadda Mullah, crossed the border, nearly 6,000 strong, and attacked Shabkadr fort, a mere nineteen miles from Peshawar and in the plains. This made it possible to use cavalry with great success. But it had been a near thing.

The Khyber posts fell; the heights of Samana had been attacked and the Kurram valley threatened. The reinforced Malakand garrison, under Major-General Sir Bindon Blood, visited most of the unknown Mohmand country, Bajaur, Utman Khel, Swat and Buner, in operations related in fascinating detail by Churchill. A force of 40,000 men under Sir William Lockhart invaded Tirah, the Afridis' hitherto inviolate mountain home: the first and last British troops ever to penetrate there. By March 1898 all tribes from the Tochi northwards had submitted; and a policy of non-interference was definitely reaffirmed by the Secretary of State, and lasted until 1922.

## CHAPTER 23

# The Twentieth Century

THEN came Curzon (1899–1905). After 1897, there was, as always after a campaign, peace for a time; and in 1901 the changes in organization set out earlier took place. About the same time, too, Kitchener* withdrew many regular troops from small posts, replacing them by levies and Border Military Police (later called Frontier Constabulary). Road building continued; and apart from the only partially successful Mahsud blockade of 1900–2, there were seven years of almost unbroken peace. (To supplement the blockade, a series of sudden offensive raids was initiated, with success, against the Mahsuds.) Rugby,† the Chief Commissioner, a strong opponent of the forward policy, wrote in a 22-page memorandum of 1922:

> There was one great attempt to lay the ghost of the Frontier. It is hardly necessary to add that it was made by Lord Curzon, and that it showed masterly grip of the subject and a true perspective. *Nihil tetigit quod non ornavit.* It was essentially a policy of non-intervention but it needed a few years more of his watchful control, altering here, adjusting there.

Deane, whom we have met in the Malakand, was selected by Curzon over the heads of many political officers as the first and very successful Chief Commissioner of the new province; he stayed till 1908, and was succeeded by Roos-Keppel (1908-19), an exceptional officer who came to the Chief Commissionership with no experience of the plains (his service had been mostly in the Kurram and Khyber) but soon mastered district administration and proved a brilliant if unorthodox Chief Commissioner. (It was believed that, as was alleged to be done by numerous

---

* 1st Earl Kitchener of Khartoum (1850–1916). Commander-in-Chief India, 1902–9. Secretary of State for War, 1914–16.

† Sir John Maffey, first Lord Rugby (1877–1969), G.C.M.G., K.C.B., K.C.V.O., C.S.I., C.I.E.; I.C.S., Punjab, 1900. Private Secretary to the Viceroy 1916–19; Chief Secretary to H.R.H. the Duke of Connaught for his Indian tour, 1920–1. Chief Commissioner, N.W.F.P., 1921–4. Governor-General, Sudan, 1926–33. Permanent Under-Secretary for Colonies, 1933–7. U.K. Representative to Eire, 1939–49.

Provincial Service officers, he put up a tribe to 'play up' while he was away on leave, so that he could get the credit for quick pacification on his return.)

The only other trouble in this period was what was called by *Punch* 'The week-end war': an expedition against the Zakka Khel Afridis in 1908. The rest of the Afridi tribe took no part in it, and it was successful. So was a small campaign against the Mohmands, a few months later.

And so this 'Curzon policy' held sway, mostly with success. One grave problem in this first decade of the century was the arms traffic. For many years, modern weapons had been smuggled in to the Frontier from many sources, principally the Persian Gulf, via Kalat; but between 1897 and 1910 the trade increased alarmingly. In the last three years of this period, no less than 90,000 rifles were brought in, of which 30,000 Martin Henrys reached Kandahar from the Gulf in one consignment. Most of these, to add insult to injury, were perfectly good rifles sold off by the Australian and New Zealand governments when they re-armed their forces with .303s during the South African war. They were bought by 'enterprising dealers, who eventually obtained touch, through French and German armament firms, nondescript tramp steamer companies, owners of fast sailing dhows and other devious channels, with the equally enterprising customer from the N.W. Frontier.'[77]

The trade was more or less killed, thanks largely to the Royal Navy, by 1911; but the harm had been done. This was an immensely important factor in all future planning. The tribes had been rearmed, and the relative position of the opposing forces could never again be the same. We, of course, also rearmed; but not until air power redressed the balance had we much superiority in weapons: and none in the skill in their use.

Rugby, in the same note, says:

> The close border system is a far better proposition in the 20th century than it was in the 19th owing to technical developments (aircraft, motor transport). The expedition into tribal territory is a far worse proposition than it was. Heavy .303 armament has made the tribal nut extremely difficult to crack.

The same period saw a systematic policy of assassination of British officers, largely attributable to the Mullah Powindah. When, in the 1920s Barnes—nephew of Sir Hugh Barnes, the Foreign Secretary—was murdered in Fort Sandeman, he was the third Political Agent in recent times to suffer assassination. Gaisford and Finnis were similarly killed on duty, as was Duncan after Partition. Best and Bazalgette were also killed, but theirs were not cases of assassination. (Earlier, in 1897, Downes, uncle of Parsons, and Gee were both murdered in the Tochi, as were Burnes, Macnaghten and Cavagnari earlier still in Kabul.) And all along, there remained the problem of the outlaw; the proclaimed offender from a settled district who took refuge in tribal territory and whose surrender was as difficult as it was rare to secure.

But the period was on the whole one of peaceful progress, notable for the foundation of the Islamia College (now the University of Peshawar) under the encouragement of Roos-Keppel and his distinguished assistant Abdul Qayyum.* Caroe's portrait of these two remarkable men[78] is a fine summing-up.

And so we reach World War I. Though, largely thanks to Roos-Keppel (and Amir Habibullah Khan†), the province got through it with little trouble, there were anxious moments. They began with an attack on Miranshah from Khost in Afghanistan, followed by another on a post in the Upper Tochi (North Waziristan). In 1915, the Hindustani Fanatics – who deserve a book to themselves – rose, as did shortly afterwards the Mohmands, who again attacked Shabkadr. Things were not going well in France, and India was drained of troops. There was serious trouble in 1915 in the Punjab from the *Ghadr* conspiracy among the Sikhs and an agrarian rising in the Multan division. A regiment mutinied in Lahore. Altogether 1915 was an anxious year; but 1916 was better. In 1917 an expedition against the Mahsuds was at last found inevitable – they had long been asking for it.

> The expedition was remarkable for the fact that it was carried through, under every conceivable disadvantage of terrain, communications and weather, in the height of the summer, by troops unseasoned to the Frontier; and was completely successful.[79]

Then after two years of profound peace, the 3rd Afghan war broke out early in 1919. It resulted in quick and complete defeat of the Afghans, who signed a peace treaty on 8 August 1919; but in one sector alone, an

---

* K. B. Nawab Sir Sahibzada Abdul Qayyum (1866–1937), K.C.I.E. Rose from the ranks to membership of the political service, in particular was P.A., Khyber, 1918. Earlier, he had been Political Assistant with the troops in the Tirah campaign of 1897. Retired in 1919 and entered politics, leading the majority party in the Frontier Assembly till his death. First Minister, 1932. Not to be confused with Khan Abdul Qayyum, Kashmiri, who became the first Muslim League Premier in 1947, shortly after Partition. See p. 197.

† In March 1915, the Viceroy wired Roos-Keppel the text of a message received from the Amir. It was that, so long as there was no interference with the rights of Afghanistan, he would never deviate from the path of neutrality.[80]

Afghan advance in the region of Thal led to our militia garrisons of the Upper Tochi and other outlying posts being withdrawn to Miranshah. The Afridis of the Khyber Rifles had wavered from the start, and the corps was disbanded to forestall a mutiny. This collapse in morale in the north made the position impossible in South Waziristan, which might otherwise have held out.

A disaster resulted. Other tribes followed suit, though the Mohmands remembered their 1915 lesson and the Afridis did not fatally commit themselves. During 1920 there was a fairly general, gradual settlement. But as Caroe says: 'Unlike other wars, Afghan wars become serious only when they are over';[81] in Waziristan in 1920 the situation amounted practically to a general rising of the tribes, and there was no alternative to the thorough reconquest of the evacuated country. None, that is, if the frontier policy then obtaining was to be applied to Waziristan. As we shall see, there were those who had very different ideas, and felt that this was the time to pull out at least regular troops, and radically cut down commitments in Waziristan.

But for the moment, reconquest was the aim: and it led to 'such fighting as had never before been seen upon the Frontier'.[82] And, one may add, to fighting little less fierce in the counsels of Government on the heights of Simla. We may examine this campaign in the secretariat, which lasted from 1920 to 1922.

## CHAPTER 24

# Waziristan

AFTER the 3rd Afghan war of 1919, Waziristan was occupied by a large force engaged on its reconquest. In 1922 the troops were still in Waziristan, still reconquering; it had taken two years to decide what was to be done about this recalcitrant area. And they were at it again between 1936 and 1939.

One thing was clear. Waziristan was infinitely the most important and most difficult problem; the other tribal areas were in good shape and did not need any reappraisement. Let us for the moment look ahead to 1939. In that year, after discussing the case with all his expert advisers, Linlithgow\* in a 46-page printed memorandum indicated what was to be done about the Frontier, of which he had already been in charge for three years. He was clear that there were two problems:

a. Waziristan;

b. The rest. (This was: the Hazara tribes; Buner, Swat and Bajawur; Chitral and Dir; the Mohmands, upper and lower; the Afridis; the Orakzai; the Kurram valley.

As to b., he noted that the policy long since applied had for practical purposes been the close-border policy of non-interference; and that it had been successful. The occupation as against the Afridis of the Khajuri plain and the (abandoned) proposal to build a road into the Tirah, with Afridi co-operation, in 1935, were the only important exceptions to this rule. It is true that the fact that the Mohmands attacked the border five times between 1927 and 1936, and that we had to make the Nahakki and Loe Agra roads, did not appear to constitute mutual non-interference. But that was all; the other areas were quiet; Linlithgow laid them aside as undoubtedly *de facto* close-border and *de facto* successful. At the same time, he felt that he must point out that, strictly, official policy was the same for these tribes as for Waziristan (and, *ipso facto, not* close-border), and was summed up in an important pronouncement to which he several times reverted (doubtless because it was officially communicated to the

\* 2nd Marquess of Linlithgow (1887–1952). Viceroy and Governor-General of India, 1936–43.

Afghan Government, and presumably constituted a Cabinet decision).
It read:

> The policy of the Government of India in regard to their tribal
> territory is to preserve the peace of the border, foster good relations
> with the tribes, and gradually to introduce standards of civilisation
> and order into the tribal area together with the improvement of
> their economic conditions. Moreover, it is their policy to pursue
> these ends by peaceful means and in agreement with the tribes, and
> not to resort to military action except when it is necessary to do so. . .
> in order to preserve the peace, and to repel attacks on British and
> protected areas, or British forces, or on friendly tribes.

So Linlithgow was convinced that no change was needed anywhere on
the Frontier outside Waziristan; and indeed it was a conclusion that, at
any time between 1919 and 1947, would have secured pretty general
agreement. There remained Waziristan, to which he devoted forty-three
out of the forty-six pages of his minute. Looking back on the policy
adopted in 1922 from every point of view, and after consulting expert
after expert and discussing various other solutions, his considered view
was that in one and one aspect alone had there been wrong or wrongly
applied policy; and that in all other respects the cautions and gradual
policy of road-making and peaceful penetration should be pursued as
before.

The exception was welfare. 'In the improvement of the welfare of the
tribes and the extension of civilisation among them, I cannot resist the
conclusion that we have failed –or failed at any rate in a material degree.'
So he ordered an economic survey by an economist, and an educational
survey by an educationalist. And that was that. As regards education, he
was almost certainly right, since the marked improvement in relations
with the Waziristan tribes since Partition is generally admitted to be
largely due to their eager adoption of education–not excluding female
education, at that–and to the excellent results of their training at the
Canadian-sponsored Warsak project in engineering and mechanics.
Mahsuds are now found in large numbers, holding down well-paid jobs
throughout West and even East Pakistan. Schools and minor irrigation
schemes and scholarships for technical training might have been worth
their weight in gold.

When Linlithgow looked at the main problem–was the Waziristan
policy adopted in 1922 sound or could it be improved?–he seems to have
said Yes, sound, rather half-heartedly. Reading between the lines, one

has the idea that he was much–and rightly–concerned with the immin-ence of war, and had this not been so likely, he might have looked further into possible new policies. In any case, his decision was for carrying on with the current policy, and he was enthusiastic about the terms of the 1936 declaration to the Afghans quoted above, even though 1936–9 had been a period of continuous fighting. The policy certainly survived World War II well; the Frontier was surprisingly quiet, with all kinds of temptations to the contrary.

We have looked ahead from 1922 to 1939 to see how the policy adopted in 1922 appeared to one uniquely qualified to appraise it. Now let us revert to the great debate.

We have commented on the length of the viceregal minute just dis-cussed. In July 1921, Rawlinson* went into action with a 21-page note recounting in detail the history of our relations with Waziristan. He queried–as we all do–what might have been had Sandeman lived; he recounted the strong support that Sandeman got from Lansdowne, Roberts, and Durand, and the value that Sandeman was to the army in the second Afghan war. 'Sandeman always declared,' he remarked, 'that, in his policy, he was only following in the footsteps of and on the principles acted on by Edwardes and Nicholson.' In 1895, it was decided to hold Wana and a post in the Tochi, to keep open the Gomal and Tochi routes and to overawe the Mahsuds–a policy that held the field till 1919. (Would Curzon have agreed? In 1899 he minuted that one reason for holding Wana and the Tochi post had gone–the army had decided that they were not feasible routes for invading Afghanistan with regulars. And in 1921, Md. Shafi† noted that another argument had gone: Imperial Russia.) Rawlinson observed that Barnes, Foreign Secretary to Curzon, disagreed with Curzon and was for holding these posts. And that when everything went up in 1919, Roos-Keppel was for disarmament of the tribes and occupation up to the Durand line. So, surprisingly was Barton‡–one of the ablest politicals of this century: the man who fought and beat the Nizam. But, as Churchill had pointed out in 1898, it could not be done: shortage of troops and of finance ruled it out. More weightily, Linlithgow in 1939–with whom Cunningham agreed–said that the presence of the

* General Lord Rawlinson of Trent (1864–1925). Commander-in-Chief, India, 1920–5.

† Mian Sir Muhammad Shafi (1869–1932). Education member of Executive Council, 1919–22; Law member, 1923–4.

‡ Sir William Barton (1871–1956), K.C.I.E., C.S.I.; I.C.S., Punjab, 1894. Served in N.W.F.P., 1899–1916. Later, Resident in Mysore, 1920; at Hyderabad, 1925–1930.

Afghan kingdom behind the Frontier forbade it. Tuker* was pressing for it again in 1945. So the debate went on.

So there we were, in 1921, with thirty battalions in Waziristan, the Germans and the Afghans beaten. Rawlinson pleaded–how rightly!–for a fixed and long-term policy (and he got it). Whether it was the best one is another matter. The policy he advocated was roughly what was adopted: roads, roads, roads; regular troops well forward, at Wana and Razmak, and Scouts widely placed in Mahsud country.

Where was the money to come from? The controversy turned almost entirely on finance, and indeed narrowed down to a particular road with its particularly heavy bill. Hailey† was at this time Finance Member to the Government of India. A successor of his as Governor of the Punjab once said to the author that the only post Hailey held in which he was not a conspicuous success was that of Finance Member; 'Only a man as great as Hailey could have done so comparatively badly as Finance Member and gone on to such successes.' However that may be, faced by this claim of Rawlinson, he wrote a 38-page printed note in opposition to it. He pointed out that both sides claimed Roos-Keppel's support. Roos-Keppel's recommendations were odd, and inconsistent with each other. Hailey's budget was before the Indian Legislative Assembly, and a period of acute financial stringency was on. Rawlinson's figures of startlingly increased cost were alarming. Md. Shafi, who with Vincent,‡ was touring the frontier as a sub-committee of the Viceroy's Council in November 1921, took the same view. We just could not afford it: India's figures of illiteracy and ill-health suggested a better use for her money; she had lost, 7,767,684 lives in the 1918 influenza epidemic. Shafi emphasized that the Russian *military* danger had gone, and said that nearly all the Hindus and Muslims he had met in the N.W.F.P. were for a close-border policy.

A striking exception to most Frontier officers, who seem in this period generally to have supported a forward policy, was Maffey (later Lord Rugby), Chief Commissioner from 1921–4 when he resigned on this issue. He was a dyed-in-the-wool close-borderer. In August 1922 he

---

* Lt.-Gen. Sir Francis Tuker (1894–1967), K.C.I.E., C.B., D.S.O., O.B.E. Chairman, Frontier Committee, India. General Officer, commanding in chief, Eastern Command, India, 1946–7.

† Lord Hailey of Shahpur and Newport Pagnell. *See* p. 27.

‡ Sir William Vincent (1866–1941), G.C.I.E., K.C.S.I.; I.C.S., Bengal, 1887. Member, Executive Council, 1919–22.

wrote a 22-page note entitled 'Unsolicited views on an unsolved problem'; it was written in Kasauli, a significant address to anyone who knows the Punjab. (It was where one went for a long and unpleasant course of anti-rabies injections if one had been bitten by a mad dog or one suspected of madness.) However, the gloom which was endemic to Kasauli does not seem to have affected the author's style which is witty and exceedingly readable. He summed up his recommendations with 'Give up surgery and try a poultice.' The Viceroy asked for something briefer, and in October 1922 got a 3-page note giving a précis of his views. Bray, the Foreign Secretary, in a covering note to the Executive Council agreed with much that Rugby wrote, but complained that he spoilt his case by overstatement. Bray rightly pointed out that, though Rugby claimed that his policy was, 'Keep clear of the tribal area and hold it by good roads and good dispositions on *our* side of the border along the whole length,' he made so many exceptions (Khyber, Malakand, Tochi and others) that his policy really amounted to: 'Keep out of South Waziristan.'

And that really was what this immensely drawn-out controversy in 1920–2 amounted to. The Commander-in-Chief wanted to clear up Waziristan while a large army was still there. The Finance Member, briefed by the Chief Commissioner, wanted to adopt the Chief Commissioner's proposed close-border policy and thereby cut down expenditure on Waziristan which was appallingly high at a time of financial stringency. All the civilian members of Council agreed, as did, unofficially, Inchcape,* (the most eminent of British business men concerned with India–P. & O. line, etc.) A unanimous despatch supporting retrenchment on road works had gone home–signed by Rawlinson, the Commander-in-Chief–when there was a strange volte-face. Rawlinson went home, approached the Committee of Imperial Defence and next we find the Secretary of State writing that a sub-committee of that powerful Committee had fully discussed Waziristan and that he and they agreed that 'the Rs. 396 *lakh* scheme was faulty for lack of lateral communications, and that the Rs. 469 *lakh* scheme should be adopted'. Road construction must be pushed on with. Our fixed policy, he wrote, must be permanent control of Waziristan by military occupation, 'if it is not possible to suggest any other means hereafter'. The Secretary of State also enquired whether the Commander-in-Chief really agreed with the unanimous despatch; and then he and the Viceroy, Reading, resiled from it. Since the whole of the rest of the Council dissented from them, a curious position arose. It had some

* 1st Earl of Inchcape (1872–1932). Chairman, Indian Retrenchment Committee, 1922–3.

time back been laid down that if an official member (i.e. a civil servant nominated as a member of any of India's legislative bodies) felt conscientiously unable to support some Government motion, he was entitled to make his opposition clear in a personal statement though he was required to cast his vote for Government. But here we were faced with the whole of Council except the Viceroy and Commander-in-Chief disagreeing with the latter's demands for funds. The legislative Assembly was sitting and discussing the budget; it would have been a scandal without precedent for them to get up, one by one, led by the Finance Member, and say that though they disapproved of the inclusion of these heavy extra credits in the defence budget, yet they would have to vote for them. A compromise practically involving a surrender to the Commander-in-Chief followed.

But though the whole business was kept secret, there was one voice that would not compromise. Rugby found that a decision had been taken over which he, the responsible authority for the N.W.F.P., had not been so much as consulted. When the Frontier was cut off from the Punjab by Curzon without the Lt.-Governor of the Punjab being consulted, he protested but did not resign (though one of his officers, the Commissioner of Delhi, did). History did not, however, repeat itself; Rugby was content with no mere protest but, on the day his pension was due, sent in his papers, and resigned from the service. Hailey describes Rugby as 'the real begetter of the policy I advocated as Finance Member'. His resignation—in his own words, 'very much under a cloud'—was almost unique in the Political Service. He went on to a distinguished career as Governor-General of the Sudan, Permanent Under-Secretary for the Colonies and finally Representative to Eire. And to a peerage, living till 1969.

Waziristan, and more particularly South Waziristan, was thus the crux of the Frontier problem from 1920 onwards. What is sometimes called the semi-forward policy was adopted. Large sums were spent on roads, Wana and Razmak were garrisoned by regulars, and Scouts posts were established up and down the country. There was no question of disarmament or advance up to the Durand line. Nor, again, was there any idea of retreat to the old border, let alone the Indus; it was a compromise policy but not a mere compromise: self-consistent and widely supported by frontier officers. Most of them thought it turned out a success; but one—perhaps the greatest of them: Cunningham, Governor from 1937–46 and from 1947–8–three times gave his opinion on this point. Early on, it was: Yes: it has been a success. In June, 1937,* he wrote: 'I do not agree with

* At that time, we were engaged in a bloody and costly campaign in the Ahmadzai salient which, arising out of the Islam Bibi case, dragged on for three or more

those who say it', our Waziristan policy, 'has completely failed.' After Partition, when he returned as Pakistani Governor, he wrote: 'Razmak has been occupied by regular troops for 25 years, Wana for a few years less. The occupation has been a failure.' Then at last, on his and Iskander Mirza's recommendation, the regulars were withdrawn from both Razmak and Wana; a small force of Scouts was retained in Waziristan; and a great peace broke out.

That does not necessarily mean that Reading and Rawlinson were wrong. World War II might well have found a very embarrassing position awaiting us, had we had no regulars on the spot. That alone – the external menace, which one feels lay behind Linlithgow's strong support of the *status quo* in 1939 – was perhaps sufficient justification for the 'semi-forward' policy. And again, though post-1947 policy has led to profound peace at small cost, it must never be forgotten that since Partition, there have been no Hindus nor British left to kidnap, and uniformity of religion and culture, though not alone decisive, are important weapons in the hands of Pakistan. Lately, a senior Pakistan official, speaking of the remarkable improvement in the Mahsud question – thousands of them now are earning an honest living as soldiers, shopkeepers, emchanics, drivers, etc., in the plains – said that, yes, it was true that the coming of Pakistan had made this possible, 'But it would not have been possible had it not been for the century of the policy which you British enforced beforehand.'

To a layman, the arguments seem closely balanced, even when seen with the hindsight which the years and the success of the Pakistan policy reveal. If they had known how well Mahsuds would behave once the Army moved out, would those then responsible have replaced the Army with Scouts, forty years back? Auchinleck* thinks, Yes; but adds[83] that the generals would have taken a lot of persuading! He feels that Pakistan has got the final answer to the problem: more heavily armed Scouts (they now even have mortars and light artillery). Great progress, he adds, has been made in Mahsud country, also in Dir, by Pakistan engineers who have tapped underground water. With small electric pumps much ground has been irrigated. Chetwode admitted to Liddell Hart† the truth of the

---

years and tied up numerous troops during the war. Indeed, the Faqir of Ipi's continued immunity to capture or defeat was a great argument against the official Waziristan policy.

* Field-Marshal Sir Claude Auchinleck (b. 1884), G.C.B., G.C.I.E. Commander-in-Chief, India, 1941 and 1943–7. Supreme Commander in India and Pakistan, 1947.

† Captain Sir Basil Liddell Hart (1895–1970). Military Historian and writer on strategy.

charge[84] often made against the Army and usually hotly denied – that they welcomed the continuence of the frontier problem because it provided them with so fine a training ground. Possibly if the Home Government – policy, ultimately, was always made in London, not in India – had listened more to the politicals and less to the soldiers, a more consistent and long-term policy might have been evolved and stuck to.

But Waziristan was not an easy problem at any time, for any person. As Minto* once briefly noted on a file – he succeeded Curzon who prided himself on his decisive minutes – 'This is going to be a hard nut for someone to crack.'

* Earl of Minto (1847–1914). Viceroy, 1905–10.

# CHAPTER 25

# The Red Shirts

So far, in our discussion of the Frontier and its problems, we have dealt mostly with the trans-border tribesmen and the issues raised by their love of raiding and of independence. But what of the plainsmen, living a life and sharing aspirations not unlike those of their Punjabi co-religionists across the Indus?

In the first place, the whole province had been excluded from the constitutional changes – timid though the nationalist Indian considered them – introduced by the Montagu-Chelmsford reforms in 1919. There was no local assembly, let alone dyarchy; there was no election to District Boards; the province was represented by two members nominated, not elected, in the (exclusively legislative) Assembly at Dehli. Executive authority rested in the hands of the Chief Commissioner, himself constitutionally under the control of the Viceroy acting through the Delhi Foreign Office or, as it was later called, the External Affairs Department.

The Montagu-Chelmsford report of 1918 had advised that the Frontier for strategic reasons, stay entirely in the hands of the Government of India, though they proposed an Advisory Council with limited authority. This latter suggestion was not adopted, and the Government of India Act, 1919, left the constitution unchanged. In 1930, the Simon Commission recommended a cautious advance: executive control would remain with the Chief Commissioner, but a local legislature with indirectly elected representatives with control over the purse should be established.

The Government of India, in their despatch of September 1930, went rather further, and recommended a unitary scheme similar to that to be ntroduced in other provinces, but with less devolution of powers. For example, the legislature would be only half elected, and of the two Ministers who were to assist the Governor, one would be an official. The province being a deficit one, there would be a large subsidy from the Centre; and certain subjects peculiar to this province, e.g. the Frontier Constabulary, the Scouts, frontier allowances and strategic roads, would remain Central, i.e. controlled by the Chief Commissioner.

At the Round-Table Conference, Nawab Sir Abdul Qayyum pleaded strongly for further advance, and succeeded in getting agreement to a constitution almost identical with the provincial autonomy decided on for the rest of British India. And since there would be some delay before the new constitution came into force–five years, it turned out to be–the Prime Minister announced at the close of the second conference in December 1931 that the provisions of the existing Government of India Act relating to Governors' provinces would be applied to the Frontier forthwith. This decision was widely welcomed and quickly implemented; the Viceroy visited Peshawar in April 1932 and installed Griffith,* the Chief Commissioner, as the first Governor; Abdul Qayyum became the first Minister, a position which he held for some five years. In 1937, the Government of India Act, 1935, was introduced, here as elsewhere; and its much wider franchise resulted in Abdul Qayyum's rejection by the electorate. He died shortly afterwards.

Abdul Qayyum was succeeded by a remarkable personality, Dr. Khan Sahib† who, with his younger brother, Khan Abdul Ghaffar Khan,‡ led the Congress movement–locally known as the Red Shirt movement–in this province. This party, which commanded a majority of voters until its dramatic collapse in 1947, deserves careful attention. Its leaders were 'the small Khans': landlords, but middle-class men who could be said to have stood on a left-wing ticket, particularly as leaders of the non-Pathan helots in the towns and villages. So much for its local attachments. More important were its links with the Indian National Congress, an almost exclusively Hindu body elsewhere which only here, surprisingly,§ in this overwhelmingly and somewhat fanatically Muslim province, received a majority of Muslim votes as well as extra-parliamentary support. We shall recount, shortly, some of its extra-parliamentary activity; but first we may briefly examine its rise and fall in the legislature.

Khan Sahib, who had formerly held a commission in the Indian Medical Service and was married to an Englishwoman, was a politician of ability and integrity. After partition, in spite of a period of detention

* Lt.-Col. Sir Ralph Griffith (1882–1963), K.C.S.I., C.I.E. Army, 1901–8; Political, 1908. Served almost exclusively on the N.W. Frontier. Chief Commissioner, 1931. Governor, 1932–7.

† Dr. Khan Sahib (1887–1958). Indian Medical Service. Resigned 1920, and became Congress politician. Chief Minister, N.W.F.P., 1937–9 and 1945–7.

‡ Khan Abdul Ghaffar Khan (b. 1889). Congress politician. Founded 'Red Shirts', 1925. Imprisoned, 1921–4, 1930–1, 1931–4, 1934–6, 1942–5, 1948–54 and 1961–4.

§ Not so surprisingly if one remembers that the Hindus were so small and weak a minority that the Muslims never dreamed that there could be such a thing as Hindu raj. When, in 1946, they realised that it had all but arrived, they quickly switched allegiance.

by the Government of Pakistan, he made his peace with them, returned to politics and was Premier of the new unitary province of West Pakistan when he was murdered: a lamentable end to a career which showed signs of being even more distinguished towards its end. His younger brother, Khan Abdul Ghaffar Khan, known as 'A.G.K.', was more of a stormy petrel, and led the militants. After Partition he remained in opposition and was imprisoned for a fairly long period.

After Khan Sahib had replaced Nawab Abdul Qayyum, the unexpected occurred, and a Cabinet with an extreme anti-British record settled down to some years of constructive work, enjoying excellent relations with Cunningham, the recently (1937) appointed Governor. Cunningham was a man of exceptional tact and charm; his use of the bridge table as a link with his anti-British Premier even when, during the war, he was in opposition, was typical.

So things went on till the Congress Ministry was required to resign by the Congress high command during the war; they were replaced by a short-lived and not very successful Muslim League ministry under Sardar Aurangzeb Khan,* a not very impressive personality and a strange choice for Pakistan's first ambassador to Burma. The League suffered from this period of office—almost any government in power during a war is likely to acquire unpopularity. And so when 1947 came, and the vital decision for or gainst Pakistan had to be taken, the strange position existed that there was again a Congress Government in power though everyone knew that the great majority of public opinion had swung round to the League. (They realized, at last, that the British were going and that the choice lay between the Muslim League and the Hindu raj.) Everyone that is, except Pandit Jawaharlal Nehru, the Foreign Minister, who insisted in spite of the strong advice of Caroe,† the Governor, on paying a visit to his new charge in the winter of 1946–7. He was lucky to have escaped with several stonings and not to have lost his life, and only did so because Curtis, the Deputy Commissioner of Mardan, insisted on smuggling him in a lorry out of his district, where his life certainly was not safe, by a devious route under a guard of Mullagori tribesmen.

* Sardar Aurangzeb Khan (1899–1957). Entered Politics 1930. Muslim League politician, Chief Minister, N.W.F.P., 1944–5. Pakistan Ambassador to Burma, 1949.

† Sir Olaf Caroe (b. 1892), K.C.S.I., K.C.I.E.; I.C.S., Punjab, 1919. Political 1923. In 1937–8 officiated as Resident, Waziristan. Foreign Secretary, 1939–45; Governor, N.W.F.P. 1946–7. Political Resident, Persian Gulf. A.G.G. in Baluchistan.

The strange history of the Red Shirts ended with the dismissal of the Congress Ministry, a few days after the establishment of Pakistan; the return as Governor of Cunningham—one of the four British Governors* appointed by Qaid-i-Azam Jinnah; and the appointment of Khan Abdul Qaiyum Kashmiri,† a very able Muslim League parliamentarian, as Premier.

We must now consider the 'extra-parliamentary activities' of the Red Shirts. To revert to their rise, we must go back seventeen years, to 1930, when we see the beginning of this strange alliance between the Congress Party and this new Pathan movement. Its leaders were known first as 'the Afghan Jirga', and its shock-troops as the 'Khudai Khidmatgaran' (Servants of God). Soon the nickname 'Red Shirts', from the informal uniform which they wore, became their usual designation. And soon in spite of the dotty journalists' description of their leader, Abdul Ghaffar Khan, as the 'Frontier Gandhi' (it is difficult to imagine two people less alike), it became clear that this movement was a grave menace to law and order and very far from non-violent.

The outburst which occurred in 1930 started quietly, with the visit of a Congress committee to look into the working of the Frontier Crimes Regulation. The situation in Peshawar became very tense, and on 23 April warrants were issued for the leading dissidents. While these were being served, a large and dangerous crowd assembled. Metcalfe,‡ the Deputy Commissioner, called in troops which included armoured cars— vulnerable weapons for use in a crowded city. A despatch rider was killed, an armoured car burnt, and the Deputy Commissioner and an Assistant Superintendent of Police knocked out by bricks. The troops eventually opened fire, and about twenty rioters were killed. More troops were sent in, and control of the city was recovered by the afternoon of 23 April. On 29 April 1930, after a conference between the Chief Commissioner§ and leading citizens, all troops were withdrawn. Control of

* Sir George Cunningham (N.W.F.P.), Sir Francis Mudie (Punjab), Sir Frederick Bourne (E. Bengal), Sir Ambrose Dundas (N.W.F.P.).

† Khan Abdul Qayyum (b. 1901). Lawyer. Congress Politician in Central Legislative Assembly, 1937. Joined Muslim League, 1945. Chief Minister, N.W.F.P., 1947. Minister for Industry, Government of Pakistan, 1953. Arrested 1960 and 1962.

‡ Sir Aubrey Metcalfe (1883–1957); I.C.S., 1907, Punjab; Political, 1914. Foreign Secretary, 1932–9. A.G.G. in Baluchistan, 1939–43.

§ Sir Norman Bolton (1875–1965), K.C.I.E., C.S.I.; I.C.S., 1898, Punjab; Ch. Commr. N.W.F.P., 1923–30. He was a most distinguished revenue officer but failed in the 1930 crisis. He had, or was declared to have, a nervous breakdown and was packed off hurriedly to England.

Peshawar was thereafter completely lost until 4 May when troops and the police reoccupied the city.

Meanwhile, hell broke loose over a great part of the province. Murphy, the Assistant Superintendent of Police of Mardan, was lynched on 25 May in an unsuccessful attempt to carry out some arrests. Similar troubles occurred in Kohat and Bannu; slightly less in Dera Ismail Khan. Indeed, only Hazara district remained reasonably law-abiding. But these events, grave and unprecedented as they were, did not stand alone. What was even more alarming was the fact that tribesmen from over the border intervened. On 4 June 1930 an Afridi *lashkar*\* of some 3,000 men invaded the Peshawar *tahsil*, entering the outskirts of the city, and causing great excitement in the villages. Troops and the R.A.F. saw them off, and the whole *lashkar* left by 7 June; but on the night of 7 August they re-entered the district in groups of 150 to 200 strong. Unsuccessful attempts were made to enter Peshawar city and cantonment. All revenue officials were withdrawn from the villages to the city, and martial law had to be declared on 16 August. That led to an Afridi withdrawal, and all had left by 20 August; but owing to the smallness and mobility of the gangs, the good cover and the co-operation of the villagers, they were difficult to locate and expel. Things quietened down in the whole province from early September.

But while they lasted, these days in the summer of 1930 (of which we have mentioned only the major outbreaks) were the nadir of British rule in the province. There was a sudden recrudescence of the movement in July 1931, aided by the Halifax–Gandhi pact. All this activity was, of course, a reflection of what went on in other provinces – when there was a Civil Disobedience movement there, the Frontier followed suit. But the Frontier was armed and naturally violent, even the plains area. And this move by certain tribes to join in was dangerous indeed. The Afridis had for long been quiet, and even now were somewhat half-hearted in their 'invasion'. But no such action by such a tribe could be ignored; and it was found necessary to occupy permanently the Khajuri plain: the approach to their homeland, the Tirah. At Christmas, 1931, Government struck, swiftly, surprisingly. Here and in the Punjab the anti-Government movement was crushed rapidly, not without casualties: fourteen persons were killed in Kohat.

So much for the 'extra-parliamentary activity' which the opposition could lay on. We must not ignore the routine history of the Frontier in the nearly fifty years from Curzon's creation of the province, when the

\* Raiding gang.

political service took over from the Punjab Commission. This was a period of progress all over India, and the Frontier was no exception. Roads, schools, agriculture–in many directions there was real advance, for all the political difficulties. But these difficulties were very great, e.g. by comparison with the Punjab. At Christmas, 1930, I was travelling to Lahore with the Financial Commissioner* and the Commissioner† of Multan. They were discussing Frontier affairs, and Townsend remarked: 'Metcalfe has written to ask what we do when people won't pay their land revenue–apparently not a penny has been paid in the whole of Peshawar district this year.' 'What did you reply?' 'Oh, we said that we had never allowed such a state of affairs to arise, so we couldn't advise.' The Punjab civilian took the view that general administration–what was known in India as 'revenue' and included land taxation, survey, local self-government etc.–had slipped badly in the N.W.F.P.; and from 1931 till the war, the Frontier revenue staff was stiffened by the post of Revenue Commissioner being filled by two senior Punjab civilians, Thomson‡ and Salusbury,§ who did much to pull things together.

A criticism often made of our policy towards the tribesmen of Waziristan (and, indeed, of other areas) is what one may call the economic one. It is suggested that the country simply could not feed the mouths it held and that they had to raid to live. That is an exaggeration. There is much good soil in Waziristan and it was not the Government's fault that they spent so much on buying arms and building watch-towers. The blood feud is an expensive luxury.

But there is no doubt that the economics of the matter pointed to the value of employment outside the tribe. Settlement on the land in the plains was always advocated, seldom really successful. But many Frontier Pathans sought and got good employment in a variety of ways. Earlier Powindahs took their camels to Australia and opened up the interior. Then there were the Black Mountain tribesmen from Hazara, who had a semi-monopoly of night-watchmen's posts in the Far East : Hong Kong, Singapore, etc. Their pensions were a valuable invisible import; and when, during the war, the Japanese overran their source, the N.W.F.P. Government paid up instead.

Again, there was a big Pathan colony in Bombay, forty thousand strong, mostly consisting of Orakzais; and they and the Mohmands provided

* C. A. H. Townsend (1874–1954), C.I.E.; I.C.S., Punjab, 1898.
† B. H. Dobson (1881–1945), C.I.E., C.B.E.; I.C.S., Punjab, 1904.
‡ J. S. Thomson (b. 1888), C.I.E.; I.C.S., Punjab, 1912.
§ C. V. Salusbury (1887–1969), C.S.I., C.I.E.; I.C.S., Punjab, 1911.

numbers of stokers, particularly on the boats of the British India Line and on tramp steamers. The Khalils, from near Peshawar, provided domestic servants all over India: and one small area–the village of Nawagaon in Peshawar district–produced in profusion a galaxy of the finest players of squash racquets in the world. Mostly closely related, the Pakistani squash champions, who regularly sweep the board in Europe, constitute a remarkable phenomenon. Lastly, the Afridis seem to have achieved a footing in Karachi: as you arrive in Pakistan, an Afridi taxi-driver may well be your first contact with the Frontier.

Towards the end, there was widespread recognition of the need for planning for development–it was usually 'post-war development', and in 1945 a 450-page 'Five year post-war development plan' was issued by Mallam,* the Development Commissioner. It is interesting to note that it was a plan 'for the N.W.F.P. *and tribal areas*'. Linlithgow's recognition of failure adequately to civilize the tribes was repeated here; the plan dealt with agriculture, animal husbandry, co-operation, medicine and public health, industries and marketing, forests, education and public works including hydro-electric schemes.

'Province *and* tribal areas.' There lay the sign post for the future. Cunningham, after his return to Pakistan, felt that the time was ripe for a closer link. When the Government in Peshawar was no longer that of one or two fiercely rival parties, but supported by an assembly pretty unanimously based on the Pakistan ideal, there were good hopes for a solution of the tribal problem. That solution was union with the plains–one never attempted in British times. Let us hope that Pakistan will evolve such a solution. The signs look propitious. But let us remember that Curzon said: 'No one who has ever read a page of Indian history will prophesy about the Frontier.'

---

* Lt.-Col. the Rev. G. L. Mallam (b. 1895), c.s.i., c.i.e., Bar at law. Army, 1916; Political, 1921. Served almost wholly in N.W.F.P.

# CHAPTER 26

## The Work of a Frontier Political Officer

How did the life of a Deputy Commissioner in charge of a Frontier district differ from that of his brother officers in other provinces? There is no simple answer, because the circumstances of the six Frontier districts differed greatly.

The duties of the Deputy Commissioner of Hazara did not differ much from those of any administrator in charge of a Himalayan sub-montane district; but he had one responsibility which was not shared by his down-country colleagues. He was responsible for the conduct of relations with the tribes who lived beyond the border on and around the Black Mountain, and who inhabited the deep valleys of Allai, the country which lay between the left bank of the Indus and the border to the west of Kagan. These were Pathan tribes, but they did not share the common Pathan characteristic of insisting that all men are equal. This area was a stamping ground for small Khans who were, in fact, successful bandits. They were perpetually at war with one another, but they rarely, if ever, led their men across the borders, and the Deputy Commissioner's responsibilities did not weigh very heavily on him. He was also responsible for relations with the Nawab of Amb and the Khan of Phulra, rulers of two small states.

The districts of Mardan and Peshawar were originally one, but the two eastern *tahsils* of Mardan and Swabi were cut off to form a new district in 1936. The problems of both Deputy Commissioners were similar. The border mountains formed the western boundary and swept in a broad arc from north to south, their summits in the winter glittering with snow, while the river Indus formed the eastern boundary. Between these two features stretched a plain which, since the extension of the canal system, had become highly productive. In the neighbourhood of Peshawar there were many acres of orchards. Elsewhere, in the summer, the plain was diversified by blocks of sugar cane. These were quite impenetrable. The maize, which was also widely cultivated, grew taller than a man. Anyone who happened to get into trouble with the police could seek refuge across the border in tribal territory. Now the life of an outlaw in tribal territory was not a bed of roses; and when circumstances permitted, and particularly in the late summer and early winter when the maize and sugar cane crops provided cover,* the outlaw returned to live near home. Since in many cases he had nothing to live on, he had to help himself to other people's goods. The presence of outlaws, desperate men with little to lose, who might be met with at any time in any part of these districts, constituted a heavy responsibility for the Deputy Commissioner.

It was a humiliating fact that in these two districts it was never safe to be out at night, and motors and lorries were frequently stopped and robbed and passengers killed and wounded within a few miles of the leading towns. Many roads were 'closed' as unsafe until, a year or two after the creation of Pakistan, the Inspector-General of Police (still an Englishman) was able to report that every road in the province had remained 'open' for the whole year. (As we have already remarked, there were no British officers or Hindu merchants left to kidnap.)

The Deputy Commissioner of Mardan was responsible for relations with the Gaduns, a small tribe at the northern end of Mardan district. The Deputy Commissioner of Peshawar was responsible for relations with the Mohmands, who lived to the north of the Afridis. The Mohmands were a formidable tribe against whom it was from time to time necessary to take military action. Since Partition, the Government of Pakistan has created a separate Political Agency for the Mohmands, with headquarters at Peshawar.

While any district officer who had a large Indian city in his charge carried a similar load, Peshawar was an exceptionally wicked city. In the murder stakes year by year, it usually ran first or second with New York City. The annual murders in Peshawar roughly equalled those in all the other five N.W.F.P. districts, which equalled all the twenty-nine Punjab districts, which equalled all the rest of India. It was also the headquarters of the drug trade, drugs being brought down from the Central Asian tableland by caravan, and carried forward by rail to a large extent by Anglo-Indians (formerly known as Eurasians), travelling between Peshawar and the seaport, Calcutta. The criminal elements in the city population, when allied with political malcontents, were a formidable proposition and in 1930, as we have seen, for some ten days in the summer the British Raj did not extend to Peshawar city. That matters had once come to such a pass was a fact that every officer later in charge of the Peshawar district remembered.

The lot of the Deputy Commissioner of Kohat was regarded with

* As others besides outlaws knew. There is a Punjabi love-song which goes: 'Careful, now, careful. Your husband is watching. But when the sugar cane is full grown, there we shall meet.'

envy. Not that climatically his district had much to commend it, but it was not so far from the capital as Bannu and Dera Ismail Khan, and it was generally reckoned that some of the most attractive tribes, the Khattak and the Bangash, lived within its borders. He was responsible for relations with the Kohat Pass Afridis, who were distinguished by the fact that they manufactured rifles in a crude but, to some extent, effective manner. He was also responsible for relations with the Orakzai. This large tribe gave extremely little trouble and beyond paying their allowances and inter-viewing their *jirgas* from time to time, the Deputy Commissioner had few problems with them.

While everyone fancied himself for the position of Deputy Commis-sioner in Kohat, there were never many volunteers for the post of the Deputy Commissioner of Bannu. From their earliest contact with them, the British never much varied from Herbert Edwardes' opinion of the Bannuchis: 'Cowardly, bigoted, of poor physique but of different types, all reduced to a harmonious whole by the tint of universal dirt.' The dis-trict occupied a salient into Waziristan, and its villages harboured wealthy Hindu communities engaged in the agricultural distribution trade. These made attractive targets for raiding parties from across the border. The border was studded with Frontier Constabulary posts and incessantly patrolled, but the broken nature of the terrain made it rela-tively simple for gangs to slip through. The Deputy Commissioner's attention, therefore, was much engaged in the problem of the mainten-ance of security. It was not by any means unknown for large scale raids to be mounted against Bannu itself, protected though it was by a canton-ment of troops. The Deputy Commissioner was responsible for relations with the Ahmadzai Wazirs, who lived within Waziristan but along the British border. The raiding took place through their territory, and they were technically responsible, but in fact, had they wished, they could not have controlled raiders from more powerful tribes, particularly after the Faqir of Ipi had risen to fame.

The story of how he attracted such a reputation for saintliness illus-trates the type of difficulty that a British officer administering British law among people who had many contacts with tribal territory had to face. Islam Bibi was born a Hindu girl, but she was courted by a Muslim who carried her off, not against her consent, converted her to Islam and married her. A legal battle for her possession between her rival Hindu and Muslim claimants broke out in 1936. When, towards the end of the summer, the final Court of Appeal decided that she must be returned to her Hindu relatives, it was obvious that to implement the decision openly would result in grave disturbances. She had, therefore, to be smuggled out by night to her Hindu relatives. Thus ended for her a remarkable adventure in matrimony, an adventure which for us was to lead to three years of the bitterest and most costly tribal warfare under the inspiration of the Faqir of Ipi.

For the situation developed into the Waziristan war which cost many valuable lives and set back the peaceful development of tribal territory by at least a quarter of a century. Indeed, the prolonged operations in the Ahmadzai salient were as long and as savage a business as any Frontier expedition. There is no time to recount it in detail; but the Faqir of Ipi, like his predecessor, the Mullah Powindah, provided a focus–and a very efficient and dangerous one–for Waziristan 'hostiles' which dragged on well into post-Partition days. (He lived on till 1960.)

Next lay the district of Dera Ismail Khan, where, as we have seen, the summer was long and trying, and the post so unpopular that officers were changed too frequently. The district embraced large areas of virtual desert, parts of which came under cultivation when, from time to time, torrents from the hills passed over them. The Deputy Commissioner had a problem which was shared by only one other, in Dera Ghazi Khan. He had within his borders very large encampments of *powindahs*. These were nomad Ghilzai tribesmen from Afghanistan who migrated with their flocks and families every autumn from the tablelands of the Ghilzai tribe to India. Passing through tribal territory, they often had to fight their way. Mahsuds and Wazirs used to take any opportunity which presented itself for plunder, and the passage to and from India each year was in the nature of a military operation. A *Powindah* caravan on the march, with its camels heavily laden with red-faced Ghilzai tribesmen with their enormous shaggy dogs, was a picturesque sight. They camped in the plains and the young men went on to India, where some of them traded as purveyors of cloth, carpets and the like. Others worked as labourers.*
The old men and women remained to look after the flocks. The *Powin-*

---

* The *Powindahs* also acted as money-lenders all over India, despite the Islamic ban on usury. They specialized in middle-class Indians and Anglo-Indians and recovered their debts with a big stick–no civil suits for them. Some penetrated with their camels so far as Australia, the interior of which they helped to open up in the pre-railway age; they often married there and brought their Australian wives back to their wild hills. Poulton† once met a *Powindah* who, to his surprise, greeted him in broad Australian. 'What is your name?' 'Roz Gul.' 'That's an unusual name.' 'Oh it's really Riaz Gul, but them Austrylian boogers calls me Roz Gul, and I've got used to it.' He had an Australian wife.

† Lt.-Col. H. M. Poulton (b. 1898), c.i.e. Army, 1917; Political, 1922. Resident for Central India, 1946.

*dahs*, on entering British territory were searched and disarmed. Neverthe-less, it was not uncommon for them to take part in pitched battles in which rifle fire was a feature and it was rare that, if ever, the crime of possessing arms could be brought home to them.

The Deputy Commissioner of Dera Ismail Khan had in his care a tribe, the Bhittanis, who inhabited the foothills between Waziristan and the plains. Raiders necessarily passed through their areas, and under tribal law they were responsible. It was rare that they themselves originated trouble, and the Deputy Commissioner had to fight their battles with his colleague, the Political Agent of South Waziristan, who was respnsible for the more powerful tribes, the Wazirs and Mahsuds, on their western borders.

Scattered in the country towns and villages of the Dera Ismail Khan district, as in Bannu, there were Hindu communities of size and wealth who were always exposed to the hazard of raids from across the border. Apart from loot, raiders found it profitable to kidnap and hold to ransom men, women and children. The telephone might well ring as the Deputy Commissioner was settling down to dinner on a winter's evening; it would be a police or civil official reporting a raid, and as a background to the man's voice could be heard the reports of rifle fire. It was difficult to do much to relieve such a situation at night, but the Frontier Constabu-lary would be alerted and pursuit parties made up from the nearest police posts. The tribesmen being mountain people were more inclined to raid in the winter than in the summer, when their return home at speed would be a terrible experience in the fierce heat. Occasionally, however, in the rains, which fall in the late summer, they would take advantage of the breakdown of communications; and there were one or two notable occasions when tribesmen penetrated far into the district, carried out a raid, and regained their home territory at a speed which would have been credible in the winter but in the fierce heat of summer called for phenomenal endurance.

In addition to the six districts which constituted the administered part of the North-West Frontier Province, there were six Political Agencies (counting the Mohmand Agency, created after Partition). These Political Agencies were not administered, and their original function had been to secure an area on the borders of administered country where British in-fluence, i.e. indirect rule, could be used to hold the indigenous anarchy in check, and thus reduce the danger of raids on administered territory.

The most northerly of the Political Agencies was that of the Malakand. Here, the Political Agent was the British envoy to three chiefs who were under British protection but who were left to rule their dominions much as they pleased. The senior of them was the Mehtar of Chitral. The Political Agent was represented at Chitral by an Assistant Political Agent, who was in practically independent charge; and until the concluding years of British rule, Chitral had a small garrison of Indian regular troops, later replaced by Scouts. South of Chitral lay the dominions of the Nawab of Dir, and further south lay those of the Wali of Swat. In the south of the Malakand Agency was a small area where the Political Agent was directly responsible for the maintenance of order, but there were no police and no courts and tribal law ruled. The task of the Political Agent of Malakand, which consisted of conducting the relations with three chiefs of varying importance, was obviously quite different from that of the other Political Agents who were one and all concerned with tribes. In many respects, it was less arduous, as decencies of order were observed in Swat and Chitral and usually in Dir. The Political Agent enjoyed wonderful opportunities for sport, both shooting and fishing, and was able in the course of his duties to seek higher altitudes in summer.

The Political Agent, Khyber, looked after the Afridis, perhaps the most important tribe on the Frontier. If relations with them turned sour, the consequences along the whole Frontier soon made themselves felt. The Political Agent, who lived in Peshawar, was directly responsible for the safety of the celebrated pass. After the dissolution of the Khyber Rifles, the pass was garrisoned by Indian troops and its security was, therefore, doubly guaranteed, because the allowances paid to the Afridis were given in order to assist them to keep the pass clear from interference by bad characters. The system worked admirably.

South of Afridi country came the valley of the Kurram. The position of the Political Agent of this valley was much more comfortable than that of any of his colleagues, in that the British had occupied the valley at the request of the inhabitants, the Turis. The Turis belonged to the Shia sect of Islam and had been oppressed by Afghan officials and by their neighbours who belonged to the Sunni sect. The Kurram valley was scenically and climatically delightful, and the Political Agent lived the life of a country gentleman administering justice according to the notions of tribal law with the assistance of tribal *jirgas*, and amusing himself with shooting and fishing according to the season. His principal worries were the incidents which took place on the Afghan border. These would lead to protests made by the Government of Afghanistan to the British legation at Kabul whence they would be seriously considered by both the Government of India and the Foreign Office in London. In fact, they were rarely more than quarrels about grazing, complicated by the fact that the grazing grounds were situated on an international frontier. From time to time, arrangements would be made through the legation for the Political Agent and his Afghan counterpart to meet on the border with their tribal elders; and after much bargaining, the contending tribes would reach a monetary settlement; monetary because every life on the Frontier had an ascertained value in a rupee which, in those far off days, had a stable value. It was rare for a Political Agent of Kurram to be involved in tribal disputes resulting in the intervention of the Army. He had his own militia in the form of the Kurram Militia, and this force, backed as it was by the good-will of the tribes, was usually sufficient to maintain the peace within the Kurram valley.

Further south lay the tangle of infamous hills called Waziristan. This country was divided into two agencies, North Waziristan and South Waziristan, and the activities of these two Political Agents were, in theory at any rate, co-ordinated by the Resident in Waziristan.

Waziristan was inhabited by tribes whose vigour and fertility a barren country could not support. Consequently, during the whole time when the British were responsible for the Frontier, they never ceased to be worried by the truculence of the Wazirs and Mahsuds. In earlier years, they had attempted to contain them within their own country by a system of border posts; but the Wazirs and, even more, the Mahsuds were much too formidable to be controlled by militia. The occupation and administration of a country, which consisted in the eastern half at any rate of barren hills, was too expensive to be undertaken. A compromise was reached by which roads were driven into the highlands of Waziristan and a big military camp established at Razmak in the central highlands. The main line of communications between Razmak and India lay through North Waziristan, and the routine duties of the Political Agent were to assure the uninterrupted passage of military traffic to and from Razmak. The Political Agent himself had his quarters in Miranshah, which was the headquarters of the Tochi Scouts.

The Political Agent of South Waziristan was concerned with the Mahsuds, a very formidable tribe who were attempting to expand at the expense of their cousins, the Wazirs, and who had frequently impressed upon the army their high military value. There was only one cantonment in South Waziristan, at Wana, where it was situated in Wazir country and where its presence was not entirely resented as it did provide some sort of security to the Wazirs against Mahsud aggression. Communications with this garrison had to be kept open and, as they lay across Mahsud country, the Political Agent had to ensure that the Mahsud tribe kept their bad characters under control. When he failed to do so, a convoy might be ambushed with loss of valuable life and material, as occurred at the sinister Shahur Tangi in 1937.

The Political Agent himself lived in the winter in the plains at Tank. In the winter, too, the Mahsuds left the highlands and moved to the lower hills. They would be called to Tank by the Political Agent to receive their allowances during the winter.

Allowances were given to a tribe to reward them for carrying out on behalf of the Government unpopular tasks such as the restraining of criminal elements, which might otherwise cause trouble to tribes in Waziristan or inhabitants of the plains. In the summer, the Political Agent would spend his time between the various Scouts posts, taking advantage of propinquity of tribes to pay the half-yearly allowances.

It was the custom of each allowance holder to interview the Political Agent. This was quite an arduous matter, as each man had his own particular favour to ask, and it was necessary to humour as many as possible and to offend as few, otherwise there might be trouble. The Political Agent or his officials might be sniped at or the Scouts on their patrols ambushed or the roads blocked so that military convoys could not use them. But of course the resources at the Political Agent's disposal were limited, and it was by no means easy to send everyone away satisfied. The leaders of the tribe having seen the Political Agent individually, the tribal *jirga* then saw him collectively and made their requests. These would vary from asking for the establishment of a village school to the supply of a set of false teeth to the tribal *mullah*,* the grant of a contract for the supply of vegetables to the military, a gift of land in the plains or the enhancement of allowances and the creation of a large number of paid tribal militiamen. Proceedings were usually good-humoured, but arguments developed between the Political Agent and tribal leaders which sometimes became heated. The Political Agent had to steer a careful course. It did not do to be too clever in argument. A tribal leader defeated in debate and made to look a fool might well become a dangerous enemy.

In addition to the allowances which were paid to tribal *Maliks*,† the Government also paid a tribal militia called *Khassadars* who occupied posts of a rudimentary kind along the main roads. The inspection and payment of the *Khassadars* was a duty carried out by the Political Agent's subordinates, and through them he was kept in touch with what was going on in the agency. We shall now examine more closely the role which they and other irregular forces exercised.

* Muslim religious leader.          † Petty chiefs.

CHAPTER 27

# Frontier Patrol: *Khassadars,* Constabulary, Militia, Scouts, Frontier Force

IN addition to the normal police force to be found in all provinces, the Frontier had what may be called para-military forces which require notice. In recent times, there were three such bodies: the *Khassadars,* the Frontier Constabulary and the Scouts. Earlier, different names were used and there was some difference in their function. The word 'militia' is generally used for trans-border tribesmen recruited for service in their own tribal area–a system found lacking and almost entirely replaced by the Scouts' formula to which we shall return. But for special reasons it was a success in the Kurram. The Border Military Police, Jazailchis, Khyber Rifles–these are all terms which dropped out though the thing remained. In 1913, Roos-Keppel changed the name of Border Military Police to Frontier Constabulary; and in 1919, the Kurram Militia and Khyber Rifles were reorganized and called Scouts.

The *Khassadars* were the most down-to-earth of these bodies. (The term is used by the Amir Abdul Rahman in his autobiography.)* Something like the 'levies' in Baluchistan, they provided their own arms, wore no uniforms and were paid not as individuals, their section of the tribe being instead paid to supply a theoretical number of men who might in fact not always turn up. It was alleged that they would not fire to kill when their own tribesmen attacked, e.g. government transport which they were escorting; and altogether in Waziristan, which most concerns us, they were regarded (especially by the army, who did not love them) as having a long way to go before they could be regarded as satisfactory, even in the limited role that they were required to play. Yet they were undoubtedly an opening into the tribe, and as years went by, liaison became more and more satisfactory. Caroe[85] quotes Cunningham† as saying that, towards

* Howell believes that the origin of this word is the Portuguese *caçadores* (Spanish, *cazadores*) literally, 'hunters': irregulars who were raised in the Peninsularwar. According to this theory, Wellington's officers who later served in India brought the word to India.

† Sir George Cunningham (1888–1963), C.G.I.E., K.C.S.I., O.B.E.; I.C.S., Punjab, 1911. Political, 1914. Private Secretary to Viceroy, 1926. Otherwise served almost exclusively in N.W.F.P. Governor, N.W.F.P., 1937–46 and 1947–1948. Rector of St. Andrews University, 1946–9.

the end, the political officers 'got to know the tribes better and better, till at the end they knew them better than ever before'. The *Khassadars* were the chain, however feeble some of the links, which joined the political set-up and the tribe. Writing in 1934, Howell says:[86]

> The Khassadar is completely mobile and almost equally unreliable. The regular is his exact opposite in both respects. Half-way between the two you have the Scouts.

Next came the Frontier Constabulary. These were armed police, and were housed in barracks in the administered area–often very close to T.T., as tribal or unadministered territory was called, but not, like the Scouts, *in* T.T. Their duty was to catch the raider when he came out of his hills: preferably before he made his attack, but more probably on his way home. They were mostly Pathans drawn from cis-border tribes, with much the same background as those regular soldiers who were recruited from the N.W.F.P. plains. They co-operated loyally with the Scouts; all Frontier Constabulary posts in the south were instructed to inform Jandola, the South Waziristan Scouts headquarters, at once of any raids in their area.

The Frontier Constabulary were staffed with officers, mostly British, seconded from the Indian Police (who had a joint officer cadre for the Punjab and the N.W.F.P.). Similarly, the Scouts got their officers from the Indian Army–again, overwhelmingly British in composition, though there were enough Muslim officers with Scouts experience gained before Partition to provide Pakistan with qualified officers to take over. Pettigrew, in a brilliant, privately published monograph[87] on the South Waziristan Scouts, mentions Captain Mohammed Yusaf Khan, M.C., later a political officer, and Sahibzada Khushwaqt-ul-Mulk, brother of the Mehtar of Chitral, who after Partition became Inspecting Officer, Frontier Corps–the title held by the officer who commanded all the Frontier Scouts. The men were all Pathans, but drawn almost entirely from an area other than where they served. It seems to have taken our policy makers a little time to learn the lesson which Roman history should have taught–that you should not post soldiers in the area from which they are recruited.* The Romans sent their Celts to Syria and their Spaniards to Britain; but it is surprising how often this obvious precaution has to be learned afresh.

---

* Pettigrew (*op. cit.*) compares the procedure in Spain where the *Guardia Civil* are never stationed in the areas in which they are recruited. We may add that exactly the same rule applies to the Carabinieri in Italy.

Pettigrew's account of the South Waziristan Scouts gives a clear picture of what was the most important tribal area on the Frontier (always excepting the well-behaved but potentially dangerous Afridis), and of the organization of the Scouts. With his permission we will quote freely from it:

It was after the Mutiny in 1857–58, when India had been taken over from the East India Company, that the British met the Wazirs and Mahsuds. . . . There was serious trouble with the Mahsuds in 1860 and 1870 following large scale raiding including attacks on Tank, which was looted in 1870 while the British were preoccupied with the Second Afghan War. Large scale military operations had been necessary and Mahsud country had been penetrated, though not occupied. In 1893 the Mahsuds were angry over two things–that they had not been consulted over fixing the Durand Line and over the occupation of Wana–and no sooner had Wana been occupied than they attacked it under their fanatical leader, the Mulla Powindah. One dark November night about 3.30 a.m. five hundred of them rushed the camp with swords and knives, and fierce fighting went on till dawn between the attackers and the infantry battalions of the garrison. Only when daylight came and the army cavalry and artillery could go into action, were the Mahsuds driven off. The same year a third punitive expedition was organized.

It was in 1899 that the first real steps were made towards solving the Mahsud and Wazir problem, by giving them money-earning service in their own country, without losing their independence, as an alternative to raiding and looting. Tribal militias were formed to take over the Tochi posts and Wana and the Gomal posts from the regular army. . . . Yet it was all based on a mistake, the mistake being in thinking that sufficient loyalty and esprit-de-corps could be instilled into such self-centred and independent tribes as the Mahsuds and Wazirs, so that real reliance could be placed on them in time of trouble in their own areas. It would have been far better to have offered them service in other militias outside Waziristan, or to have recruited more of them into the Regular Army than just the single company in the 124th Baluch Infantry, which was raised in 1898.

The Mahsuds in the South Waziristan Militia only lasted from 1899 until 1905. A dramatic series of murders ensued, one of which is well told by Howell in Appendix D of Caroe's *The Pathans*. Thereafter, Roos-Keppel, the Chief Commissioner from 1908 to 1919, kept the Frontier remarkably quiet, till disaster occurred in 1919, when Afghanistan made war. Even though our forces available were not up to strength in quality or quantity–demobilization and war-weariness between them weakened British and Indian troops–the Afghans were very soon defeated. But, as we have already quoted Caroe as saying, it is after, not during, a war with Afghanistan that real trouble occurs. In this case, we lost lives, arms and prestige to an extent which affected the great debate on Frontier policy of 1922.

Pettigrew gives a vivid account of the 1919 disaster. Briefly, as the Afghan army advanced, the North Waziristan militia posts in the Upper Tochi were withdrawn on 25 May 1919, which left the Southern Waziristan militia stranded. A gallant attempt was made to evacuate the posts and retreat to Fort Sandeman, in Baluchistan, but it failed; the officers were nearly all killed and out of the 400 men who started on this retreat, only 150 reached Fort Sandeman.

Thereafter, in 1922, the militia was reformed under a new name, the South Waziristan Scouts (S.W.S.), with a strength of about 1,000, but never again any Wazirs or Mahsuds–and very few from other transborder tribes. They gradually built and occupied a number of posts, and by 1924 were properly organized. They patrolled the country extensively, assisting the slower-moving and perhaps slower-reacting army when they carried the flag through this infamous country, as Curtis calls it.

Pettigrew sums up their organization as follows:

> The South Waziristan Scouts (and also the Tochi Scouts, the Kurram Militia, the Chitral Scouts and later on other Scouts and Militias) were under the Inspecting Officer, Frontier Corps, who was answerable at Peshawar to the Chief Commissioner (later to become Governor) of the North-West Frontier Province. They were a political force and not an army one, though their British officers were drawn from the regular Indian Army on secondment for three years at a time. They were employed in a variety of tasks at the discretion of the Commandant in close cooperation with the Political Agent for South Waziristan, to support whose authority was the main reason for their existence. The Political Agent was under the Resident in Waziristan (when the appointment was later created), who in turn was responsible to the Governor of the N.W.F. Province. The Scouts were only placed under the Army when major operations against the Wazirs or Mahsuds, involving large scale Army action, became necessary; though naturally, small detachments of Scouts

operating as Scouts with Army mobile columns would be under the direction of the column commander.

And this was how officers were recruited:

... Vetting was a vital and invariable part of the method of selection of Scouts' officers. With only fourteen British officers, five at head-quarters and three with each of the wings, there could be no misfits. So all apparently suitable officers who applied to join, and who were recommended by their commanding officer, were asked to take a week's leave and spend it with the S.W.S. During that time they visited a good number of the posts and met all the officers, were taken out on *gasht*,\* encouraged to talk to the Pathan officers. They joined in the usual fun at Jandola in the Mess, were talked to, and listened to, and observed. Sometimes they were accepted and sometimes they weren't. The Commandant and the Wing Commanders, all experi-enced Scouts on their second tour of duty with the S.W.S., decided. But every one's opinion was asked and considered. If anyone did not take to the applicant he was probably rejected. It could easily so happen that the two of them would be at Ladha or some other post for weeks and weeks, with no other company in the Mess than each other's. Any real dislike, or even a serious clash of personalities, could disturb the whole post. The risk was not worth it. There were plenty more pebbles on the beach, with the Scouts' reputation so high and the attractions of the outdoor life so strong towards the right men.

What the Scouts thought of the Army is interesting:

How good or bad British regiments were on the frontier depended on just one thing, and that was how ready they were to learn. All the Indian and Gurkha regiments spent two years in every six on the frontier and had a large proportion of older men experienced in fron-tier warfare and the ways of the Pathan. Brigadiers and Staff of the Razmak, Bannu and Wana Brigades had all spent many years in Waziristan or elsewhere on the frontier. They all said the same, and we all came to know it. If a British regiment arrived at Razmak, or better still at Bannu prior to its march up to Razmak, and said: 'We are new to this. You are not. Please teach us!' then it would soon be a regiment well able to look after itself and take its share of responsibil-ity in the mobile columns, piquetting and so on. But let a regiment

\* Patrol.

think it knew, that it was too famous to have to learn, think that the Highlands of Scotland bore any real resemblance to the mountains of Waziristan, and that regiment would have trouble. And during its year in Waziristan it would be of little use to anyone, and often a liability.

And of their own role:

Scouts were not meant to work with the Regular Army and it was far better that they should not. They could do their own particular jobs on their own. And to do them it was often easier and happier for everyone if relations with the Mahsuds were fairly good, if not exactly cordial. But to the Mahsuds the Army meant the enemy and so Scouts working with the Army became enemy too.

The Scouts' role was to back up the Political officers in their main task of keeping the peace in Waziristan; keeping the road open, preventing raids into the plains, escorting the Powindahs, and constantly *gashting* to show the flag so that the tribes would see that their territory was not inaccessible. And if the Political officers needed force to round up outlaws, or enforce fines on recalcitrant sub-tribes or villages, then the Scouts were there to provide it. Once, however, that tribal lashkars gathered, or a powerful sub-tribe showed open hostility and defiance, then the matter would probably become too much for the Scouts to handle. With all their other normal commitments still to be met, and with no other weapons than their rifles, except a few small guns and machine guns in the larger posts, the Scouts could not bring a real strength to bear. They were after all Scouts and not soldiers.

How did the Scouts set about one of their important roles – of co-operating with the Frontier Constabulary to stop the Mahsuds raiding the plains?

Any Mahsud raiding party was pretty certain to emerge from the hills somewhere between the Shuza river in the north and the Gomal in the south. A distance of at least twenty-five miles in a straight line. And unladen as they would be, under cover of dark, they could cross at a hundred places and never be seen or heard. It was obviously impossible to prevent them getting down into the open plain. But getting back again was different. Provided that information of a raid could be received fairly quickly, and with telephone and wireless in the frontier constabulary posts as well as in the Scouts' posts this should not be too difficult, then the area through which the raiders would withdraw could be cut down to a few miles instead of twenty-five. And Scouts' *gashts*, moving faster than the Mahsud or Wazir raiders, encumbered now with loot and captives too, probably, could seal off the main escape routes in the area. Of course sometimes they would be too late, and the raiders would be gone. At other times they would be unlucky and the raiders would be able to avoid them through an informer. Sometimes there would be a successful ambush with many raiders killed or wounded, and prisoners and loot recovered. More often the raiders were surprised and scattered, one or two perhaps wounded and most of the loot recovered. Hostages, the raiders' prisoners, would be left, alive if they were Moslems, more often dead if they were Hindus. But the raiders returned home as empty handed as they had set out, angry and tired and, the Scouts hoped, doubting the value of raiding any more. At least for some time.

We must always remember the changes brought about by the arms traffic which led to the whole Mahsud tribe being armed with modern precision weapons and fairly ample ammunition. What happened at Tank in 1860 could scarcely have been done in 1910:

It was right back in 1860, when the Mahsuds were very cock-a-hoop and sallied forth from their hills three thousand strong to attack and plunder Tank. Tank itself was held by a single troop of cavalry under Saadat Khan, but when he got word of the approach and intention of the Mahsuds he collected all the horsemen he could, regular and irregular, from the outposts round about, and moved out with nearly two hundred *sowars** to meet the raiders. He found them drawn up a bare half-a-mile the Tank side of the *tangi*,† so to draw them further into the plain he ordered his sowars to fall back. With their enormous superiority in numbers it was not surprising that the Mahsuds thought the cavalry were afraid, and they came on after them with shouts of derision, until they had gone another mile away from the safety of their hills. Then Saadat Khan's men turned and charged, having first sent a party wide on the open flank to get behind the Mahsuds. The tribesmen, individually strong and tough and brave, lacked the discipline and training to fight cohesively and deter-minedly in the open plain. When the cavalry galloped over them with lance and sabre, several of their leaders among the first to fall, their morale went and they fled towards the safety of the *tangi*. But

* Troopers.　　　　　† Gorge.

three hundred of them were killed, including six *maliks* and their chief leader, and many more were wounded, while only one cavalry-man was killed.

When, after the first Sikh war, the first British arrived on the Frontier, they realized that something else was needed besides regular troops. So early as 1846, the Resident, Henry Lawrence, deputed Harry Lumsden to raise a force of cavalry and infantry known as the Guides. Later, other units were added, similarly organized, and all were known as the Punjab Frontier Force. This force was under the ultimate direct orders of the Punjab Government, and so remained until 1902, when Kitchener re-organized the Indian Army. This change was, doubtless, to the advantage of the army; it was certainly a blow to frontier administration.

The Frontier Force consisted at first of the Corps of Guides, five regiments of cavalry, five battalions of infantry, three light field batteries of artillery, two garrison batteries and two companies of sappers and miners. Later, there were some changes of composition and constitution; but basically it retained its character as an irregular force until 1903. Towards the end of the nineteenth century, the Frontier Force had to some extent, through filling the role of regular troops, lost the rough and ready character which it originally had. A more loosely constituted local organization was needed for the everyday work of raids and tribal incidents. This was supplied by raising levies and militia (Scouts).

The peculiar feature of the Punjab Frontier Force, or 'Piffers' as they were familiarly known, was that the permanent headquarters of all units was in the N.W.F.P.; and though sometimes they might serve in other parts, the Frontier was their home, and preservation of the peace of the border their expertise. The Guides, in particular, had their permanent headquarters at Mardan–then in Peshawar civil district but, since January 1937, a district of its own–and early on their C.O. seems to have acted *ex officio* as the local civil or political administrator. Lumsden, who raised them and commanded them from 1846 to 1862, was a remarkable man. He realized that what had to be filled was a role something between that of regular troops and what, as we have seen, the Scouts later provided. The Guides, which were composed of a cavalry regiment and infantry battalion cantoned side by side, had to be ready to turn out instantly for action; their uniform was adapted for this, not for the barrack square. It was, in fact, khaki, and they were the first to wear this later world-famous dress. Their name indicated their role: they were to be the eyes and ears of the regulars whom they were to guide to their goal. Mardan lies in the heart of the great Yusufzai tribe–rich plains dwellers for the most part, who have not lost the qualities of tribal Pathans; and they and their neighbours, the Khattaks (perhaps the most dependable and 'satisfactory' of all frontier tribes) provided the majority of the men of the Guides.

CHAPTER 28

# The Royal Air Force

MENTION must be made of the role of the Royal Air Force. There was constant friction between them and the Army, and this is the case for the R.A.F.[88] They were a very young organization and only appeared for the first time on the Frontier – and that in minute numbers – towards the end of World War I. (The very first plane to reach India arrived in 1919.) They never had more than eight squadrons of twelve planes each. The Army were very powerful; their head, the Commander-in-Chief in India, commanded all three forces – military, naval and air – was *ex officio* a member of the Governor-General's Executive Council, and had the ear not only of the Governor-General but of very influential circles in England, such as the Committee of Imperial Defence. The R.A.F. were virtually under the Army at first; it was only in 1939 or so that they were able to strike out. The local Army commander approved the whole tactical set up, once it was decided to attack a recalcitrant tribe: the R.A.F. were not even consulted on where they should operate. All R.A.F. officers felt that they could have done their job cheaper and better.

Gould,* in his *Jewel in the Lotus* makes a strong case for precision bombing. He describes how, in the Kurram, survey and mapping was done with such accuracy that the R.A.F. could pick out one individual house for attack, punishing only a hostile tribesman and leaving his neighbours untouched. Dundas,† another Frontier expert (he was the last British Governor of the N.W.F.P. after Partition), also felt strongly that the R.A.F., properly used, provided a cheap, humane and efficient weapon for tribal control.[89] Villages were never attacked until an elaborate warning system – the dropping of different coloured leaflets – had been gone through; and it was generally felt that this procedure, valuable though it was when cited before a critical world-opinion, in particular at the League of Nations, was not a very effective way of overawing a hostile

---

* Sir Basil Gould (1883–1956), C.M.G., C.I.E.; I.C.S. 1907–47; Punjab, 1907, Consul Sistan, 1918–25, Counsellor, Kabul, 1926–9, Political Officer, Sikkim, and for Bhutan and Tibet, 1935–45. He spent 1929–35 in various posts in the N.W.F.P. and Baluchistan, and had an unusually wide variety of postings. Collaborated with H. E. Richardson in books on the Tibetan language.

† *See* p. 167.

tribe or section. A less known, but, according to Dundas, effective method was air patrol of the cultivated ground near a settlement, so that the threat of machine-gunning kept the 'hostiles', as they were called, away from their fields. Sometimes it drove them into caves, where they were much troubled, it is said, by fleas and other vermin.

But what would the Army have said? Surely, that this plea for a different method of control was basically a cry for economy. The old Government of India has been defined as 'a magnificent organization for promoting economy in peace time'. How they could fall down on bigger tasks – as they did notoriously in World War I in Iraq – was sometimes apparent. The Army protagonist would go on to say that, however much Sandeman-policy supporters would claim to get results without force, however much the close-border men would insist that they could pull right out and police the country to the extent of stopping raids by air action, one came back eventually to the hard fact that a strong garrison of regular troops was needed close at hand: and that when a tribe was really defiant there was no substitute for the p.b.i. – 'poor bloody infantry' – as it was called in World War I.

We will not attempt to settle an internal controversy (or feud) of these dimensions. It remains, however, to be said that while, shortly after the turn of the century, the tribes reached a standard of equipment, thanks to the arms traffic with the Gulf, which equalled that of our regular soldiers and sometimes surpassed that available to police, levies and so on, in the air arm they were up against quite another proposition. In World War II the R.A.F. in India was still indifferently armed, with obsolete planes. Had the British remained on for more than those short two years which separated V.E. day from Independence day, they might have developed air control a very great deal. Indeed, though Pakistan promptly removed the garrison of regular troops from Razmak and Wana, the Scouts who police Waziristan to this day carry out *gasht* (patrols) and when necessary call on the Pakistan Air Force for assistance in the old way. And an R.A.F. officer who revisited the Frontier in 1961 formed the impression that the Pakistan Air Force hit much harder than their predecessors. Ruthlessness may be merciful, in the long run.

# CHAPTER 29

## Aden

VARIOUS posts outside India were filled by Indian political officers. It is not always easy to see on what principle this was done, but finance must have played a large part. That is to say, when the opening of a consulate or political agency seemed to the British Government desirable at most, while to the Government of India it seemed essential, it would be arranged that the latter should bear all the costs of the post. Its holder would, if in an independent foreign country, report to both the London Foreign Office and the Government of India. Protocol-wise, London had the last word; but he who pays the piper calls the tune; and the posts which we shall now discuss were of far greater importance to India than to England. And most were staffed by our service.

There were different reasons for this interest. In some cases it was pure strategy; in the Persian Gulf, the need to check the slave and arms trade: later to encourage the oil trade and to secure an air route. In a trans-Himalayan post like Kashgar, the needs of a small Indian commercial community played a minor role to that of watch-dog over the recurring problems of Russia and China. Afghanistan was important both as a buffer against Russia and as a power always concerned with, and apt to intrigue among, the tribes on the hither side of the Durand line.

Aden, the first of these posts which we will consider, owed its importance to its position as a coaling station on the way to India. Early in the nineteenth century, it was realised that the route round the Cape of Good Hope was needlessly lengthy, and two short cuts were devised. The first was the sea route up the Persian Gulf to Basra, then up through Iraq and across the Syrian desert to the Mediterranean. The other was that via the Red Sea to Suez, whence a short land route by camel or horse took the mail-carrier or other light-loaded traveller roughly along the route later to become famous as that taken by the Suez Canal.

In 1839 this route was already so important that it was felt necessary to occupy Aden. A plausible excuse was found, a local tribe was attacked and conquered, and Aden was British. Here there was no question of indirect rule; it was direct government which was installed and the Indian Political Service did not come into the picture until 1932. As we left in

1937, there is little more to be said of this tenuous link. However, during the later years of our relationship with Aden, much closer interest was taken in the Protectorate, as the large tribal area in the interior was called, and indirect rule was there the order of the day. Previously, attention was more or less confined to the tiny Settlement, i.e. the Crown Colony area consisting of little but the town of Aden. Ingrams's* work in Mukalla offers many analogies with Sandeman's in Baluchistan.

So late as 1966, the future of the States comprising the Federation was hotly disputed. Bell's† article,[90] 'A constitution for South Arabia', in the Royal Central Asian Society's Journal for October 1966 well sums up the problem and explains its difficulty. He writes in it:

> Let me begin in 1839, the year of the occupation. The story of Britain's relationship with Aden and the states or tribes of the South Arabian coast during the 100 years following 1839 is simply this. Britain needed Aden as a base; she was not interested in the hinterland or the tribes save to the extent that she was determined that they should not fall under the influence of any other external power. She therefore signed a series of treaties by which in exchange for protection, the Rulers undertook not to dispose of their territory without United Kingdom approval. But bases have a habit of involving their occupiers, whether they will or not, in affairs often far removed from the original strategic purpose of the base. And this is, indeed, what happened. The Italian occupation of Ethiopia in 1937 marked the beginning of just such a development, reflected in the first of the Advisory Treaties. This was signed by the Sultan of Mukalla,‡ and it provided that the British Government would appoint a Resident Adviser to Mukalla and that the Sultan would accept his advice. Two years later the Kathiri Sultan signed a similar agreement, and between 1944 and 1954 Advisory Treaties were concluded with thirteen Western Protectorate Rulers.

* W. H. Ingrams (b. 1897), C.M.G. Colonial Service, 1919. In Aden 1934–49. From 1937–40 was Resident Adviser at Mukalla, and completely pacified the Hadramaut, an area formerly a prey to the blood feud.

† Sir Gawain Bell (b. 1909), K.C.M.G., C.B.E. Sudan Political Service, 1931. Political Agent, Kuwait, 1955. Governor, Northern Nigeria, 1957. Joint Constitutional Adviser to the Federal Government of South Arabia, 1965. It is interesting to note how, after the winding up of the Indian Political Service, experts were drawn from other sources.

‡ This Sultan had also a long link with Hyderabad State in India, where his ancestors had settled with many of their tribesmen who served in the Hyderabad irregular forces. He had a *jagir* (tax-free property) there whose income exceeded that of his State in Arabia.

Having regulated her relationship with the individual states, Britain was inescapably faced with a responsibility for the relationship of the States one with another. In other words, for developing those institutions that would–rightly–lead both Aden and the states to seek self-government and independence. Of all the Arab countries, South Arabia must surely be the most difficult to weld into a united whole. This welter of stark and barren mountains ranged behind a narrow coastal plain; these bitter traditional tribal feuds and political suspicions; poor communications; poverty. And a great gulf, social and economic, separating Aden itself from the hinterland, as if the rock and its crater were physically an island set apart from the mainland.

It must be remembered, however, that, until a few years back, Aden was merely a bunkering station, first for coal and then for oil. It was never a naval base and had no repair facilities. It had a large oil refinery and, up to 1927, a very small garrison from the Indian army, replaced in that year by the R.A.F. plus a battery of guns. This skeleton force protected the frontier with the Yemen and occasionally intervened in internal tribal policing. But in 1955 relations with the Yemen, long strained, got much worse; and a battalion of British troops was added, the R.A.F. base at Khormaksar being simultaneously speedily enlarged. By 1959 Aden, now the headquarters of 'British Forces, Arabian Peninsula', was equipped for intervention in the Gulf and East Africa. Local forces were expanded and modernized. With the decision of Her Majesty's Government to withdraw from Aden by 1968, a vast and expensive set up has been moved or abandoned.

The connection of our service with Aden though short, included the tenures of two Governors from it: Reilly* and Hickinbotham.† The latter was re-employed, some years after the partition of the sub-continent.

Before we pass on to consider the Persian Gulf, we may remark that a language problem arose in both of these areas. The lingua franca in India was Urdu, in which all officers of our service had passed examinations before joining. English was used much more than Urdu in the States and Pushtu largely replaced Urdu on the Frontier. But holders of posts in the

* Lt.-Col. Sir Bernard Reilly (1882–1966), K.C.M.G., C.I.E., O.B.E. Military Political, 1908. Resident and Commander-in-Chief, Aden, 1931–7; Chief Commissioner, Aden, 1932–7; Governor and Commander-in-Chief, Aden, 1937–40.

† Sir Tom Hickinbotham (b. 1903), K.C.M.G., C.I.E., O.B.E. Military Political, 1930. Served in Aden at intervals, 1931–9. Chairman, Aden Port Trust, 1948–51; Governor and Commander-in-Chief of Colony and Protectorate of Aden, 1951–6.

Muslim areas outside India were thrown up against the necessity of speaking–and speaking well–at least one more language. Arabic was the language of Aden and of most of the Persian Gulf posts, as we shall shortly see. It is a difficult language, and practically no one in the service knew any on his arrival in those parts. Persian, which is much easier, is spoken on the east coast of the Persian Gulf, of course in consular posts inside Persia, and in Afghanistan (alongside Pushtu). Thus there tended to be some specialization by officers who knew one or both of those languages well; and after Partition they were in demand by the London Foreign Office to fill posts on contract in this area.

Not that there were not some colourful linguists earlier. A notable example was Claudius James Rich (1787–1820). After learning Arabic at fourteen, and many other languages later, he was nominated a cadet in the service of the East India Company in 1803, and subsequently writer on the Bombay establishment. He was, however, posted to Egypt to improve his Arabic and Turkish, and told to report to the consul general there. He started in 1804, was shipwrecked off Spain and went to Italy where he learned Italian. The consul general in Egypt having died, he was allowed to switch to Constantinople and Smyrna. He arrived at last in Bombay in 1807, and next year married the Governor's daughter. Before he was twenty-four, he was made Resident at Baghdad, 'by mere merit' it is recorded. He travelled much and wrote much; Mountstuart Elphinstone selected him for 'an important office in Bombay'; but he caught cholera and died on 5 October 1820.

# CHAPTER 30

## East Persia, the Persian Gulf and Iraq

WE have now to consider an area of the greatest importance to India's external policy: one with which our service was closely concerned over a very long period, and where, some good authorities believe, the most valuable work of the service was done, at least in this century. We refer to the Persian Gulf, Iraq and East Persia.

To take first the East Persian posts. The consulate general at Meshed, the consulate at Kerman, the vice-consulates at Zabul, Zahedan and Ahwaz, and sometimes Birjand, were all, in theory, staffed from our service, though not always in practice, particularly in peace-time.

Usually work was not heavy. Noel,* a consul at Kerman, on transfer to the North-West Frontier Province, stayed with the author in the early thirties. He described his work: 'No, it could not be called heavy. Last year, I took a few weeks off to pay a sight-seeing visit to the Caspian. No one acted for me, and when I returned, I found that all my files had piled up and awaited me on my desk. It took me till luncheon to dispose of them.'

Earlier, Persia had been (as it became again later) a bone of contention between Great Britain and Russia. In 1907, the Anglo-Russian agreement, the conclusion of which was an inevitable feature of the Triple Entente, removed this bone, to the great annoyance of various watchdogs, including Curzon.

Meshed came into prominence during the two world wars. During the first, Haig† was Consul-General there and, in an unfinished MS. deposited at St. Antony's College, Oxford, gives a vivid account of his experiences. Our allies the Russians had a prisoner-of-war camp not far across the border, where a number of Austrians were confined. Discipline among the guards was lax, and the prisoners escaped in large numbers, crossed into neutral Persia and eventually reached the Austro-Hungarian

---

* Lt.-Col. E. W. C. Noel (b. 1886), C.I.E., D.S.O. Military Political, 1912. Served in Persia and Iraq and was one of our greatest Persian experts.

† Sir T. Wolseley Haig (1865–1938), K.C.I.E., C.S.I., C.M.G., C.B.E. Albany Herald 1927–35. Professor of Arabic, Persian and Urdu, Trinity College, Dublin. Indian Army, 1887; Berar Commission, 1892; Military Political, 1901; served in Persia, 1910–20. One of the co-editors of *Cambridge History of India*.

legation at Tehran. Haig arranged to kidnap them *en route* and send them back to Russia. He had a dozen or two Indian troopers and considered this ample for holding off the Persian army which, it was rumoured, might attack the consulate.

A great deal happened in Persia during World War I. Our position there was often precarious, especially after the Russian revolution. In World War II, there were similar difficulties until the German invasion of Russia, when the wholly unexpected problem of helping to get supplies through to Russia was added to the duties of our political consuls. While Haig's account is confined to Meshed, Gould's memoirs *The Jewel in the Lotus* and Skrine's* *World War in Iran* range further. Indeed, Gould's book is perhaps the most varied account in existence of the career of an Indian Political Service officer. He seems to have served everywhere.†

Harold Nicolson[91] well sums up the situation in Persia during and after World War I. He writes:

> Persia, during the war, had been exposed to violations and sufferings not endured by any other neutral country. In the earlier stages of the war the Turks, and then the Russians, had been mainly responsible for rendering Persian territory an area of hostilities. The British were dragged into the business mainly against their will. Yet after the Russian retirement in 1917, the British alone were left in occupation, and upon them alone fell the full force of Persian indignation. . . . in the north the Turks were the first to cross the Persian border and were at once countered by Russian troops. Our own intervention in the south was provoked by the disturbances and outrages organized by German residents and agents: of such men as Wassmuss, Zugmayer, and Niedermayer. . . . the local German agents, isolated and in hourly danger of their lives, never abandoned confidence. They armed the Austrian and German prisoners who had escaped from the concentration camps at Tashkend; they provoked countless incidents in the hope that these incidents would force the British Government to reprisals; they undermined our influence and prestige by every means within their power, contending even that William II had been converted to the Muslim faith. It is impossible not to admire the ardent courage and inventiveness of these devoted patriots. Nor were they unsuccessful. Their propaganda was so

---

* Sir Clarmont Skrine (b. 1888), o.b.e. I.C.S., U.P., 1911. Political, 1915. Served long in Persia and took H.I.M. Reza Shah into exile.

† *See* p. 218 n.

efficient that it induced Mustaufi-ul-Mamalek, the Persian Prime Minister, to sign a secret treaty promising Germany the full support of the Persian administration. It was so dangerous that it obliged the British Government to intervene in Persian affairs, to recruit the 'South Persia Rifles' and to send armed forces to occupy Bushire and other points of strategical necessity.

Although, therefore, we had only violated Persian neutrality to protect ourselves against our enemies, and although the Persian Government had placed themselves entirely in the wrong by concluding secret treaties with one side, while accepting subsidies from the other, yet the fact remains that Persia emerged from the war in a mood of innocent but violated rectitude.

Curzon concluded an agreement with Persia in 1919 which, had it been quickly ratified, would have given both parties many advantages. But negotiations were allowed to drag on and it was before long repudiated by Persia's Mejlis or Parliament.

Before World War I, our consulates had guards supplied by India, which, though not numerous, had an important influence on morale. Wilson* in his brilliant book *South West Persia*, not to be confused with his much less readable *The Persian Gulf*, draws a picture of the life of a subaltern seconded for political intelligence work in a remote region before World War I. Though the story it tells is very different, it compares with T. E. Lawrence's *Seven Pillars of Wisdom* as an absorbing account of a young man's reaction to the Middle East.

Generally, consular posts in Persia, as in other independent southwest Asian countries, were staffed from the Levant Consular Service. But the few posts mentioned above, presumably because of their comparative proximity to India, were staffed from the Indian Political Service. The same was true of the Persian Gulf posts, to which, with their fiendish climate, we shall now turn.

The Persian Gulf means, strictly, the inner sea north and west of the narrows formed by the Straits of Hormuz, the outer and easterly sea being correctly called the Gulf of Oman. However, the broad term 'The Gulf' has normally been used to describe the whole area, and we shall follow suit. Right back in the early sixteenth century, the Portuguese established

---

* Lt.-Col. Sir Arnold Wilson (1884–1940), K.C.I.E., C.S.I., C.M.G., D.S.O. Indian Army, 1903; Political, 1909. Served mostly in Persia, Iraq and Persian Gulf. Acting Civil Commissioner and Political Resident 1918–20. In oil company, 1921–1932. M.P., Killed in action 1940. Numerous publications.

themselves in these waters, being driven out of Hormuz by the Persians and their allies the British in 1662. In 1650, the Arabs drove the Portuguese out of Muscat, and thereafter the scene was set for a century of opposition between the British and the Dutch. In 1763, we first hear of a British resident at Bushire. (From 1862 he was known as the political resident–a term not used elsewhere.) Bushire, though on Persian soil, ever after remained the headquarters of our service in these parts until, in 1946, it was moved to the island of Bahrain. (Our naval base had already, in 1936, moved there.)

It is of interest to see how and why this change was made in 1946. Weightman,* the Foreign Secretary, as he was still usually known (the correct title was Secretary, External Affairs department, India) wrote to Hay,† the political resident-designate, in April 1946, to break the news that the Cabinet at home had taken a decision that the Persian Gulf residency must move out of Bushire forthwith. This, he presumed, was evidently very much a snap decision on a (British) Foreign Office representation, taken without normal inter-departmental procedure in London being observed. Nevertheless, it was a Cabinet decision and as such must be accepted. Delhi was clearly of the opinion that the residency could not function except in the Gulf itself, and consequently they had indicated pretty plainly to London that if the residency was to move at all in the near future to temporary quarters while consideration of permanent construction continued, then His Majesty's Government must let the Government of India have the whole or practically all of the property that they owned in Bahrain, including the Senior Naval Officer's new house and probably a good deal of the Air Ministry property too.

He went on to say that he feared that this news would be most unwelcome to Hay, as indeed it was to them. The (British) Foreign Office claimed that it was essential to eliminate all hostages to fortune in Persia if the (British) Foreign Secretary was to be able to handle the Russo-Persian situation adequately, and listed (with astonishingly little justification, in Weightman's view) the retention of the resident at Bushire as one of our weakest positions in Persia.

From an early date, we had officers in Iraq, at Baghdad and at Basra, the former being known as the 'British resident in Turkish Arabia'–a

* Sir Hugh Weightman (1828–1948), C.S.I., C.I.E.; I.C.S., 1922, Assam. Political, 1929; Foreign Secretary, 1946–7.

† Lt.-Col. Sir Rupert Hay (b. 1893), C.S.I., C.I.E.; I.C.S., Military Political, 1920. Served mostly on North-West Frontier; Resident, Persian Gulf, 1941–2 and 1946–53.

style unwelcome to the young Turks but justified by the capitulations. Similarly, the staffing of the Basra post by Indian politicals was unwelcome to the British mercantile community in Basra, since they normally knew no Turkish and had no commercial training. It was therefore decided early in this century to replace them and their Baghdad colleagues by members of the Levant Consular Service.

The set-up in the Gulf varied from time to time, but basically the usual picture was of a first-class resident at Bushire, three political agents at Bahrain, Kuwait and Muscat*, a consul at Kerman and a vice-consul at Mohammerah (later re-named Khorramshahr). There was a vice-consular post at Bunder Abbas, but it was often left unfilled. That at Bam was long since closed. After the Partition of India and Pakistan in 1947, when all such posts were taken over by the London Foreign Office, two new political agencies were created. Sharja, created originally as a temporary war-time measure, was moved in 1954 to Dubai, and another post opened at Dohah, the capital of Qatar (pronounced Gutter), oil discoveries having brought increased importance to them.

Oil is, of course, now by far the most important thing in the Gulf, but it was not struck in south-west Persia till the opening years of this century. Shortly before World War II, its existence was proved in several Gulf areas, but its commercial development was postponed till after the war. The importance of the Gulf in earlier times was four-fold: strategy, piracy, slaves and arms. The importance to India of this fairly easy approach route was obvious – the barren coast was no obstacle to Alexander the Great's army as it returned from what is now Pakistan. Some writers have denied the seriousness of the threat presented by Napoleon, especially during his alliance with Russia and occupation of Holland; those responsible for the security of India had every reason to take the threat of an attack through Persia seriously. Whether made the basis of a full-scale invasion or a mere raid in force, the effect of such an attempt might well have been disastrous to internal security in India. (Similarly, nearly a century and a half later, when Japan had control of the sea in the Bay of Bengal, a few scattered landings on the east coast of India would have caused enough panic to justify the step.)

In 1807, when France made a treaty with the Shah of Persia and was temporarily allied with Russia, Minto, the Governor-General, sent envoys to Persia, to Afghanistan and to Ranjit Singh at Lahore; Malcolm,

* The Muscat post is correctly described as a consulate (later elevated to a consulate general) not a political agency, since the Sultan is responsible for his own foreign relations and not, like the trucial Shaikhs, ruler of a protected state.

one of the most distinguished early politicals, made his mission to Tehran famous by his squabble with the British Ambassador (i.e. home-based). About the same time, the French islands of Bourbon and Mauritius came into prominence from their link with the neutral Muscat, which provided with a flag of convenience many ships which took refuge there from British attacks.

Thus the importance of the Gulf as commanding the principal land approach to India should not be underestimated. It certainly was not by Curzon who, in 1903–4, personally toured the area in great state, with a large naval escort, much impressing the various Shaikhs but falling out with the Persians on a point of protocol.

In modern times the broad strategic argument for our presence in the Gulf was reinforced by particular administrative problems. The first was piracy. A great increase in piracy accompanied the spread of Wahabi power from their home in the interior to the Gulf coast early in the nineteenth century. Many attacks were made on the shipping of the East India Company, necessitating expeditions in 1809 and 1819; the latter led to all the Shaikhs of the Trucial Coast as well as the Shaikh of Bahrain signing a general treaty of peace. By the terms of this treaty, they bound themselves to refrain from piracy except as a part of wartime operations. This was found inadequate; and in 1833 all the Shaikhs of the Trucial Coast further undertook not to make war on one another by sea. This was known as the Maritime Truce; the term 'Trucial Coast', which still applies to the very small states between Qatar and Muscat, is derived from this truce. Later, in 1853, a Perpetual Maritime Truce replaced the series of extensions which had been customary between 1835 and 1853, and not merely bound the Shaikhs to keep the peace in the waters of the Gulf, but included the British Government as enforcement-authority.

Next came the slave trade. From the earliest times, slaves had been acquired in East Africa by dealers from Muscat and the Trucial Coast and taken in dhows for sale in the Gulf and for export to elsewhere in Arabia and Persia. Between 1822 and 1873, the Shaikhs (including the Rulers of the larger and more important states of Muscat and Bahrain) were persuaded to sign documents requiring them not to import slaves. More, they provided that British warships should have the right to search dhows and to confiscate them and any slaves which they might be found to be carrying.

So far, so good. But it is easier to collect signatures than to stop a long-established way of life; and it is clear that the few ships of the British and Indian navies which succeeded in catching slaves or slavers had a problem which was far from easy. Apart from the consciousness that they were only dealing with a small part of the problem, these warships had an almost impossible task. The slaves, probably in a filthy or even dying condition when taken aboard a warship, were an insoluble problem. How were they to be looked after? Where were they to be taken? Many writers emphasize the comparatively good treatment of the slaves at their destination and contrast this with the journey there, in tropical heat and cramped quarters. It seems likely that the Rulers, when they signed the agreement, did not expect it to be too strictly enforced. But we plodded away. Zanzibar, originally part of the State of Muscat and Oman, broke away from its parent State in about 1860. In both these areas the slave problem was acute. The degree of cooperation, unwilling though it must have been, which we received both at Muscat and Zanzibar over a long period, right down to the most recent times, seems remarkable.

Lastly comes the arms traffic. As we saw when discussing the North-West Frontier problem, the smuggling of arms from the Gulf via Persia and Baluchistan to the tribal areas of the North-West Frontier was a major difficulty in this, the twentieth century. In the last century, broadly speaking, our troops were much better armed than the tribesmen whom they opposed. The tribesmen might have the advantage of knowledge of the terrain and of numbers but when, ultimately, it came to rifle fire, our arms were always much superior. The opening up about 1900 of this route via the Gulf to the arms dealers[*] of the whole world was a grievous handicap; and steps, ultimately successful, to suppress it were taken in the first two decades of this century.

What was the authority which enabled us to tackle the arms trade? This is how Hay[92] describes it:

> The most important agreements with the States of the Persian Gulf and those on which the British position at present rests are what are known as the 'exclusive' agreements. Great Britain having acquired, more or less fortuitously, a dominating influence in the Gulf, became anxious to retain it, primarily to safeguard her communications with India. At that time nothing was known of the great oil wealth underlying the barren sands of the States and the sole importance of the Gulf to Great Britain lay in its position on the flanks of these communications. During the last decade of the nineteenth century she

[*] The cooperation of the foreign government concerned could not always be relied upon. In particular, until the *Entente Cordiale* cleared up this and other sources of friction, the French government were far from cooperative over this matter.

obtained agreements from Bahrain, Kuwait and the Trucial States whereby the Rulers undertook not to have direct relations with any other foreign power, and not to sell, lease or cede land to any such power. Great Britain thus became responsible for conducting the foreign relations of these States, and, incidentally, for their protection against foreign aggression. The Rulers entered readily into these agreements because they realized that their continued independence could only be ensured by British protection. The Sultan of Muscat, however, is bound by no such agreement and is responsible for the conduct of his own foreign relations.

During most of the nineteenth century a vague control was exercised over Kuwait by the Turkish authorities at Basrah. In 1898 Shaikh Mubarak of Kuwait, anxious to avoid any extension of this control, turned to Great Britain and in 1899 signed a comprehensive treaty which contained most of the provisions included in the various agreements with Bahrain and the Trucial States. The Turks continued to exercise a nominal suzerainty over Kuwait until they entered the first World War on the side of the Germans in 1914.

When the Turks occupied the province of Hasa in 1871 they extended their control over the Qatar peninsula which they continued to occupy until 1914. On their withdrawal, the British recognized the Shaikh who had been their local Deputy Governor as Ruler, and in 1916 they entered into a Treaty with him embodying the provisions of their agreement with the other Gulf States.

Until the discovery of oil, the economy of the Gulf depended, to a considerable extent, on pearl fishing. Early in this century, 4,500 boats and 74,000 men depended on this trade. The ports of Qatar and the Trucial Coast existed for this trade alone. Bahrain and, to a lesser degree, Kuwait also depended on it. But after oil was struck work in the oil fields proved far more attractive. Kuwait and – a recent discovery – Abu Dhabi, have achieved enormous wealth from oil. Bahrain has only a small quantity but indirectly, through a huge refinery, depends on the same source of income. Since these States form part of the sterling area, Great Britain and other members of this area benefit greatly from their membership.

But this is a matter of recent, post-1947 history. During the period when our service served there, the Gulf's importance was still mainly strategic: it was one of the gates to India. We had ceased to man posts in Iraq – Turkish Arabia until World War I – but the proximity of this Turkish province had been a threat so long as Turkey's friendship or neutrality was not guaranteed. Turkey joined Germany very soon after the outbreak of war in 1914; and there followed the invasion of Iraq by an expeditionary force sent from India. After many reverses and a scandalous breakdown in the medical arrangements, Iraq was conquered by British and British-Indian troops; and then there ensued a regime in Iraq which lasted some years, Great Britain receiving a League of Nations' mandate which was in force until the treaty which made Iraq an independent power under a king drawn from the Hashemite family of the Sharifs of Mecca.

Earlier, very different ideas prevailed. In Petrie's life of Austen Chamberlain[93] we read:

> The Cabinet appointed, in the middle of March 1917, a small committee to deal with this question' (the future of Iraq). . . . The conclusions of this body were that the territory roughly corresponding to the Basra *vilayet* should be incorporated in the British Empire, and should be directly and openly administered as such, while in the Baghdad *vilayet* British influence should be exercised through a Resident working behind an Arab façade, and as far as possible with Arab officials, but supplied with such British officers as might be necessary for good government. . . . It would be more conveniently administered by the Foreign Office than by India, though the Resident at Bushire would continue to control both shores of the Persian Gulf.

These ambitious ideas were abandoned and, as is well known, Churchill, advised by T. E. Lawrence, worked out the different solution actually adopted in Iraq in 1922. What is not so well known is that, though Churchill was minister and Lawrence adviser, Lloyd George asked Lawrence whom he would like appointed as his chief, and Lawrence chose Churchill. Liddell Hart[94] had this direct from Lloyd George.

This period in Iraq, first of military government and later of mandate, was one of great difficulty. Development had to start almost from scratch; the Turkish Civil Service had fled or declined cooperation, and India had to supply personnel under almost every head. Numbers of Indian Civil Servants, Indian Police and other officials were seconded for service in Iraq. The Political Service had comparatively few officers who could be spared, but mention must be made of two who were outstanding: Cox and his assistant, Wilson. Both had served in the Gulf as military political officers for long periods; both became High Commissioners in Iraq, Wilson replacing Cox when the latter was sent as Minister to Persia. Cox was probably the most distinguished of all political officers in this century. Wilson was the scribe of the adventure: when we were 'getting out of Iraq', and there was little official recognition of what our men had done, Wilson single-handed[95] set out to make a complete record of their achievement. Shakespeare and Leachman were other outstanding officers who met an early death; Howell and Wingate are still flourishing. Philby* whose career in Iraq and Saudi Arabia was an extraordinary one, was a Punjab Indian Civil Service officer, not a political.

What the Iraq expedition, and later the mandate, illustrated, was how our service, aided–for its numbers were always minute–from other services in India, could be turned to at short notice, to establish indirect rule in new and unexpected places.† Though control was from London, not from India, and the political officers mentioned were seconded, India and its Political Service supplied the tradition which was followed during the Iraq mandate.

We now turn to another Muslim region where the political undertook new tasks: the Kabul Legation.

* H. St. J. B. Philby (1885–1960). I.C.S., Punjab, 1908. Seconded to Iraq administration, 1965. Retired from I.C.S., 1925. Chief British representative, Transjordan, 1921–4. Explorer and author. Father of 'Kim' Philby, the spy.

† During World War II, nine political officers and two sloops of the R.N. kept the Gulf quiet–which shows of what the personal influence of a few individuals was capable.

# CHAPTER 31

# Afghanistan

WE have seen how Salisbury insistently pressed for the establishment of a proper diplomatic mission, staffed by British officers, in Kabul, and how the Government of India and the Government of Afghanistan, agreeing in this if in little else, opposed this project. After the tragic experiences of the first two Afghan wars, there was no diplomatic mission either in Kabul or in London, though a comparatively lowly Indian official lived in Kabul and sent out such information as he could pick up – neither in quality nor in quantity did it seem usually to amount to much.

By 1919 things had changed. King Amanullah, though his lamentable and unjustified attack on India's frontier defences failed, was – wisely – treated with generosity in the peace-treaty. He pressed above all, and successfully, for complete independence, i.e. the right to establish diplomatic relations with countries other than Great Britain, with whom alone his predecessors had had them. Afghanistan opened missions in Paris, Berlin, Moscow, Rome, Tehran, Ankara and later London; and it was only natural that, along with the Afghan legation in London, the British, not the Indian Government should open one in Kabul.

This was done, and no pains spared to house it in some degree of splendour. Curzon, who, as Foreign Secretary, had by no means lost his old interest in Indian frontier affairs, was anxious that our Kabul legation should be the finest building in Central Asia. A large area was laid out, containing, in an attractive garden, houses for the Minister and his staff. (His staff consisted of a counsellor and a secretary, always drawn from the Indian Political Service, and a military attaché from the Indian army.) Opinions vary as to the quality of the architecture; more than one Minister has been known to inveigh against the legation as a horror. Gould's *Jewel in the Lotus* and Mayne's *Narrow Smile* give a good account of life there.

Amanullah, having secured a free hand through 'independence' set out to modernise his country. He meant well, but he was a weak man and an ass. It was not long before his campaign of modernisation caused great discontent, leading to the Khost rebellion of 1924. Though this was suppressed, conditions in the country were far from stable when Anamullah set off, in December 1927, for a European tour of seven months' duration. He arrived back in Kabul on 1 July 1928, with wind in the head, an empty treasury, and a dissatisfied army. By the end of September, a well-known brigand, one Habibullah Khan, nicknamed Bachha-i-Saqao (son of the water-carrier), a Tajik highwayman who had been eighteen months in the Afghan army and later a tea-seller in Peshawar, rose against the government in the neighbourhood of Kabul. This movement soon subsided, but the formidable tribe of the Shinwaris rose on 14 November and had soon invested Jalalabad. The Mohmand tribe's attitude was also threatening. The Soviet and Turkish Ambassadors urged the King to fight to the end; Humphrys* the British Minister, urged conciliation in an interview with the King on 24 November 1928. The latter seems to have taken the advice to heart, and sent the Foreign Minister to reason with the rebels. But by 10 December Bachha-i-Saqao and his men reappeared on the scene, seized a fort and moved on Kabul. On 14 December he passed the British Legation, where the gates were shut and he was warned against attacking any of the foreign missions. For some days there was heavy fighting round the British Legation which was cut off from the outside world and was under heavy fire from both parties. The military attaché's house was burnt down, and on 23 December the women and children were taken by night to the aerodrome and flown out to Peshawar. On 14 January 1929, when the royal forces surrendered, Bachha-i-Saqao had control of the aerodrome and Amanullah abdicated in favour of his brother, Inayatullah, and fled to Kandahar. Inayatullah lasted only three days, and was then with his party flown out in British planes to Peshawar. Humphrys, the British Minister, assisted by Kuli Khan, a very able Pathan extra assistant commissioner, arranged for a cease-fire to enable the British planes to perform this mission. They also flew out the staffs of the various other diplomatic missions, Humphrys being the last to leave, with the legation's flag. This evacuation was a distinct diplomatic success; British prestige probably stood higher than it had for many a year.

Bachha-i-Saqao was not recognized by us, nor was Nadir Khan, a collateral of Amanullah who arrived from France to restore Amanullah, it was stated: in fact, to seize the throne for himself. A policy of neutrality was adopted, which operated strangely but successfully; though Afghan-

* Lt.-Col. Sir Francis Humphrys (b. 1879), G.C.M.G., G.C.V.O., K.B.E., C.I.E.; Military Political, 1904. Served mostly in North-West Frontier Province; son-in-law of Sir Harold Deane, its first Chief Commissioner. Minister, Kabul, 1922–9; High Commissioner, Iraq, 1929–32.

istan and the outer world believed that we were secretly supporting Nadir Khan, this was not so. He gained the throne by his own and his brothers' strong arms, and the assistance of the Wazir and Mahsud tribes, from the Indian side of the frontier, whom he had, incidentally, to pay by permission to loot Kabul. Till Nadir entered Kabul, in October 1929, there was a vacuum; and nothing was done in Britain or India to fill it.

Thereafter, the present dynasty has held the throne. H.M. King Nadir Shah (to give him the new name which he adopted on succession) ruled with wisdom till his lamentable assassination in 1933. He was succeeded by his young son, H.M. King Zahir Shah, who has ruled ever since, ably assisted by his numerous uncles who have shown a degree of loyalty and unity all too rare in the history of this country.

Few but distinguished have been the British representatives in Kabul since the establishment of normal diplomatic relations. The third Afghan war was followed by the Treaty of Rawalpindi, in 1919, which was, after some delay, followed by a mission under Dobbs,* the Foreign Secretary, in January, 1921. After long drawn out negotiations, a treaty was signed, and Humphrys was appointed minister and arrived in 1922, serving there until 1929. He was followed by Maconochie,† an outstandingly able frontier officer, who served until succeeded by Fraser-Tytler‡ in 1935. Fraser-Tytler's great claim to record in the story of Kabul is his work *Afghanistan, a study of political developments in Central Asia*.

He was replaced in 1941 by Wylie who was sent to Kabul to take a strong line over the evacuation of Germans and other aliens from Afghanistan. He, in turn, was followed by Squire§ whose six years of tenure saw both the winding up of our service, and the raising of the post from legation to embassy.

* Sir Henry Dobbs (1871–1934), G.B.E., K.C.S.I., K.C.M.G.; I.C.S., North-West Provinces, 1892. Political, 1899. Served in Persia and Iraq and Afghanistan. High Commissioner, Iraq, 1923–9.

† Sir Richard Maconochie (b. 1885).

‡ Sir Kerr Fraser-Tytler (1886–1963), K.B.E., C.M.G., M.C., Indian Army, 1910. Military Political, 1921. Secretary, Kabul, 1923–5; Counsellor, Kabul, 1930–2; Minister, Kabul, 1935–41. Writing of Maconochie, he said: 'To him I owe ... the stimulus during much of my service of working with one of the clearest and most acute minds that ever tackled the problems of Asia.'

§ Sir Giles Squire (1894–1959), K.B.E., C.I.E. British Army 1914–19; I.C.S. Central Provinces, 1920; Political, 1924; Minister 1943–8 and Ambassador, 1948–1949 to Afghanistan.

CHAPTER 32

# The Himalayan Frontier: Gilgit, Kashgar, Nepal, Assam, Sikkim, Bhutan

D URING the whole long period when our service acted as guardians
of the glacis of India, its eyes were turned to the west. True, there
had been political agents in such spots as Penang, Mauritius and Canton;
Warren Hastings had sent George Bogle on a mission to Tibet in 1774;
someone looked after the Chinese frontier with the Shan States after the
acquisition of Burma. But Afghanistan, Persia and the Gulf–those were
the main points of interest and of danger. It was not till after Partition,
in 1947, that the relations of China with India and with Pakistan became
of vital importance.

It was partly the height and breadth of the Himalayas and adjoining
ranges, partly the decadence of China, followed by the fall of the Manchu
dynasty, which led to a certain neglect of this frontier. There were
always officers conscious that the Karakorum had been crossed by a
Chinese army and could be crossed again: aware of the problems raised
by the episode of Yakub Beg's quick rise and fall from power in Chinese
Turkestan; but the service had posts only in Gilgit, Kashgar, Katmandu,
Gangtok (Sikkim) and Gyangtse. These posts would seem to have been
adequate, as in fact nothing very much did happen on this northern
frontier until the post-1947 period, except for Tibet.

In a much earlier period, the first half of the nineteenth century, when
fear of Russia was perhaps at its height, the mountain approaches to
India were by no means neglected. It was felt, e.g. by Ellenborough* in
1829, that the Russians were likely eventually to invade India, and would
come either via Persia, Herat and Kabul or by Turkestan, up the Oxus
and across the difficult passes of the Hindu Kush, via Bamiyan and
Kabul. Later, Alexander Burnes seems to have felt that the Russians
would more probably move east, behind the Hindu Kush, Pamirs and
Himalayas, and would then strike towards Kashmir, behind Chitral
(which he regarded as a key position) and Gilgit, even passing through
Sinkiang to infiltrate Tibet. Wild though such a project sounds if we

* Lord Ellenborough (1790–1871). Governor-General, 1841–4. Created First
Earl, 1844.

think in terms of large European armies, it was very far from utopian if we think rather in terms of a cavalry raid into and through Chitral. We were late in occupying the Malakand and Gilgit agencies, and very thin upon the ground when we did so. Early on, very little was known of this area, and perhaps even less of the tracts further east.

Professor H. W. C. Davis, in his classic *The Great Game in Asia* (1800–1844) shows how numerous and on the whole how successful the attempts were to survey and otherwise report on this vast area, which we may call the Himalayan frontier. He is inclined to ignore the existence of the Indian Political Service and to call the various travellers who were employed as spies 'political agents' which, in our modern sense of the term, they mostly were not. What a list he gives us! Bogle, whose mission to Tibet in 1774–5 was wholly commercial; Jonas Hanway; George Forster (1783); Mehdi Ali Kahn; Mohan Lal; the brothers Alexander and James Burnes; Mir Izzet Ullah; Moorcroft; Talamash; the three Gerard brothers; John Wood; Percival Lord; Eldred and Henry Pottinger; John McNeill; Claud Wade; Christie; Morier; Fraser; Vigne; Macnaghten; D'Arcy Todd; Stoddart and Conolly, who died miserably in a Bokhara goal.*

Some of these men were soldiers: some even identifiably 'politicals'. Several were surveyors or doctors (human or animal), several half-castes:† many were low-paid Indian subordinates, known often in the records by initials only, but brilliant and faithful intelligent agents. Davis sums up the list:

> They were on the whole an ill-fated race; for even the most successful of them–Sir John Malcolm and Sir Henry Pottinger–hardly attained to positions worthy of their great merits and still greater public spirit. For the majority there were inadequate rewards if they succeeded, while disgrace was certain if they committed any slip. But the Government of India had no servants more resourceful or more gallant than the best politicals of this period.

In the mountains behind Peshawar the frontier takes a turn and, near the roof of the world, as the Pamirs have been called, runs east-west instead of north-south. At the same point, the neighbour ceases to be Persia or Afghanistan and becomes China. In this tremendous tangle of

---

* There is a good account of this and other events in nineteenth-century Bokhara in Fitzroy Maclean's *A Person from England*.

† Among fictional characters, we must not forget Rudyard Kipling's 'Kim' who, incidentally, was not a half-caste but a 'poor white'.

mountains, in healthy and beautiful country just under 5,000 ft. high, lies Gilgit: a political agency which looks on to Chitral and the North-West Frontier Province on the one hand, Kashmir on the other, while it straddles the route to Sinkiang or Chinese Turkestan.

One of the most popular postings with officers who did not mind a certain remoteness, Gilgit was an agency *sui generis*, technically part of Kashmir State. The political agent was subordinated to the resident in Kashmir; Hunza and Nagar, states in political relations with the political agent, only acknowledged a vague suzerainty of Kashmir over them. They paid a small tribute in gold or grain to Kashmir. After Partition, the Agency made haste to break away and join Pakistan. Since its population is nearly 100 per cent Muslim, this reaction to Partition was not surprising, though its handling by the two British army officers in charge of the small garrison is a remarkable story. A certain suzerainty over Hunza was also exercised by China, with whom Hunza and Nagar's relations are now, in 1970, excellent. China has recently withdrawn her Hunza frontier in response to a long-standing claim by that state which has acquired some good grazing lands and a valuable salt mine.

Gilgit, originally a *wazirat* of Kashmir, came into prominence at a time, in the last century, when fear of Russian aggression was acute, and the loyalty of the Kashmir darbar was not always taken for granted. Durand's* *Making of a Frontier* is a fascinating account of the occupation of this wild country in 1889, the year in which the agency was established. Apart from Hunza and Nagar, the agency controlled the outlying districts or petty states of Ashkuman, Yasin and Ghizar, the little republic of Chillas and other bits of territory. The country soon became, and remained, peaceful; its importance lay in its being on the western of the two routes–the other goes through Ladakh and the Karakorum–to Sinkiang from the Punjab.

The agency was noted for two things–the complexity of its languages (usually classed together under the name Dard, though Shin is that most spoken) and the ubiquity of its polo grounds. Lorimer† and his wife, after retirement, devoted themselves to the study of numerous languages and dialects in Gilgit. Polo, as in Chitral, is the national sport. The story is told of a political agent who, finding himself on tour one day at a village which lacked the normal amenity of a polo ground, gave orders for one

* Lt.-Col. Algernon Durand (1854–1923), C.B., C.I.E. British Agent at Gilgit, 1889–93. Military Secretary to the Viceroy 1894–9. His brother was Sir Mortimer Durand of the 'Durand Line'.

† Lt.-Col. D. L. R. Lorimer, C.I.E., brother of the author of the *Gazetteer of the Persian Gulf*, also a political officer.

to be laid out at once. This was done; but there were complaints when it transpired that he had strayed over the border and was in another agency, in the state of Chitral. (Or was it *vice versa*?) *Se non è vero, è ben trovato.*

Every two or three years there would turn up from Srinagar in Gilgit a colleague of the Political Agent bound for Kashgar, where he was to be Consul General, or returning to Srinagar from Kashgar after filling this post. It was a six weeks' ride: in a bad time of the year it could be a hard ride with threats of frostbite. It was normally, however, less strenuous than the alternative route through eastern Kashmir via Ladakh and the Karakorum pass. But everything in Gilgit was large-scale. The glaciers are numerous and enormous, and probably unrivalled, a glacier ice-bed extending for about ninety miles. The mountains behind Hunza and Nagar average above 20,000 feet, and never fall below 15,000 feet.

One of the strangest of our outposts was the consulate general at Kashgar, in Sinkiang or Chinese Turkestan. This post, founded late in the nineteenth century, was attractive climatically and also socially when politics were favourable. The consular district was large, and included towns—Kashgar, Yarkand and Khotan being the principal ones—where a number of Indian traders had homes. 'Mixed' trials, in which one party was British and the other Chinese, included the consul general who had to sit alongside the Chinese judge. These enterprising traders were almost exclusively Hindus from the town of Shikarpur, a subdivision of Sukkur district in Sind on the way to Quetta. They would go to Sinkiang and also to Bokhara in Russian Turkestan, for some years at a time, leaving their wives and families behind. In early days, there was always a British I.C.S. officer as Assistant Commissioner at Shikarpur; and these traders looked to him to see that their families came to no harm. They were a rich, fair, handsome caste and laid great weight on fair complexions in their children. After three or four years in Sinkiang, they would return to find a number of olive branches added to their families. They raised no objections to this, but hoped that the Assistant Commissioner had intervened if any dark-skinned lovers presented themselves. Their Penelopes were not expected to be wholly faithful to these modern Odysseuses; and the richest or handsomest of the wives was expected to be the particular care of the British official.

When, about the end of the nineteenth century, Shikarpur lost its importance and was demoted from a subdivision, so that it no longer had a resident Assistant Commissioner, there was consternation among the Sinkiang traders. But what had gone had gone; and there was normally no remedy.

Normally, but not invariably. On at least one occasion in the 1930s a handsome, blond British subaltern was travelling by train to Quetta. The train stopped at Shikarpur, and a local Hindu, on behalf of an absent merchant's wife, whispered to the officer's servant that, if the officer in question could see his way to break his journey till the next train, he would be greatly welcomed and helped to renew an old tradition. The invitation was passed on and accepted.

Kashgar, we have said, was attractive when politics allowed. This depended on world-wide developments: sometimes Chinese influence was supreme, sometimes Russian; sometimes that of local war lords (like the tyrant General Ma, 'self-styled King of Kashgar', whose fall in the 1920s Skrine describes in his *Chinese Central Asia*. Skrine was fortunate in his timing. 1922 was a period when a British official with a taste for exploration could travel freely and add to our knowledge of these remote mountains. Peter Fleming, in the early thirties, accompanied for part of the way by Ella Maillart, made the grim overland journey to India from Peking by this route. His *News from Tartary* and her *Turkestan Solo* are fine records of a remarkable journey.

At other times (as now), politics would make a visit to Sinkiang impossible, or nearly so, to Western geographers. But the Kashgar post (though occasionally staffed by a member of the Chinese Consular Service instead of from our Service) was always kept filled, sometimes with a vice-consul as well as a consul general. Even when, as happened to Thomson Glover,* the building was under sporadic fire for a matter of weeks (the consul general's wife being wounded), the flag was kept flying literally and metaphorically.

Perhaps the most extraordinary Central Asian episode in which our service was concerned was the mission on which Bailey† was sent in 1918. This colourful character was serving in south Persia in March, 1918, when he received orders to lead a mission of two officers, a small party of the guides and a small civil staff to Chinese Turkestan. The reason was that, at the Russian Revolution, the line of the eastern front, which had stretched from the White Sea to the Persian Gulf, collapsed. It had

---

* Lt.-Col. J. W. Thomson Glover (1887–1943), C.B.E. Commissioned, 1906; Military Political, 1914; Consul General, Kashgar, 1933; Resident, Kashmir, 1937; retired 1940.

† Lt.-Col. F. M. Bailey (1882–1967), C.I.E. Indian army, 1901; Tibet expedition, 1903–4; Political, 1905; Trade agent Gyantse 1905–9; explored widely in Tibet; Central Asian Mission, 1918–20; Political officer, Sikkim 1921–8; Resident in Kashmir 1932–3. Minister to Nepal 1935–8. King's messenger, S. America 1942–3.

previously, with Russian troops in the north and British in the south, successfully staved off German infiltration towards India through Persia and Afghanistan.

No one knew precisely who controlled what in central Asia. Very large numbers of German and Austrian prisoners, released by the Russians in November 1917, were wandering in search of work and food, and were a potential danger to the allied cause. Nothing was known of the state of affairs in Russian Central Asia, but it was rightly guessed to be chaotic. Bailey, therefore, proceeded to Kashgar where Macartney,* the British Consul General, was about to retire. He had been there for the astonishing period of twenty-eight years. Bailey pushed on in August 1918 to Tashkent where he found an American Consul General functioning, but a Bolshevik government. He and his American colleague had several interviews with Damagatsky, the Foreign Commissar, but in October 1918 Bailey found it necessary to go into hiding. He had first, however, made contact with one Manditch, a Serbian lieutenant who had deserted from the Austrian army to the Russians and now had a high post in the Bolshevik military intelligence organisation. Manditch's sympathies were wholly anti-Bolshevik, and it was he who warned Bailey to go underground. In November 1918 Bailey moved to the foot-hills, returning in the spring of 1919 to Tashkent. There was a price on his head, but he evaded capture by disguise, in succession as a Galician, Lett and Rumanian prisoner, and finally as an Albanian–a nationality of which no representative was likely to turn up.

At this stage it was clear that no purpose would be served by his remaining in Tashkent, so with the aid of Manditch he was recruited into the Bolshevik counter-espionage service. One of his duties was to find Colonel Bailey; another, to establish relations with Bokhara, a State whose status in Russia was surprisingly like that of Indian States in India. The Russians had sent fifteen agents there to see what was going on. (There was a story that British officers were organizing the Bokharan army–actually, there were two Indian sepoys who later joined Bailey and escaped with him.) All these fifteen agents were believed to have been strangled by the Bokharan secret service, so volunteers were hard to come by. Bailey, however, volunteered, and in October 1919 he moved to Bokhara where he disclosed his real identity to the Bokharans and

* Sir George Macartney (1867–1945), K.C.I.E. His father was secretary to the Chinese Legation in London and a K.C.M.G.; his mother, Chinese. Never formally a member of the Political Service, he served the Government of India in Kashgar from 1890. His position was regularized in 1908 as Consul; in 1910, as Consul General.

eventually, in December 1919, with seventeen companions, made the long ride across the Persian frontier to Meshed, where he arrived in January 1920.

When we turn to Nepal, the position is, technically, much simpler. It is now, in 1970, an independent country with diplomatic representatives in several countries, and its status, it would claim, has always been such. However, at an earlier period, there is no doubt that its status was, *de facto*, much nearer that of an Indian State. The British diplomatic representative (drawn always, until 1947, from the Indian Political Service) was called resident from 1816 to 1920, envoy from 1920 to 1934, minister from 1934 to 1947, and ambassador from 1947 up to the present.

Before World War II, no other country had a permanent mission there, and Nepal's mission in London was not established until 1934.

Nepal, a country rather over 500 miles long and 100 miles wide, has records which date back to A.D. 1324. The northern part consists mainly of high mountains, including Everest, with a few fertile valleys; the southern part or *terai* is a fever-ridden plain adjoining India. The population is over six million, partly Hindu and partly Buddhist. The Gurkhas, its best known component, are a stocky race descended from Rajputs who were driven out of India by the Muslims. For more than a hundred years they have supplied very good recruits for the Indian army and still do, others being, since Partition, supplied direct to the British army.

In 1791, the Gurkhas made a commercial treaty with the British, having shortly before invaded Tibet and, surprisingly, been soundly beaten in a Chinese counter-offensive. Another commercial treaty was ratified in 1792, and yet another in 1801, when a resident was sent to Katmandu, the capital, only to be withdrawn in 1803. In 1814, Britain declared war on Nepal and an inconclusive campaign ended in 1816 with the treaty of Segauli, by which Nepal relinquished much of her newly-acquired territory and agreed to the establishment of a British mission in Katmandu, the capital.

In 1845, Jang Bahadur, the strong man of Nepal, nephew of the king, killed his uncle, massacred his enemies and ruled admirably till his death in 1872. He visited England in 1850, and helped Britain in the Mutiny of 1857, in gratitude for which some territory was returned.

In 1923, a new treaty with Great Britain replaced the 1816 treaty and recognized the complete independence of Nepal. No doubt that was largely in recognition of the great help given to the Allies in World War I. In both wars, apart from the large Nepalese recruitment to the Indian army, the Nepalese army lent a contingent for internal security duties, for which they were particularly well adapted, in India.

Thus relations were, in practice, not very different from those with the larger Indian States, such as Hyderabad and Gwalior, save for two things. The first was the complete isolation of Nepal. As in Tibet, there was an effective ban on visits by Europeans to Nepal. The British minister and his very small diplomatic staff could invite their own personal friends as guests; tourists were completely forbidden entry.

The other peculiar feature in Nepal was the arrangement that, while the king, or His Majesty the Maharajadhiraj, to give him his Nepalese title, was in theory a despot, in practice he was quite powerless, the absolute ruler being the prime minister, or His Highness the Maharaja, as his title was.* This 'mayor of the palace' came from a remarkable family, the Ranas, who succeeded from brother to brother and produced a number of able rulers. Wholly unexpectedly, this peculiar but long-standing system was put an end to, doubtless at Indian instigation, soon after Partition in 1947, and an uneasy semi-democratic system has since held the field, with many anxious glances to Peking on the one side and Delhi on the other.

While the royal family followed the normal rule of succession by primo-geniture, succcession in the prime minister's family followed a complicated course similar to that which obtained in the other end of India, in Cochin. This is how the Nepal succession is described by Falconer† in a privately printed note:

> This is a complicated affair created by Jang Bahadur. Descent is through the eldest legitimate agnate, in order of priority of birth from one brother to another, or one cousin to another, until all survivors of a generation have succeeded in turn. This succession is not from father to son nor necessarily to the eldest son of the eldest of a line of brothers. Jang Bahadur's object in devising this plan of succession was to ensure that the Government of Nepal should never be in the hands of an immature member of the family. But what he did not foresee is that age alone is not a qualification for office, nor the expansion of the number of eligibles in each succeeding generation, so close together in that age that they are jealously tumbling over one another, and that none would eventually attain office in the ordinary way until well over 60 years of age.

* This dates from the time of Jang Bahadur.

† Lt.-Col. Sir George Falconer (b. 1894), K.B.E., C.I.E. Military Political, 1923; Minister to Nepal, 1944–7; Ambassador, 1947–51

A convention existed that an officer selected (invariably, as we have seen, from our service up to 1947) for the post of minister to Nepal should retire on the completion of his five years' tenure of the post. In other words, since the emoluments of the post were roughly equal to those of a second-class residency he was debarred from promotion to a first-class residency, which the holder of a second-class residency in India was not.

Though the same convention obtained in Kabul, this caused no difficulty as the emoluments there were roughly equal to those of a first-class resident. One could not, therefore, post to Nepal officers of outstanding talent who expected further promotion.

A Himalayan area, now of considerable importance to India, with which however our service had no dealings, was that lying north of Assam and now called the North-East Frontier Agency. This large area, so lately as in the mid-1930s unadministered and little known, became front-page news through the Japanese invasion of Burma and India, and remained so when China and India fell out more recently. Writing as late as 1932, Sir George Dunbar in *Frontiers*, a book of memoirs, shows how limited was the contact which Indian army officers seconded to the military police battalion known as the Assam Rifles, had with the Abors, Daflas, Hill Miris, Akas, Pasis and similar tribes. Baron C. von Führer-Haimendorf, a serious anthropologist writing in a light vein, gives, in *The Naked Nagas*, a charming account of a people whose differences with the post-Partition Government of India have been grave and internationally noticed. The 1946 issue of the list of the Indian Political Service shows the Governor of Assam as also Agent to the Governor-General (*cf.* the Governor of the North-West Frontier Province), and assisted by six political officers only one of whom, Mainprice, belonged to our service. This was in keeping with the 'forward policy' adopted just before, during and after World War II in these parts. But it must be noted that activities in the North-East Frontier Agency do not concern our service.

The remaining Himalayan areas for which our service was responsible were Sikkim, Tibet and Bhutan. We established an agency in Sikkim many years ago, and though for some reason the holder of this post was called a political officer and not a resident, his work was not markedly different from that of any second-class resident in India. The status of Sikkim was not very closely defined, still less was that of Bhutan, a much larger but very backward and remote state. Bhutan's status would approach nearer to that of some of the Persian Gulf Shaikhdoms; but no one cared, as for scores of years little if anything happened. Since 1947, a great deal has happened and the China-India quarrel has brought these states into the foreground. But that is another story.

A treaty with Sikkim in 1817 led to no important results, but that of 1861 certainly did. Sikkim, though small and of minor importance as a State, was the doorway to Tibet. Sikkim had close political relations with Tibet (in an outlying province of which the Raja of Sikkim spent much of the year), as did Bhutan also. Bhutan was at war with Britain in 1865, and it was quite hard fought. For a long period approaches to Tibet were made through these two States, though some people thought the converse preferable. However, though many, including the Chinese, were against the opening up of Tibet, trade with Tibet, especially in tea, was optimistically thought to be easily established. Indeed, several Chambers of Commerce in England petitioned Government to take action to enable them to engage in this trade.

# CHAPTER 33

## The Himalayan Frontier (*continued*): Tibet

THE problem of Tibet can be summed up in the question: Was China's relationship with Tibet one of sovereignty or one of suzerainty? Now, as is well known, China's attitude to foreign countries has always been that they are either outer barbarians or tributaries of China. Limitrophe countries such as Burma and Indo-China she seems to have regarded as tributary; Tibet rather as an integral part of China. Sikkim and Bhutan might fall in either category. China never considered nationality or sovereignty in the same way as Western countries, and we have by no means heard the end of this problem.

It has been fully discussed by three writers, of whom T. T. Li (Li Tien-tseng) in *The historical status of Tibet* broadly follows the Chinese view; H. E. Richardson\* in *A Short History of Tibet*, the Tibetan view; while Alastair Lamb in *Britain and Chinese Central Asia* adopts an intermediate one.

In considering the relations which our service maintained with Sikkim, Bhutan and Tibet, it seems necessary to stress the wide difference between them and the countries in the Muslim world which we have been discussing: a difference due to religion. These three countries were not only overwhelmingly Buddhist by religion but, at least in the case of Tibet, religious to a degree which affected all their attitudes to the outer world.

In early years, Tibet was ruled by kings whose close relationship to the Chinese Emperor (beginning in the seventh century A.D. and discussed at length in the books just mentioned), though its exact nature is disputed, was at least partly a religious one. Later, in the seventeenth century, Tibet became a theocracy as complete as Mount Athos, governed by a priest-ruler, the Dalai Lama. By the middle of the eighteenth century he had supplanted the king. Not only was he, until the recent Chinese invasion, effectively the ruler of Tibet: he was regarded by many Buddhists outside Tibet as a religious leader or pope. Apart from Sikkim and Bhutan (Buddhist states with close relations to their neighbour, Tibet)

---

\* H. E. Richardson (b. 1905), C.I.E., O.B.E.; I.C.S., 1930, Bengal. Political, 1934. In charge of the Mission – first British, later Indian – to Lhasa, 1936–40. and 1946–50.

the Dalai Lama was regarded with the greatest reverence in areas so varied as Outer Mongolia, the Indian borderland and various regions of western China.

Tibetan belief was that, when the Dalai Lama died, he was forthwith reincarnated in a child born about that time and recognized by certain traditional signs and omens. But all power was exercised by a regent until the child came of age: which, for several generations before the 13th Dalai Lama came of age in 1895, he failed to do. The 8th Dalai Lama died in 1804, aged forty, the 9th to the 12th, inclusive, died young before attaining majority. All, it is believed, were assassinated.

The Panchen Lama, similarly an incarnate being, had no constitutional status, though very influential over his own area, and often mixed up in political intrigue. It was he who welcomed the first British envoy, George Bogle, sent on a commercial mission by Warren Hastings in 1774.

The foreign policy of Tibet, supported enthusiastically by monks (a huge proportion of the people) and laity alike, can be very shortly summed up. They were against foreign powers. The three whom they knew were China, Britain and Russia; they wanted no contact, save the meagre traditional commerce, with the outer world, since, they felt, it would eventually lead to the weakening of their religion. Britain and Russia they could hold off – extremely few citizens of either power visited Tibet from the date, at about the end of the eighteenth century, when contacts began. China was not so easy; though Tibetans usually did all that was possible to keep their country free from any interference by China, China had certain privileges. At the lowest, Tibet was required to receive a resident Chinese official known as the Amban at Lhasa, their capital. His status was surprisingly like that of a resident in an Indian state, though residents were seldom so weak and ineffective as he often was. (The Chinese sent their less well regarded officials to Lhasa, which was regarded as a penal posting.) The Tibetans usually succeeded in inhibiting any action which he contemplated, and he often cuts a rather ridiculous figure in history. But he was there, with a small staff; and not all Tibetans rated his position so low. The Panchen Lama, writing in 1775 to Warren Hastings, says:

> As this country is under the absolute Sovereignty of the Emperor of China, who maintains an active and unrelaxed control over all its affairs, and as the forming of any connection or friendship with foreign powers is contrary to his pleasure, it will frequently be out of my power to despatch any messengers to you.[96]

While the extreme Tibetan view regarded the Amban as a mere diplomatist, watching over an ill-defined and grudgingly admitted suzerainty, the Chinese regarded themselves as exercising full sovereignty, and he was to them perhaps analogous to the Governors-General in the British Dominions before they acquired dominion status. The Chinese did not recognize any right, for example, for the Dalai Lama to correspond with foreign powers or issue passports to foreigners. No agreement was, in their eyes, valid unless countersigned by the Amban. They were always ready to assert their claims, and they would have been more successful had they not been so unfortunate as to have varied trouble at home or on other frontiers from the mid-nineteenth century up to the other day. Encroachment by Russia; several unsuccessful wars—with Britain and Japan; the Boxer and other rebellions; the fall of the Manchu dynasty, and the early collapse into a regime of war-lords of the republic which followed it—all these troubles left China with little power and less inclination to adopt a forward policy towards Tibet.

In the nineteenth century the Government of India began to be seriously concerned with Tibet. Numerous visits to the Tibetan border by British or Indian officials took place from time to time about the '70s, aimed at encouraging trade. Cooper, a businessman, Houghton, the Commissioner for Cooch Behar, and various Indian assistants paid such visits. In 1876, the Chefoo Convention between Britain and China provided that, once at least, a full British mission should visit Tibet. It was, however, not fully ratified till 1886, and no use was ever made of it. The British legation in Pekin was constantly if not enthusiastically in touch with the Chinese Government, attempting to secure passports which would be accepted in Tibet. In 1884, Macaulay, Finance Secretary to the Bengal Government, visited Sikkim and the Tibetan border, the Bengal Government and not the Government of India being responsible for relations with Tibet. Just as Afghanistan was the immediate concern of the Punjab Government until Curzon created the North-West Frontier Province in 1901, so Bengal was responsible to the Governor-General for relations with Tibet as well as Sikkim and Bhutan. Curzon described in 1901 a certain failure of the Bengal Government as 'one of the most eloquent results of handing over political functions to local governments who have no aptitudes, no taste, no experience and no men for the job'.[97] He resolved to take control of Anglo-Tibetan relations into his own hands.

Curzon had come out, two years earlier, with a reputation for being likely to favour a vigorous, not to say aggressive, foreign policy. He acted, however, with great circumspection over Tibet. He inherited several annoying but essentially petty disputes which had been pending since 1890.

The far from exigent terms of the Convention of 1890 and the Trade Regulations of 1893 were ignored (by Tibet). An illegal tariff continued to be levied on the trickle of trade entering Tibet from India. The boundary remained undemarcated. A situation had arisen – had, indeed, existed without showing any improvement for ten years – which the Government of India could not, without dereliction of its duty, tolerate any longer.[98]

Curzon intervened in August 1900, and sent a friendly letter to the Dalai Lama. It apparently did not reach him and was returned six months later. A second letter, curter in tone, was sent through a different intermediary in January, 1901; it, too, was returned. Curzon appears to have taken this incident of the letters as a personal insult; and after long correspondence with Whitehall, it was decided to send a political officer with an armed escort to insist on Tibetan soil that Tibet should discuss the matters in dispute.

These petty measures remained the excuse for the mission; but what in fact was alarming Curzon was the evidence that was accumulating of Russian activities in Tibet. The home government shared his anxiety though, on account of the South African and Russo-Japanese wars, storm clouds over Somaliland, a gradually growing aim at a diplomatic settlement with Russia and public opinion in England, they could not go all the way with the Viceroy.

Above all the activities of one Dorjieff, a Buryat Mongol who was a Russian national as well as being a Buddhist and a close intimate of the Dalai Lama, caused consternation. He was received in audience by the Emperor of Russia and stories flew around of secret Russo-Chinese and Russo-Tibetan treaties and of Russian supplies of weapons. When our mission eventually reached Lhasa, no Russians and no Russian armoury were found. Interest in Russia seemed to cease. Historians appear still divided on the importance of these Russian activities. Whoever is right, the Anglo-Russian agreement of 1907 put an end to the majority of them. So late as 1939, Younghusband* wrote:

* Lt.-Col. Sir Francis Younghusband (1862–1942), K.C.S.I., K.C.I.E. Commissioned, 1882. Much exploration in Central Asia, crossing the Muztagh range in 1886. Political, 1890. Mission to Lhasa 1903–4. Resident in Kashmir, 1906–9. Resigned early, at the age of forty-seven. After retirement wrote extensively, and founded the World Congress of Faiths.

The acting Russian Ambassador during the Great War told me that he was a Secretary in the Russian Foreign Office during my mission to Tibet and could assure me that the Russian Government were in no kind of communication with the Dalai Lama. What, he said, did happen was that the Dalai Lama's tutor, Dorjieff, through Rasputin, got into personal touch with the Tsar and Tsarina. There was an interchange of presents between the Tsar and the Dalai Lama. The Tsar seemed to acknowledge some kind of spiritual guidance from the Dalai Lama; and the latter thought he was under the political protection of the Tsar.

Although uncorroborated, this version of affairs may well be close to the truth.[99]

Whatever the principal motive of the British and Indian Governments was, a mission was sent to Tibet, in 1903, under Younghusband, with a military escort which eventually exceeded 8,000 men under the command of Brigadier-General J. R. L. Macdonald, R.E. The relations of these two officers, after an initial friendly period, could not have been worse. This was hushed up in contemporary blue books and memoirs, but is fully brought out by Peter Fleming in his *Bayonets to Lhasa*.

Curzon, meanwhile, had gone home on leave and his strong arm was not available to help Younghusband through. The Secretary of State, Brodrick,* whose relations with Curzon were as bad as could be, seems to have been suspicious of and unsympathetic to Younghusband.

Younghusband was a remarkable political officer who was badly treated by his masters. His mission failed to find anyone with whom to negotiate until they reached Lhasa, permission to go there having grudgingly been given by the home Government. They fought three engagements on the way, the Tibetans suffering severe casualties, the mission almost none. On arrival at Lhasa, they found that the Dalai Lama had fled;† for good measure, the Chinese Emperor deposed him. They concocted a Government with whom to deal, based on a Regent whom the Dalai Lama had

---

* St. John Brodrick (1856–1942), 9th Viscount and 1st Earl of Midleton. Secretary of State for India, 1903–5.

† Later, in 1910, the Dalai Lama fled again: this time from a Chinese attack, and to India where he was the guest of the Viceroy, Lord Minto. His stay was prolonged, and it was getting difficult to entertain him. Someone, however, suggested a newly received invention, the cinematograph. He was shown a documentary of agricultural improvements, after which the Viceroy asked, through an interpreter, what he thought of it. 'Most interesting.' After several such films, with reactions of this sort, the 1910 or so equivalent of a strip-tease was shown. 'And what did His Holiness think of *this* film?' 'Vastly auspicious', was the reply.

nominated (leaving his seal, for what that was worth), and surprisingly quickly, agreed on a treaty, known as the Lhasa Convention. Very much was due to Younghusband's firm and patient diplomacy; the position had looked hopeless a few weeks earlier. Once at Lhasa, he secured co-operation in a brilliant manner.

The home Government insisted on the omission of two clauses in this convention. One, technically a Separate Agreement, allowed the agent who would now be sent to Gyantse to visit Lhasa 'to consult with high Chinese or Tibetan officials on such commercial matters of importance as he has found impossible to settle at Gyantse'. (Curzon had, before the mission started, pressed strongly for a permanent agent in Lhasa, and the Cabinet had as strongly turned him down.) The other clause allowed the British to occupy the Chumbi Valley until the indemnity was paid, which was to take seventy-five years. These conditions, included in the Government of India's proposals to the home Government but not accepted by the latter, were not objected to by the Tibetans, and were essential if the mission were to prove of any use. It is arguable that H.M.G. were right in insisting on their omission, as they were at the time negotiating with Russia, and to send an agent to Lhasa (as the offending clause practially permitted) or to make such terms in regard to the indemnity as would involve many years of occupation would have been asking for trouble.

> ...in the early summer of 1904 while Younghusband was being besieged at Gyantse, Lansdowne was hinting to the Russians that he might be prepared to make some modifications in British claims as to the status of Tibet, which the Younghusband Mission could not fail to alter in practice if not in theory, in exchange for Russian acceptance of the principles of the recent Anglo-French agreement over Egypt.[100]

The tragedy was that the man on the spot was not kept sufficiently informed of developments in the much wider field of international diplomacy. Younghusband claimed that there was no time, before winter set in and raised the problem of feeding and otherwise supplying 8,000 troops, to negotiate a revised convention; and, disobeying orders, he executed one which the Tibetan Regent may or may not have been competent to sign, and which the Chinese Amban refused to countersign. Later, in 1906, China's adhesion to the convention was negotiated, with the result that Britain lost all the advantages gained by this costly* mission and China, the *tertius gaudens*, was the one power to gain from it.

* It cost £10,000,000; but of course the Indian, not the British, taxpayer paid.

Younghusband was let down very badly, but not before a curious episode occurred. 'Younghusband', wrote the Secretary of State for India, 'has got hold of someone near the King, and it will do him no good in this crisis.' It did, however; Brodrick failed in his intention to do down Younghusband in regard to honours. True he only got the K.C.I.E. while the King wanted him to have the K.C.S.I., a higher order. But the K.C.I.E. was at least the highest honour normally awarded to our service. The personal interest of King Edward VII was enlisted, not for the first or last time, in such matters.

In the years immediately following the Younghusband Mission the gains, implicit and explicit, of Curzon's Tibetan policy were further whittled away. Curzon had hoped to do away with the 'fiction' of Chinese suzerainty over Tibet; but in 1906, as the price for the Chinese adhesion to the Lhasa Convention, Chinese control over the administration of Tibet was reaffirmed and the British bound themselves not to interfere at all in the internal affairs of that country. The Anglo-Russian Convention relating to Persia, Afghanistan and Tibet of 1907 further tied British hands across the Himalayas. Even in the matter of the indemnity, the British felt obliged to make further concessions to China; and they agreed to its payment by the Chinese Government on behalf of Tibet, though they were able to insist that the actual transfer of funds should be made by the Tibetans to British representatives. This did not prevent the Chinese from representing themselves as the true friends of Tibet.

> Hence the most apparent result of the Younghusband Mission, which undermined the authority of the Dalai Lama, was to lay Tibet open to a reassertion of Chinese authority. This process began almost immediately after the withdrawal of Younghusband from Lhasa, when anti-Chinese risings in Eastern Tibet gave rise to strong and effective Chinese counter-measures. Under the energetic leadership of Chao Erh-feng the Chinese reduced Eastern Tibet, which they proceeded to incorporate into China proper; and in 1910 a Chinese army entered Lhasa.
>
> Tibet was saved from complete dismemberment as a group of Chinese provinces by the outbreak of the Revolution of 1911 and the collapse of the Manchu Dynasty. The outcome of the Revolution was the expulsion of the Chinese from Lhasa and from all of Tibet to a point between Chamdo and Batang.[101]

Thereafter, there was a tripartite conference at Simla in 1914 which ended in an agreement signed by the British and Tibetans but only initialled by the Chinese delegate, whose action in even initialling it was not approved by his Government. The Government of India always placed great store by this 1914 agreement, but foreign powers, including the U.S.A. which seems to have taken considerable interest in these matters followed the Chinese lead of not recognizing it.* The Government of India however

> considered that the Simla Conference not only cancelled the Anglo-Chinese agreement of 1906 and the Anglo-Russian agreement of 1907, but also the restrictions of the Trade Regulations of 1908; and after the First World War a number of British Missions visited Lhasa, culminating with the permanent removal of the place of residence of the British Trade Agent from Gyantse to Lhasa. The last British Trade Agent, H. E. Richardson, then in the service of the Indian Republic, left Tibet in 1950.[102]

Relations with Tibet, between the Younghusband Mission in 1904 and the demission of British power in 1947, were essentially on a personal level. The 13th Dalai Lama was a close friend of Bell,† who was the first of a line of politicals who visited, but theoretically were not permanently stationed in, Lhasa. He was followed notably by Gould and Richardson, whose relations to the Regency and, later, the 14th and present Dalai Lama remained close; more briefly, by Weir, Williamson and Hopkinson.

The Government of India were not over-worried by the theoretically strong position of China *vis-à-vis* Tibet provided that, in practice, the theocratic regime kept the country quiet and provided a complete buffer state. Towards the end, Gould and Richardson, whether based in theory on Sikkim or Gyantse, effectively provided an agent to the Tibetan authorities, visiting Lhasa for long periods. (A good picture of how the set-up appeared to an outsider is given in Heinrich Harrer's *Seven Years in Tibet*.)

* During World War II, the Indian Agency General in Washington was surprised to find that the State Department, and the maps current in America, regarded Tibet as under Chinese rule. When American pilots crashed over Tibet, however, they found that whatever the *de jure* position, they must deal with the Dalai Lama's government if they wanted action.

† Sir Charles Bell (1870–1945). I.C.S., Bengal, 1891. Later, Political. From 1904 onwards served in Tibet, Bhutan and Sikkim. Listed his recreations in *Who's Who* as: 'Long travels and short walks.'

CHAPTER 34

# Washington, Chungking, Pondicherry, Goa

IN Chapters 4 and 5 we mentioned briefly the most recently created political posts. There is not much more to be said about them. The necessity for the posts at Washington, D.C., and Chungking (China's wartime capital, which, after the defeat of Japan, moved back to Nanking and, later, to Peking) was self-evident. Bajpai's record in Washington has already been mentioned. To Chungking, Zafrullah Khan,* another former member of the executive council of the Governor-General, was sent as first Agent-General, in 1942. He was succeeded in September 1943 by Menon, of our service. The junior diplomatic staff in both of these posts was drawn mostly from our service, supplemented by Indian army officers (the author was first secretary at Washington from 1941–4; Richardson, who later specialized in Tibet, was first secretary at Chungking in 1942–3).

The Goa and Pondicherry posts were, for many years before 1936, the care of the Provincial governments concerned – Bombay and Madras. Placed on the political service cadre a few years only before Partition, they did not play a conspicuous role, save that it was a matter of some importance that the French administration in Pondicherry followed General de Gaulle and not the Vichy Government; and this was achieved by the Viceroy through the agency of our Consul General.

Goa, the quite large former Portuguese colony on the west coast, forming an enclave in Bombay, had two extremely small patches of outlying territory: Diu, an island two or three miles square off the coast of Kathiawar, and Daman, a slightly larger coastal area in Surat district, Bombay, with a separate inland enclave called Nagar Haveli.

Pondicherry, an enclave in the district of South Arcot, on the coast south of Madras, and the last survivor of the former French possessions in India, was architecturally perhaps the most handsome town in India. It was the seat of a Governor-General and controlled the few other French

---

* Sir Muhammad Zafrullah Kahn (b. 1893), K.C.S.I. Advocate. Member of council for Law and Commerce. After Partition, Foreign Minister of the Government of Pakistan, 1947–53. Thereafter, Judge of the International Court of Justice, The Hague.

possessions : the small settlement Chandernagore, inland in Bengal, and the even smaller ones of Mahé, Karikal and Yanaon, Mahé on the west and the two others on the east coast of the Province of Madras. All these territories were acquired by the Government of India after Partition, the French ones by negotiation, the Portuguese by force.

# CHAPTER 35

# Conclusion

WE have seen that the Service had three roles: diplomacy in the States, administration on the Frontier, and consular functions in limitrophe countries. These might all, more or less, be described as aspects of indirect rule. How well did the Service fulfil its task?

In the States, until the last few years when federation became an issue, there was in this century less scope for action than in the last one. The Residents resided; critics from British India would have said that this was all that they did. From the States, it will be remembered, came instead complaints that they interfered too much, not too little. On the whole, the balance was held fairly, and the Service need have nothing to be ashamed of in its handling of the routine problems of diplomacy with the States.

The one great problem in this century was the attempt to organize a federal system, and after its failure, to release the States with honour from their obligations to the British Crown. That the federal scheme failed utterly was not the fault of the Service. The whole business was taken out of the hands of the men on the spot, and handled at a higher level. Many officers have thought that steady, quiet persuasion by Residents and Politial Agents would have been more successful. It seems doubtful; federation was doomed from soon after the 'first, fine careless rapture' at the Round-Table conference.

As for the Frontier, in which we here include Baluchistan, there was steady progress during the hundred years which preceded independence. In 1901, about half-way through, our Service took over the Frontier Province; and despite two new difficulties – the arms trade and later the Red Shirt movement – on the whole it achieved its aims. Indirect the rule had to be outside the settled districts; and this formula, in spite of minor differences in interpretation, long filled the bill. The work of the Service as wardens of the marches deserved Curzon's encomiums, not Linlithgow's criticism.

But perhaps the greatest scope for achievement in this century was offered by the posts outside India. The area was vast; the problems, though changing, were often formidable. Consider the glacis of north-west India where, from Tibet to Afghanistan and on to the Persian Gulf, without armed forces in peace time or more than a handful of political officers, India possessed a look out which kept her interests in view and secured friendly relations with a variety of people. Indeed, the term indirect rule, here, would be something of an exaggeration: we are dealing with foreign countries, where there could be persuasion but not rule, even indirect. Yet how far our relations were removed from mere diplomacy: the Government of India were always subordinate to the British Government, yet their policy was recognized, whether liked or disliked, by generations of neighbours who knew and respected its interpreters. If you came across a 'Political Agent' whether in Muscat or Meshed, you would know whom he represented and what the role of his service was. Even though, in Meshed, he would be called a consul-general, his background would be quite different from that of a member of H.B.M.'s Consular Service.

The service is wound up; closed down; consigned to the archives. In but a short time, the hundred-odd surviving members of the Service will have joined their precursors. May this brief account of the nature of their work serve as an introduction for fuller studies; the best memorial of their deeds lies in the institutions which they helped to create.

# Table of Salutes
## to Ruling Princes

### SALUTES OF 21 GUNS

Baroda, The Maharaja (Gaekwar) of,
Gwalior, The Maharaja (Scindia) of,
Hyderabad and Berar, The Nizam of,
Jammu and Kashmir, The Maharaja of,
Mysore, The Maharaja of,

### SALUTES OF 19 GUNS

Bhopal, The Nawab of,
Indore, The Maharaja (Holkar) of,
Kalat, The Khan (Wali) of,
Kolhapur, The Maharaja of,
Travancore, The Maharaja of,
Udaipur, (Mewar), The Maharana of,

### SALUTES OF 17 GUNS

Bahawalpur, The Nawab of,
Bharatpur, The Maharaja of,
Bikaner, The Maharaja of,
Bundi, The Maharao Raja of,
Cochin, The Maharaja of,
Cutch, The Maharao of,
Jaipur, The Maharaja of,
Jodhpur (Marwar), The Maharaja of,
Karauli, The Maharaja of,
Kotah, The Maharao of,
Patiala, The Maharaja of,
Rewa, The Maharaja of,
Tonk, The Nawab of,

### SALUTES OF 15 GUNS

Alwar, The Maharaja of,
Banswara, The Maharawal of,
Datia, The Maharaja of,

Dewas (Senior Branch), The Maharaja of,
Dewas (Junior Branch), The Maharaja of,
Dhar, The Maharaja of,
Dholpur, The Maharajrana of,
Dungarpur, The Maharawal of,
Idar, The Maharaja of,
Jaisalmer, The Maharawal of,
Khairpur, The Mir of,
Kishangarh, The Maharaja of,
Orchha, The Maharaja of,
Partabgarh, The Maharawat of,
Rampur, The Nawab of,
Sikkim, The Maharaja of,
Sirohi, The Maharao of,

## SALUTES OF 13 GUNS

Benares, The Maharaja of,
Bhavnagar, The Maharaja of,
Cooch Behar, The Maharaja of,
Dhrangadhra, The Maharaja Raj Saheb of,
Jaora, The Nawab of,
Jhalawar, The Maharajrana of,
Jind, The Maharaja of,
Jungadh, The Nawab of,
Kapurthala, The Maharaja of,
Mabha, The Maharaja of,
Riawanagar, The Maharaja Jam Saheb of,
Palanpur, The Nawab of,
Porbandar, The Maharaja Rana Saheb of,
Rajpipla, The Maharaja of,
Ratlam, The Maharaja of,
Tripura, The Maharaja of,

## SALUTES OF 11 GUNS

Ajaigarh, The Maharaja of,
Alirajpur, The Raja of,
Baoni, The Nawab of,
Barwani, The Rana of,
Bijawar, The Maharaja of,
Bilaspur, (Kahlur), The Raja of,

Cambay, The Nawab of,
Chamba, The Raja of,
Charkhari, The Maharaja of,
Chhatarpur, The Maharaja of,
Chitral, Mehtar of,
Faridkot, The Raja of,
Gondal, The Maharaja of,
Janjira, The Nawab of,
Jhabua, The Raja of,
Maler Rota, The Nawab of,
Mandi, The Raja of,
Manipur, The Maharaja of,
Morvi, The Maharaja of,
Marsingarh, The Raja of,
Panna, The Maharaja of,
Pudukkottai, The Raja of,
Radhanpur, The Nawab of,
Rajgarh, The Raja of,
Sailana, The Raja of,
Samthar, The Raja of,
Sirmur (Nahan), The Maharaja of,
Sitamau, The Raja of,
Suket, The Raja of,
Tehri (Garhwal), The Maharaja of,
Wankaner, The Maharana Raj Saheb of,

### SALUTES OF 9 GUNS

Balasinor, The Nawab (Babi) of,
Banganapelle, The Nawab of,
Banada, The Raja of,
Baraundha, The Raja of,
Baria, The Raja of,
Bhor, The Raja of,
Chhota Udepur, The Raja of,
Danta, The Maharana of,
Dharampur, The Raja of,
Dhrol, The Thakor Saheb of,
Jawhar, The Raja of,
Kalahand, The Maharaja of,
Khilchipur, The Raja of,

Limbdi, The Thakor Saheb of,
Loharu, The Nawab of,
Lunawadra, The Raja of,
Maihar, The Raja of,
Mayurbhanj, The Maharaja of,
Mudhol, The Raja of,
Magod, The Raja of,
Palitana, The Thakor Saheb of,
Patna, The Maharaja of,
Rajkot, The Thakor Saheb of,
Sachin, The Nawab of,
Sangli, The Raja of,
Sant, The Raja of,
Sawantwadi, The Raja of,
Shahpura, The Raja of,
Sonepur, The Maharaja of,
Wadhwan, The Thakor Saheb of,

# Notes

| PAGE | NOTE | |
|---|---|---|
| 13 | 1 | Sir G. de Montmorency: *The Indian States and Indian Federation.* |
| 15 | 2 | Sir W. Lee-Warner: *The Protected Princes of India,* 1895. |
| 19 | 3 | Sir R. Bullard (1895): *The Camels Must Go.* |
| 23 | 4 | de Montmorency, *op. cit.,* p. 65. |
| 26 | 5 | Memorandum on the Indian States, 1936. |
| 31 | 6 | K. M. Panikkar: *The Founding of the Kashmir State,* p. 132. |
| 32 | 7 | C. L. Tupper: *Indian Political Practice,* vol. I (1895), p. 63. |
| 37 | 8 | Sir M. O'Dwyer: *India as I knew it, 1885–1925.* |
| 44 | 9 | *Manual of instructions to officers of the Political Department of the Government of India.* |
| 47 | 10 | Communicated by Mr. S. C. Sutton, C.B.E., Librarian, India Office Library. |
| 47 | 11 | Dennis Holman: *Sikander Sahib,* p. 167. |
| 51 | 12 | Templewood, Lord (Sir S. Hoare). *Nine Troubled Years,* p. 76. |
| 52 | 13 | Salisbury papers. Christ Church, Oxford. |
| 58 | 14 | Sir W. Barton: *The Indian States.* |
| 58 | 15 | Sir W. Lawrence: *The India We Served,* p. 46. |
| 69 | 16 | C. L. Tupper, *op. cit.,* vol. 2, pp. 199–201. |
| 69 | 17 | Political Department Manual, *op. cit.,* pp. 57–63. |
| 70 | 18 | MacPherson's *British Enactments in force in Indian States.* |
| 71 | 19 | Tupper, *op. cit.,* vol. I, p. 75. |
| 71 | 20 | Sir C. U. Aitchison: *A Collection of Treaties, Engagements and Sanads relating to India.* |
| 71 | 21 | J. Sutherland: *Sketches of the relations subsisting between the British Government in India and the different Native States,* p. 174. |
| 71 | 22 | India Office Library, Home Miscellaneous Series, vol. 102, p. 445. |
| 72 | 23 | Tupper, *op. cit.,* vol. 2, pp. 1–22. |
| 72 | 24 | *See* Table, p. 262. |
| 72 | 25 | de Montmorency, *op. cit.,* p. 54. |
| 73 | 26 | Sir K. S. Fitze: *Twilight of the Maharajas,* p. 85. |
| 74 | 27 | A. P. Nicholson: *Scraps of Paper,* 1930. |
| 74 | 28 | E. M. Forster, *op. cit.,* p. 325 (1936 edn.). |
| 77 | 29 | See E. Thompson's *Life of Charles, Lord Metcalfe,* for the extraordinary story of the Rumbold–Palmer affair. |
| 78 | 30 | Tupper, *op. cit.,* vol. I, p. 38. |
| 83 | 31 | Sir A. C. Lothian: *Kingdoms of yesterday,* pp. 157–61. |
| 88 | 32 | E. M. Forster, *op. cit.,* p. 323. |
| 89 | 33 | Aitchison, *op. cit.,* vol. 9, p. 66. |
| 89 | 34 | Nicholson, *op. cit.* |
| 90 | 35 | H. H. Dodwell: *Cambridge History of India,* vol. 6, p. 240. |
| 92 | 36 | de Montmorency, *op. cit.,* p. 61. |
| 93 | 37 | *Ibid.,* p. 55. |
| 99 | 38 | D. A. Low: 'Sir Tej Bahadur Sapru and the First Round-Table Conference.' (University of Sussex, Conference on Indian politics and political history, August, 1965.) Reprinted in *Soundings in Modern Asian History.* |

# NOTES

| PAGE | NOTE | |
|---|---|---|
| 99 | 39 | Fitze, *op. cit.*, p. 77. |
| 100 | 40 | Low, *op. cit.* |
| 101 | 41 | J. R. M. Butler: *Lord Lothian.* |
| 102 | 42 | Lord Hailey: letter to the author. |
| 102 | 43 | Low, *op. cit.* |
| 105 | 44 | *Op. cit.*, p. 102. |
| 105 | 45 | Zetland: *Essayez*; p. 241, *et seq.* |
| 105 | 46 | Templewood, *op. cit.*, p. 87. |
| 108 | 47 | Letter to the author. |
| 108 | 48 | M. Edwardes: *The Last Years of British India*, p. 79. |
| 109 | 49 | V. P. Menon: *The Story of the Integration of the Indian States*, p. 49. |
| 112 | 50 | Menon, *ibid.*, pp. 95, 484. |
| 115 | 51 | *Ibid.*, p. 178. |
| 116 | 52 | Sir C. Corfield, letter to the author. |
| 117 | 53 | *Hansard*, 1944. |
| 118 | 54 | Fitze, *op. cit.*, p. 76. |
| 119 | 55 | Unpublished memoir. |
| 124 | 56 | Edwardes, *op. cit.*, p. 186. |
| 124 | 57 | *Ibid.*, p. 145. |
| 124 | 58 | John Connell: *Auchinleck.* |
| 125 | 59 | Corfield, letter to the author. |
| 128 | 60 | V. P. Menon, *op. cit.*, pp. 97, 98. |
| 128 | 61 | *Ibid.*, p. 108. |
| 131 | 62 | *Ibid.*, p. 151. |
| 132 | 63 | K. L. Panjabi, ed.: *The Civil Service of India.* |
| 146 | 64 | W. A. Wilcox: *Pakistan, the consolidation of a nation*, pp. 75–81. |
| 154 | 65 | Henry Thornton: *Colonel Sir Robert Sandeman.* |
| 155 | 66 | *Ibid.*, p. 317. |
| 155 | 67 | *Ibid.*, op. 32. |
| 156 | 68 | H. T. Lambrick (b. 1904), C.I.E.; I.C.S., 1927: *John Jacob of Jacobabad, passim.* |
| 158 | 69 | Oral communication to the author by General Catroux. |
| 159 | 70 | Sir O. Caroe: *The Pathans*, p. 398. |
| 162 | 71 | *Ibid.*, p. 352 *et seq.* gives an excellent account of this enactment and its use to validate the *jirga* system. |
| 166 | 72 | *Past Imperative.* |
| 166 | 73 | *Not in the Limelight.* |
| 170 | 74 | Caroe, *op. cit.*, pp. 329–45. |
| 178 | 75 | Amir Abdul Rahman's Autobiography, 1900, vol. 2, p. 160. Quoted by Caroe, *op. cit.*, p. 381. |
| 180 | 76 | Lieut. Winston Spencer Churchill: *The Story of the Malakand Field Force.* He was correspondent for the *Daily Telegraph* and the *Pioneer.* These figures are extraordinary, but Churchill would hardly have got them wrong. |
| 183 | 77 | Churchill, *op. cit.* |
| 184 | 78 | Caroe, *op. cit.*, pp. 422 *et seq.* |
| 184 | 79 | Roos-Keppel papers, India Office Library. |
| 184 | 80 | Sir E. Howell: *Story of the N.W. Frontier Province.* |
| 185 | 81 | Caroe, *op. cit.*, p. 397. |
| 185 | 82 | *Ibid.*, p. 406. |
| 192 | 83 | Oral communication to the author. |

PAGE NOTE
193 84 *Ibid.*
209 85 Caroe, *op. cit.*, p. 438.
210 86 Sir E. Howell: 'Some problems of the Indian frontier', *Journal of the Royal Central Asian Society*, vol. 21, April 1934, p. 195. *See also* his article 'Armon', pp. 468–78 of Caroe's *The Pathans*, and his 'Mizh, a monograph on Government's relations with the Mahsud tribe'.
210 87 Colonel H. R. C. Pettigrew: *Frontier Scouts.*
218 88 Oral communication to the author.
218 89 *Ibid.*
224 90 Vol. LIII, Part III, p. 266.
228 91 *Curzon, the last phase, 1919–1925*, pp. 129–131.
233 92 *The Persian Gulf States*, p. 15.
235 93 *Life and Letters of the Rt. Hon. Sir Austen Chamberlain*, K.G., P.C., M.P., vol. 2, p. 80.
235 94 Oral communication by Sir Basil Liddell Hart to a St. Antony's College seminar, 1965.
236 95 Vol. 1, *Loyalties: Mesopotamia 1914–1917*; Vol. 2, *Mesopotamia, 1917–1920: a clash of loyalties.*
251 96 Bogle papers in India Office Library (Eur. MSS.E/226), quoted by A. Lamb in *Britain and Chinese Central Asia: The Road to Lhasa, 1767 to 1905*, p. 15.
252 97 Private correspondence, India, part 2, vol. 21, Curzon to Hamilton, 5 Nov. 1901, quoted by Lamb, *op. cit.*, p. 258.
253 98 Peter Fleming, *Bayonets to Lhasa*, p. 31.
254 99 Fleming, *op. cit.*, p. 43.
255 100 Lamb, *op. cit.*, p. 306.
256 101 *Ibid.*, pp. 329–31.
257 102 *Ibid.*, p. 332.

# Bibliography

The Cambridge History of India has a very full bibliography; and Philip Woodruff, in his history of the I.C.S., *The Men who Ruled India*, discusses, in two long notes on the authorities, a number of books relative to the I.P.S. The bibliographical note in Thompson and Garratt's *Rise and Fulfilment of British Rule in India* should be seen.

The most important sources for the scholar are the records at the India Office Library subject to the ruling that official documents are available if more than thirty years old. Many of these files are duplicated by those in the archives of the Government of India in New Delhi. The Government of Pakistan, at Islamabad, and its subordinate secretariats at Peshawar and Quetta, have only a limited range of Frontier documents, the Government of India having failed to hand over, as agreed, copies of files of interest to both Governments.

The late Major W.P. Cranston, I.P.S., was appointed in April 1947 to sort out all Residency records which were secret and liable to embarrass the Princes. These were sent to the Commonwealth Relations Office in London under diplomatic seal; they covered roughly 1850–1947.

Of particular value is the private correspondence, over the whole period, between the Governors-General and the Monarchs and Secretaries of State. Much of this has been presented by the writers or their heirs to the India Office Library. Other such files are in various collections (Cambridge University, Wadham College, Oxford, Lord Halifax's Hickleton papers, etc.). Their whereabouts can be readily ascertained by reference to the National Register of Archives, Quality Court, Chancery Lane, London, W.C.2.

It was the practice of the Government of India to print about half a dozen copies of all files of any importance. These were distributed to the archives in London, New Delhi and Simla. This greatly facilitates research once the printed records can be traced.

*Authors' names marked with an asterisk were members of the Indian Political Service.*

Ackerley, J. R., *Hindoo Holiday*. Chatto & Windus, 1932

*Aitchison, C. U., ed., *A Collection of Treaties, Engagements and Sanads, relating to India and Neighbouring Countries*. Government Press, Calcutta, first published in 8 vols, 1862–5; 5th rev. ed., 14 vols., 1929–1933

Amery, The Rt. Hon. L. S., *My Political Life*, Vol. 3. Hutchinson, 1953–5

Amir Abdul Rahman, *see* Khan, Mir Munshi Sultan Mahomed, ed.

Azad, Maulana Abul Kalam, *India Wins Freedom*. Orient Longmans, Bombay, 1959

\*Bailey, Lt.-Col. F. M., *Mission to Tashkent*. Jonathan Cape, 1946

——*No Passport to Tibet*. Hart-Davis, 1957

\*Barton, Sir William, *India's North-West Frontier*, John Murray, 1939

——*The Princes of India*. Nisbet & Co., 1934

Belgrave, Sir Charles, *Personal Column*. Hutchinson, 1960

\*Bell, Sir Charles, *Tibet, Past & Present*. Clarendon Press, Oxford, 1924

Blunt, Sir Edward, *The I.C.S.: the Indian Civil Service*. Faber and Faber, 1937

Brecher, Michael, *Nehru: a Political biography*. O.U.P., 1959

\*Bruce, Lt.-Col. C. E., *Waziristan, 1936–37: the problems of the North-West frontiers of India and their solutions*. Gale & Polden, Aldershot, 1938

Bruce, Richard Isaac, *The Forward Policy and its Result: or Thirty-five years' work amongst the tribes on our North-Western frontier of India*. Longmans, Green, 1900

Bullard, Sir Reader, *The Camels Must Go:* an autobiography. Faber & Faber, 1961

Butler, J. R. M., *Lord Lothian (Philip Kerr), 1882–1940*. Macmillan, 1960

Butt, I. A., *Lord Curzon and the Indian States, 1899–1905*. Unpublished thesis for Ph.D. Degree, University of London, 1963–4

*Cambridge History of India*, vol. 6 (H. H. Dodwell). Cambridge U.P., 1922

Campbell-Johnson, Alan, *Mission with Mountbatten*. Hale, 1951

\*Caroe, Sir Olaf, *Wells of power: the oilfields of South-Western Asia* .... Macmillan, 1951

——*The Pathans, 550 B.C.–A.D. 1957*. Macmillan, 1958

Churchill, Winston, S., *The Story of the Malakand Field Force*. Longmans, 1898

Curzon, Lord, *Leaves from a Viceroy's Note-book*. Macmillan, 1926

Davies, Cuthbert C., *The Problem of the North-West Frontier, 1890–1908: with a survey of policy since 1849*. Cambridge, 1932

Davis, Professor H. W. C., *The Great Game in Asia (1800–1844)*. O.U.P., 1927

De Montmorency, Sir Geoffrey, *The Indian States and Indian Federation*. Cambridge U.P., 1942

*Dictionary of National Biography*, founded 1882 by George Smith, 22 vols. O.U.P., London, 1963–4

Dunbar, Sir George Duff-Sutherland, *Frontiers*. Weidenfield & Nicolson, 1932

\*Durand, Colonel Algernon, *The Making of a Frontier: five years' experiences and adventures in Gilgit, Hunza, Nagar, Chitral and the Eastern Hindu-Kush*. John Murray, 1899.

# BIBLIOGRAPHY

*East India Register and Directory:* first published as *East India Kalendar,* 1792. The title has changed as follows: in 1800, *The Oriental Register and East India Directory;* in 1801, *The New East India Kalendar;* in 1802, *The New Oriental Register and East India Directory;* 1803 onwards (published twice a year), *The East India Register and Directory;* in 1845, *The East India Register and Army List;* in 1861, *The Indian Army and Civil Service List,* and in 1877, *The India List*

Edwardes, Major Herbert B., *A Year on the Punjab Frontier in 1848-9,* 2 vols. Richard Bentley, London, 1851

Edwardes, Michael, *The Last Years of British India.* Cassell, 1963

*Elphinstone, Hon. Mountstuart, *An Account of the Kingdom of Caubul and its dependencies in Persia, Tartary and India: comprising a view of the Afghaun nation and a history of the Dooraunee monarchy,* 2 vols. in 1, new rev. ed. Richard Bentley, London, 1839

*Fitze, Sir Kenneth, *Twilight of the Maharajas.* John Murray, 1956

Fleming, Peter, *Bayonets to Lhasa.* Rupert Hart-Davis, 1955

Forster, E. M., *The Hill of Devi,* being letters from Dewas State Senior. E. Arnold, London 1953

Fraser, Lovat, *India under Curzon and after.* Heinemann, 1911

*Fraser-Tytler Sir W. K., *Afghanistan: a study of political development in Central Asia.* 3rd ed., O.U.P., 1967.

Freeth, Zahra, *Kuwait Was My Home,* Allen & Unwin, 1956

Fürer-Haimendorf, Christoph von, *The Naked Nagas,* Methuen, 1939

Gorwala, A. D., *The Role of the Administrator: past, present and future,* Gokhale Institute of Politics and Economics, Poona, 1952

*Gould, Sir Basil John, *The Jewel in the Lotus: recollections of an Indian political.* Chatto & Windus, 1957

Halifax The Earl of, *Fullness of Days.* Collins, 1957

*Hay Sir Rupert, *The Persian Gulf States.* Middle Eastern Institute, Washington, D.C., 1959

*Hickinbotham, Sir Tom, *Aden.* Constable 1958

Hiralal Singh, *Problems and Policies of the British in India, 1885-1898.* Asia Publishing House, London, 1963

Hodson, Henry Vincent, *The Great Divide: Britain, India, Pakistan.* Hutchinson, 1969

Holman, Dennis, *Sikander Sahib: the Life of Colonel James Skinner, 1778-1841.* Heinemann, 1961

*Howell, Sir Evelyn, *Story of the N.W. Frontier Province.* Government Printing and Stationery, Peshawar

—— 'Some Problems of the Indian Frontier', *Journal of the Royal Central Asian Society,* vol. 21, April 1934

—— 'Mizh, a monograph on Government's relations with the Mahsud tribe'. Government of India Press, Simla, 1931

*Islington Report*: Public Services Commission appointed by H.M. the King in 1912, under the chairmanship of Lord Islington. Parliamentary Papers, Session 1916, Vol. VII, Cd. 8382

Jacquemont, Victor, *Letters from India: 1829–1832*, being a selection from the correspondence of V. Jacquemont: trans. with an introduction by Catherine Alison Phillips. Macmillan, 1936

Johnston, Sir C., *View from Steamer Point*. Collins, 1964

*Kennion, R. L., *Diversions of an Indian Political*. Blackwood, Edinburgh, 1932

Khan, Mir Munshi Sultan Mahomed, ed., *The Life of Abdur Rahman*: Amir of Afghanistan. 2 vols., John Murray, 1900

Kipling, Rudyard, *Letters of Marque*. A. H. Wheeler, Allahabad, 1891

Lamb, Alastair, *Britain and Chinese Central Asia: the Road to Lhasa, 1767 to 1905*. Routledge & Kegan Paul, 1960

Lambrick, H. T., *John Jacob of Jacobabad*. Cassell, 1960

Lawrence, Sir Walter Roper, *The India We Served*. Cassell, 1928

*Lee-Warner, William, *The Protected Princes of India*. Macmillan, 1894

Li Tieh-tseng, *The Historical Status of Tibet*. O.U.P. 1956

*Lorimer, John Gordon, *Gazetteer of the Persian Gulf, Oman and Central Arabia*, 2 vols., Government Printing Press, Calcutta, 1908–15. Republished *1970*

*Lothian, Sir Arthur Cunningham, *Kingdoms of Yesterday*. John Murray, 1951

Low, D. A., ed., *Soundings in Modern South Asian History*. Weidenfeld & Nicolson, 1968

Lumby, E. W. R., *The Transfer of Power in India 1945–7*. Weidenfeld & Nicolson, 1968

*Lydall E. F., *Enough of Action*. Cape, 1949

Maclean, Sir Fitzroy, *A Person from England and other travellers to Turkestan*. Cape, 1958

MacPherson, J. M., compiler, *British Enactments in force in native states*; 2nd ed., 6 vols., Office of the Superintendent of Government Printing, India, Calcutta, 1899–1900

*Manual of Instructions to Officers of the Political Department of the Government of India, 1924*, Political and Secret Department Library, Foreign and Commonwealth Office Records

Mayne, Peter, *The Narrow Smile: a Journey back to the North-West Frontier*. John Murray, 1955

*Memoranda on the Indian States*, 1936 (Corrected up to 1st January 1936.) The Manager of Publications, Government of India Press, New Delhi, 1937

*Menon, K. P. S., *Delhi-Chunking*: a travel diary. O.U.P., London, 1947
——*Russian Panorama*. O.U.P., Bombay, 1962

# BIBLIOGRAPHY

*Menon, K. P. S., *The Flying Troika*: extracts from a diary. O.U.P., London 1963

—— *Many Worlds*: an autobiography. O.U.P., Bombay, 1966

Menon, V. P., *The Story of The Integration of the Indian States*. Orient Longmans, Calcutta, 1956

—— *The Transfer of Power in India*. Longmans Green, London, 1957

Minto, Countess of, ed., *India: Minto and Morley, 1905–1910*. From the correspondence between the Viceroy and the Secretary of State. Macmillan, 1934

*Mitchell, Norval, *Life of Sir George Cunningham*. Blackwood, Edinburgh, 1968

Moon, Sir Penderel, *Divide and Quit*. Chatto & Windus, 1961

Mosley, Leonard, *The Last Days of the British Raj*. Weidenfeld & Nicolson, 1961

Nicholson, A. P., *Scraps of Paper*. Ernest Benn, 1930

Nicolson, Sir Harold, *Curzon: The Last Phase, 1919–1925*. Constable, 1934

*O'Connor, Sir F., *Things Mortal*. Hodder & Stoughton, 1940

O'Dwyer, Sir Michael, *India As I Knew It, 1885–1925*. Constable, 1925

O'Malley, L. S. S., *The Indian Civil Service, 1601–1930*. John Murray, 1931

Panikkar, Kavalam Madhava, *The Founding of the Kashmir State*. Allen & Unwin, 1953

Panjabi, Kewal, L., ed., *The Civil Servant in India*, by ex Indian Civil Servants. Bharatiya Vidyabhavan, Bombay, 1965

Petrie, Sir C. A., *Life and Letters of the Rt. Hon. Sir Austen Chamberlain*. Cassell, 1940

Pettigrew, Colonel H. R. C., *Frontier Scouts*. Privately printed from Highcliff, Clayton Road, Selsey, Sussex, 1964

Pope-Hennessy, James, *Queen Mary, 1867–1953*, Allen & Unwin, 1959

Rawlinson, Major-Gen. Sir Henry, *England and Russia in the East*. A series of papers on the political and geographical condition of Central Asia. John Murray, 1875

*Richardson, H. E., *A Short History of Tibet*. E. P. Dutton, New York 1962. *See also* Snellgrove, D. L.

*Salisbury Papers*: Papers of Robert A. T. Gascoyne-Cecil, 3rd Marquis of Salisbury as Secretary of State for India from July 1866 to March 1867, and February 1874–April 1878

*Scott, Sir Ian, *Tumbled House: The Congo at Independence*. O.U.P., 1969

Shaw, R. B., *Visits to High Tartary, Yarkand and Kashgar*, 8th ed., London, 1871

Simon, The Rt. Hon. Sir John, Chairman, *Report of the Indian Statutory Commission*, vols. I & II, Cmd. 3568, 3569. H.M.S.O., 1930

*Skrine, Sir C. P., *Chinese Central Asia*, Methuen, 1926
—— *World War in Iran*. Constable, 1962
Smith, William Roy, *Nationalism and Reform in India*. Yale University Press, New Haven, Conn., 1938
Snellgrove, David L. and Richardson, H. E., *A Cultural History of Tibet*. Weidenfeld & Nicolson, 1968
Spear, Percival, *India, Pakistan and the West*. O.U.P., 1949: 4th ed, 1967
States Reorganization Commission: *Report of 1953–55*. Publications Division, Government of India, Delhi, 1955.
Stephens, Ian, *Pakistan*, 3rd rev. ed. Ernest Benn, 1967
Sutherland, J., *Sketches of the Relations subsisting between the British Government in India and the different Native States*. Surveyor General's Office, Calcutta, 1833

Templewood, Viscount, *Nine Troubled Years*. Collins, 1954
Terentyef, M. A., *Russia and England in Central Asia*, trans. from the Russian by F. C. Daukes, 2 vols., The Foreign Department Press, Calcutta, 1876
Thompson, Edward J., *The Making of the Indian Princes*. O.U.P., 1943
—— *The Life of Charles, Lord Metcalfe*. Faber & Faber, 1937
Thompson, Edward J. and Garratt, Godfrey T., *Rise and Fulfilment of British Rule in India*. Macmillan, 1934
*Thornton, Thomas Henry, *Colonel Sir Robert Sandeman: His life and work on our Indian Frontier*. John Murray, 1895
*Tod, Lt.-Col. James, *Annals and Antiquities of Rajasthan or the Central and Western Rajpoot States of India*. 2 vols. Smith Elder, London, 1829–1832
Tupper, C. L., compiler, *Indian Political Practice*, 5 vols. Office of the Superintendent of Government Printing, India, Calcutta, 1895–1901

*Wakefield, Sir Edward Birkbeck, *Past Imperative: My Life in India, 1927–1947*. Chatto & Windus, 1966
Warburton, Col. Sir Robert, *Eighteen Years in the Khyber*. John Murray, 1900
Wheeler-Bennett, John W. W., *King George VI: his life and reign*. Macmillan, 1958
*White Paper on Indian States*. India, Ministry of States. Government Publications, New Delhi, 1948.; rev. ed. 1950
*Wilberforce-Bell, Capt. H., *The History of Kathiawar from the Earliest Times*. Heinemann, 1916
Wilcox, Wayne Ayres, *Pakistan: the Consolidation of a Nation*. Columbia Univ. Press, N.Y., 1963
*Wilson, Lt.-Col. Sir Arnold T., *Loyalties: Mesopotamia 1914–1917*. O.U.P., London, 1930

# BIBLIOGRAPHY

Wilson, Lt.-Col. Sir Arnold T., *Mesopotamia 1917–1920: a clash of loyalties.* O.U.P., London, 1931

—— *The Persian Gulf: an historical sketch from the earliest times to the beginning of the twentieth century.* Allen and Unwin, 1954

—— *S.W. Persia: a political officer's diary, 1907–1914.* O.U.P., London, 1941

*Wingate, Sir Ronald, *Not in the Limelight.* Hutchinson, 1959

Woodruff, Philip, *The Men Who Ruled India,* 2 vols. Cape, 1953–4

Zetland, Lord, *Essayez: the memoirs of Lawrence, Second Marquess of Zetland, K.G., P.C., G.C.S.I., G.C.I.E.* John Murray, 1956

Zinkin, Maurice and Taya, *Britain and India: Requiem for Empire.* Chatto & Windus, 1964

# Index